Doing Radical Social Work

C000000631

T. P. Consich.
23·02·15

£12.99

Reshaping Social Work Series

Series Editors: **Robert Adams, Lena Dominelli and Malcolm Payne**

The **Reshaping Social Work** series aims to develop the knowledge base for critical, reflective practitioners. Each book is designed to support students on qualifying social work programmes and update practitioners on crucial issues in today's social work, strengthening research knowledge, critical analysis and skilled practice to shape social work to meet future challenges.

Published titles

Anti-Racist Practice in Social Work Kish Bhatti-Sinclair
Social Work and Spirituality Margaret Holloway and Bernard Moss
Social Work Research for Social Justice Beth Humphries
Social Work and Social Policy under Austerity Bill Jordan and Mark Drakeford
Social Care Practice in Context Malcolm Payne
Critical Issues in Social Work with Older People Mo Ray, Miriam Bernard and Judith Phillips
Social Work and Power Roger Smith

Forthcoming titles

Globally Minded Social Work Practice Janet Anand and Chaitali Das
Rejuvenating Family Support Karen Broadhurst
Social Work and Community Development Catherine Forde and Debby Lynch
A Guide to Adult Social Work Law in England John Williams, Gwyneth Roberts and Aled Griffiths

Invitation to authors

The Series Editors welcome proposals for new books within the *Reshaping Social Work* series. Please contact one of the series editors for an initial discussion:

- Robert Adams at rvadams@rvadams.karoo.co.uk
- Lena Dominelli at lena.dominelli@durham.ac.uk
- Malcolm Payne at malcolmpayne5@gmail.com

Reshaping Social Work
Series Editors: **Robert Adams, Lena Dominelli and Malcolm Payne**
Series Standing Order ISBN 978-1-4039-4878-6
(outside North America only)

You can receive future titles in this series as they are published by placing a standing order. Please contact your bookseller or, in the case of difficulty, write to us at the address below with your name and address, the title of the series and the ISBN quoted above. Customer Services Department, Macmillan Distribution Ltd, Houndmills, Basingstoke, Hampshire, RG21 6XS, UK

Doing Radical Social Work

Colin Turbett

First published 2014 by
PALGRAVE MACMILLAN

Palgrave Macmillan in the UK is an imprint of Macmillan Publishers Limited, registered in England, company number 785998, of Houndmills, Basingstoke, Hampshire RG21 6XS.

Palgrave Macmillan in the US is a division of St Martin's Press LLC, 175 Fifth Avenue, New York, NY 10010.

Palgrave Macmillan is the global academic imprint of the above companies and has companies and representatives throughout the world.

Palgrave® and Macmillan® are registered trademarks in the United States, the United Kingdom, Europe and other countries

ISBN 978–1–137–30853–5

This book is printed on paper suitable for recycling and made from fully managed and sustained forest sources. Logging, pulping and manufacturing processes are expected to conform to the environmental regulations of the country of origin.

A catalogue record for this book is available from the British Library.

A catalog record for this book is available from the Library of Congress.

Typeset by Cambrian Typesetters, Camberley, Surrey

Printed in China

Contents

List of Illustrative Material

Figures

Tables

Boxes

Practice examples

Exercises

Research boxes

Acknowledgements

This book has been inspired by colleagues who, over 35 years of frontline social work, have demonstrated how their good practice flows from core values of social justice and belief in a better world. Such workers have been drawn from homecare, residential and field social work settings, and include some managers and even a few senior managers. Many have operated this way almost unconsciously through personal belief underpinned by values stemming from the trade union and socialist traditions that are now under threat from the ideology of neoliberalism. Others, though fewer in number, have been conscious socialists keen to challenge reactionary orthodoxy. Many who entered social work in furtherance of such ideals have found professional training has helped their outlook confront reality, and those involved in this field who contribute to this process must be thanked. Out in the world of practice my present team in Ardrossan never fail to amaze me with their commitment and enthusiasm despite all the challenges they meet every day they go to work. All these colleagues have contributed to the formation of my own ideas about radical practice.

I would especially like to thank those who have contributed directly to the book: Maggie Rands, Diana Turbett, Barry McMullan and Lindsay Watson have all helped in different ways. The team at Palgrave Macmillan provided great assistance and their academic reviewers of earlier drafts came up with valued suggestions and ideas. Comrades in the trade union UNISON, especially Stephen Smellie, Convenor of the Scottish Social Work Issues Group, offered encouragement and support, as did the frequently mentioned authors of the modern 'Radical Literature'.

COLIN TURBETT

The author and publishers would like to thank Oxford University Press Canada for permission to reproduce 'The Web of Oppression' (Figure 2.1 in this book) from B. Mullaly (2009) *Challenging Oppression and Confronting Privilege*, 2nd edn, p. 198.

List of Abbreviations

ADHD	Attention Deficit Hyperactive Disorder
AOP	Anti-Oppressive Practice
BASW	British Association of Social Workers
BME	Black and Minority Ethnic
CAMHS	Child and Adolescent Mental Health Service
CDPs	Community Development Projects
EBP	Evidence Based Practice
FAS	Foetal Alcohol Syndrome
HRP	Human Rights Practice
IFSW	International Federation of Social Workers
LGBT	Lesbian Gay Bisexual and Transexual
NASS	National Asylum Seekers Support Service
NASW	National Association of Social Work (US)
NPM	New Public Management
OECD	Organisation for Economic Co-operation and Development
PCP	Person-Centred Practice
PTSD	Post-Traumatic Stress Disorder
RCTs	Random Controlled Trials
SCIE	Social Care Institute for Excellence
SMARRT	Specific, Measurable, Acceptable, Realistic, Results-Orientated and Time-Specific
SWAN	Social Work Action Network
UK	United Kingdom
UKBA	United Kingdom Border Agency
UKIP	United Kingdom Independence Party
US	United States

Introduction

In preparation for the book, I asked Jamie, who works as a children and family worker in a Scottish local authority setting, to think about a typical day and the routine tasks and challenges he faces as a practitioner in a busy office. The notes he subsequently gave me referred to constantly changing demands, difficulty in meeting his service users' needs on a day-to-day basis, undertaking detailed assessments and then recording everything almost as it happens. He also mentioned the responsibility involved not just in child protection work, but also in those situations where children were nearing the threshold for such consideration. Unsurprisingly, Jamie's account made frequent use of such phrases as 'stress' and 'pressure', the feeling at times of being overwhelmed, and the exhaustion he sometimes experiences at the end of the working day.

Despite all this, Jamie felt good about his work and was known in the office for his commitment, as well as his sense of humour. Clearly, the stress he felt was, in some senses, a coping mechanism. Jamie was usually content but was sufficiently confident to speak out if not; he felt some pride in what he did for a living and had no thought of working anywhere else. However, when he was out and about with his family, or meeting new people, he would hesitate before telling people that he was a social worker. Jamie had worked for many years in industry and had experienced unemployment and some degree of social exclusion as a young person. He was proud of his working-class heritage and values. The book's final chapter will end with Jamie's thoughts on how and why he copes with his work.

Having looked at the motives of a colleague it seems honest to locate my own position in approaching the task of writing this book. I qualified as a social worker in 1978 from Moray House College in Edinburgh. At the time, I was quite young but already a long way from my roots in the leafy South of England where I grew up. I was drawn to social work as a consequence of the radicalization that touched on my generation in the late 1960s and early 1970s – a disillusionment with a system that had not met the promise given to those who had survived World War II, and with a system whose perpetuation seemed to be based on wars such as that under way in Vietnam. Having been seconded onto professional training, I returned to Glasgow and worked for seven years in a large and busy team in a peripheral housing estate. During those years, I immersed myself in trade union activity alongside work – the two seeming entirely compatible. As a workplace, we took on board the world around us: as well as engaging in broader community social work when we could, we also identified ourselves with other groups, be they striking miners or shipyard workers facing redundancy. After this, I worked for a few years in the Strathclyde Stand-By service, continuing trade union activity for a while but, eventually, resigning my position due to the apathy and attitudes around me. At the time, I put this down to the particular colleagues I worked with but, in reality, the world was changing: in the wake of the defeat of British miners in 1985, workers in secure jobs, including social work, were becoming imbued with the values of neoliberalism (this and other keywords used in the book are described in the glossary) even if they did not realize it at the time. UK prime minister Margaret Thatcher – surely one of the most ideologi-cally-driven western political leaders in years – announced that 'there was no such thing as society' (see page 123). This seemed reflected on the ground in the way in which people became increasingly self-centred, tied into an economic system based on debt and unwilling to make personal sacrifice for others.

My own reaction was to retreat to a rural location where I then worked for many years alongside my partner as we brought up our children. Whilst we continued to live out our underlying values when we could, our focus was on other things. Social work in remote rural locations, as I have argued elsewhere (Turbett 2010), still gave opportunity for very cre-ative practice and our interest focused on this, keeping alive a belief that the job still had possibilities beyond the increasingly narrow prescrip-tions of the agendas set from above.

Following many years of rural work, I have now returned to children and family work as a team manager in an urban setting. I have been inspired here by the commitment of my colleagues and by their appre-ciation that the world inhabited by their service users and themselves is neither fair nor just. Together, we try to find ways to help those worst affected by the ravages of neoliberalism and it is here that I have begun to think again about how we might apply radical social work ideas in practice in ordinary settings encountered by workers in the real world.

The purpose of this book

There are very many books about social work theory and, probably, just as many that try to make sense of such theory for practice. Most are written from a mainstream viewpoint that sees social work as somehow detached from the processes that create the society that we live in, or, at least, that is how they can be selectively interpreted by students and practitioners: students want to write meaningful essays that will satisfy their teachers, and learn enough theory about practice to enter it with some degree of confidence. Many social workers just want to get by with their work and survive the pressures; they want a fair day's pay for a fair day's work, and to believe that they have made a positive difference to someone's life through their interventions. This, however, is where the problems start. The International Federation of Social Workers (IFSW) definition of social work states:

> The social work profession promotes social change, problem solving in human relationships and the empowerment and liberation of people to enhance well-being. Utilising theories of human behaviour and social systems, social work intervenes at the points where people interact with their environments. Principles of human rights and social justice are fundamental to social work.
>
> (IFSW 2012b)

Putting this into practice does not seem to be on the agenda of most employers.

There is a general consensus that most social work practice is based on a mixture of theoretical models that emphasize the need for individual change, but also recognize societal factors that impact on individuals and families (Payne 2005): whilst we try to treat/help individuals and hold them responsible for their situations, we take account of such factors as poor housing and unemployment, even if we cannot address such matters. Where social work theories differ is the emphasis that is placed on aspects of all of these factors, and how this reflects our values as a society and the political direction determined by governments and global systems. That said, Howe's statement in his review of social work theories that 'most social work theories preserve, in their thinking and practice, the *status quo*, that is, the interests of the dominant and established groups' (Howe 1987: 167) is still considered accurate. The consequence however, is recognition, through surveys that report the views of social workers about their work, that disillusionment often accompanies actual progress into practice as a qualified social worker, arising from incongruence between expectations and reality (Jones 2001; UNISON 2010; Community Care 2011). This book will not assume that those who are in professional training or that those who practise social work share its aspirations for social justice and, indeed, fundamental social change. Indeed, there is some evidence that a majority of people entering social work regard individuals as responsible for their own problems (Gilligan 2007). If this is the case, and if this book helps move some students and practitioners who are in doubt about this to reach a different conclusion, then it will have served its purpose: it may help them deal better with the difficulties they will face in practice (see Figure I.1).

This book is designed not only as a programme for action, but also as a call for frontline workers who want to make a difference and pursue social justice for their clients/service users. Whilst it is written from a UK perspective, the book is drawn from literature and ideas from across the English-speaking world and so should be of interest to students and frontline workers in the USA, Canada, Australia and New Zealand/Aotearea, where polices are also determined by neoliberal ideas. It rests on an analysis (essentially, a Marxist one) that considers that western capitalist societies are based on the exploitation of working classes by a ruling class whose ideology is accepted: rule and exploitation are by consensus rather than by coercion, with social work playing a part in that process. By definition, the typical reader will be one whose sympathies (perhaps in keeping with the values of social work) are with the victims of a system within which inequalities are inherent and growing. In this sense, I share the view of Paul Michael Garrett (2013: 15) in his warning to potential readers of his theoretical examination of radical social work themes: that those looking for balance should 'look away now'. The book will explain that, within a capitalist society, a welfare state can provide a more positive framework within which to operate than one where this is absent; it recognizes that welfare systems based on market models (where social work operates as if it were a business) are manifested by increases in inequality and disadvantage. It acknowledges from the outset that, within the statutory settings where many of us work (such as the workplace described in the opening lines above), the reality of day-to-day pressure can quickly subsume the motives that draw people into social work – and, indeed, can overwhelm completely. This is especially the case when the popular image of social work is negative and understanding of what practitioners do so poor.

If you take the trouble to seek them out, there are antidotes to what might seem an overburdening reality but even these, as we will see, provide little day-to-day meaningful practical guidance in many social work settings. I was drawn towards the book *Radical Social Work* (Bailey and Brake 1975) when I undertook professional training in the 1970s and tried to take its message of challenging injustice into my first work setting in a hectic social work team in Glasgow. Large areas of professional discretion for frontline workers, backed up by growing resources, gave this some reality in the 1980s but, by the end of that decade, both were being negatively encroached on. Between 2005 and 2010, several United Kingdom-based authors, whose work will be quoted, have revisited such radical themes and their efforts have drawn positive attention from many students, a number of academics, as well as some practitioners. Their efforts have resulted in a series of well-attended conferences under the umbrella of the Social Work Action Network (SWAN), a group with some international influence. I will describe these works collectively as the 'Radical Literature', meaning the writings (in order of publication) of Ferguson et al. (2005), Ferguson (2008), Ferguson and Woodward (2009) and Lavalette (2011). I must emphasize their importance to my own project: this book stands on foundations they have laid. These writers have also authored other important papers on similar themes but those listed above are their most accessible and well-read works. In addition, other social work writers have made important critical contributions to these debates, in particular: from the UK, Harris (2003), Harris and White (2009), Rogowski (2010, 2013); and, from Ireland, Garrett (2013). Elsewhere, writers such as Fook (2002) and McDonald (2006) from Australia, and Baines (2007) and Mullaly (2010) from Canada, have also made their mark on these debates. The book will also draw on other sources within the literature of social work that can help lead the reader toward a radical social work synthesis for the twenty-first century applicable to real-life practice situations.

If the core purpose of this book is to describe 'radical practice', what is meant by that term? From their conversations with frontline practitioners with sympathies towards radical practice, Ferguson and Woodward conclude that it contains the following aspects:

- Radical practice as retaining a commitment to good practice
- Radical practice as 'guerrilla warfare' and small scale resistance
- Radical practice as working alongside service users and carers
- Radical practice as collective activity and political campaigning.

(Ferguson and Woodward 2009: 153)

These are broad descriptions of a variety of activities, some of which might not seem especially radical at first view, and the last of which many practitioners would not regard as an activity they would engage in at work. However, this short list offers an introduction to the material that the book will develop and discuss.

Discretion, managerialism and spaces for Radical Practice

This book will emphasize how the space for *discretion* that, it is argued, exists within the work setting can be used in practice to deliver radical forms of social work.

The point about discretion and whether or not there is enough to permit individualized worker-determined practice is an important one. The Radical Literature tends, in general, to be light in its approach to this discussion. I searched for a quote to illustrate this point but could not find one: the problem is one of absence of coverage rather than denial of opportunity for discretion. At best, as Rogowski states in concluding a discussion on tensions, dilemmas and contradictions arising from the 'modernization' of social work, is a hope that 'the *inconvenience* [sic] of, albeit reduced, discretion will hopefully stubbornly remain' (Rogowski 2010: 187). In general terms, the Radical Literature tends towards pessimism. This is explained by the pervasive influence in the real day-to-day world of social work of *managerialism*, a force these writers tend to consider as dominant.

The creation of the welfare state in the UK in the 1940s, and the establishment of social services departments (in England and Wales) and social work departments (in Scotland) in the 1970s, was based on an aspiration to meet welfare need just as universal education would create opportunity, the National Health Service (NHS) would enable us to use such opportunity, benefits systems would create a safety net for those unable to work, and state-owned industry would ensure continuity of employment. The wartime Beveridge Report's five 'giants' – want, ignorance, disease, squalor and idleness – would be addressed through the various organs of the welfare state, and the development of social services was in keeping with this bedrock of ideas. The managerialist vision – based, as we shall see in Chapter 1, on neoliberal economics – is implicit about replacing this with social service goals that primarily concern risk reduction. These necessarily fit with eligibility criteria for services based not on need, but on risk (Parton 1998; Stanford 2010, 2011). The fact that those of us with an interest in politics cannot recall any general election anywhere when any choice was given by the main parties in western democracies on such developments is, itself, of interest. In Chile, neoliberal economics were forced on a recalcitrant population through a military coup in 1973, but elsewhere the transition has been more subtly achieved. I state these facts so starkly because they are fundamental to what is happening in social work and need to be understood.

So, is the managerialist project complete, or near complete, as suggested by Ferguson and Woodward (2009: 5), or do opportunities for radical approaches still exist in everyday practice? As the Radical Literature rightly contends, few people came into social work to care manage, or spend most of their time behind computer screens (Ferguson 2008). Informed by Lipsky, this debate is summarized by Evans and Harris (2004) by delineating those social work commentators who consider discretion in day-to-day practice has been effectively curtailed from those who believe that opportunity continues. White (2009) discusses these tensions by drawing on considerable evidence suggesting pessimism, but then considers resistance strategies, concluding that there is a place for various approaches including 'on a day to day level, subtle acts and quiet challenges' to mainstream managerially led practice (*ibid.*: 144). Stanford (2010, 2011) finds that social workers are prepared to confront the risk agendas they find themselves facing by making moral stands and consequential practical decisions that place them at risk in their work roles. Carey and Foster's research (2011) found a range of practices at frontline level that stemmed from a distrust of authority, a concern for social justice, and an empathy with service users and informal carers. Clearly, there is a practice out there that might be loosely defined as radical, but how and where does this take place and how might it be described in any detail? How does this fit into notions of the State as an entity and the place of welfare within its borders?

This book will explore the opportunities that exist within both legislation and policy at national level, and policy determined at more local level – where managerialist-driven approaches are most apparent to frontline staff. There is little within social work legislation that is absolutely prescriptive: even statutory child protection interventions to secure the safety of children depend on the interpretation of situations and the consideration of a number of options, albeit ones that might involve a high level of risk. National policy tends to be open to a great deal of interpretation by the time it reaches local authority level, which can lead to accusations of postcode determination of services – something governments try, but inevitably fail, to grapple with, especially at a time of resource scarcity (*Financial Times* 2010). Even within local authorities, senior managers struggle to know how their policies are operationalized (Munro 2010). These tensions result in the creation of areas of discretion that workers can exploit positively. Such opportunities might be described as flowing from the interface or collision of the different systems involved (a Marxist concept explained in Chapter 3) because, as Lipsky identifies (also in Chapter 3), it is here that the ambiguities and contradictions arise that make worker interpretation in practice a necessity.

There are other pressures on workers that impede or provide opportunities, or set the context for possibilities: these include the social policy setting that comes from central government, its local application (in terms of priorities, procedures and guidelines established by individual employers and agencies), the resources made available and the working environment. In late 2013, one Scottish Council advised its housing tenants in debt because of the 'Bedroom Tax' (see page 128), that they would inform Children's Services – a threat implying an oppressive role for social workers (Herald 2013). Such pressures will impact in different ways on individual workers who, in turn, will bring their own life experience, work experience and training to bear on their practice. Figure I.1

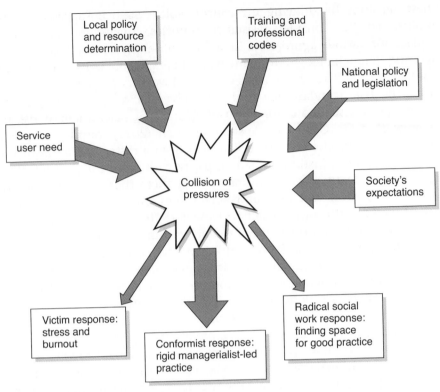

Figure I.1 Model to describe professional dilemmas and responses

provides a theoretical model to make sense of the tensions involved and the different responses that might arise from the worker. Within this theoretical model, many workers might move from one domain to another: from compliance to resistance, depending on the circumstances of a particular intervention, or perhaps vice versa. The contention, though, is that the worker who is armed with a critical view of the world and an understanding of the place of social work in western societies is in a better position to practise effective and creative social work (Mullaly 2010; Garrett 2013) – an act that is, essentially, radical. Such critical approaches are often actively discouraged by employers, who just want us to get on with the job (Garrett 2013). Sadly, as a result, many workers face dilemmas and pressures that conspire to drive some out of social work entirely; this book will attempt to provide the protective material that helps those so equipped avoid professional burnout.

The structure of the book

What this book sets out to do is to address the current state of social work in the UK (and, by implication, other countries whose social work provision is similarly based and infused with neoliberal approaches to welfare provision) in terms of the opportunities that exist for a radical practice. As described earlier in this Introduction, the background to why we are where we are is of huge importance to our understanding of what needs to be done. Chapter 1 (The Context of Social Work) provides the background for the rest of the book by setting the scene for social work policy and practice in the UK, and western democracies in general. It describes the emergence of the neoliberal economy and the change from welfare state provision to meet need, to market-based solutions to address risk. Poverty and its place will be briefly analysed and explained, as will rising inequality. The chapter will describe the language and methods used to achieve consensus. With an emphasis on the place of the welfare state in the history of social work, it will describe the transition from welfare benefit provision to workfare-based reward, and other threats to commonly accepted notions of welfare state provision. The importance of defending the welfare state will be given prominence. A view will be taken of the 2011 English riots because of what they tell us about contemporary society. The chapter will conclude with a brief look at alternatives to the current neoliberal consensus.

The premise of this book is the weakness of the Radical Literature in providing guidance for everyday practice. It would be wrong, however, to ascribe this to a dearth of alternative ideas and the aim of Chapter 2 ('Radical Theory') is to examine a range of approaches developed over the past 40 years as a foundation for the practical application that follows in subsequent chapters. A clearer definition of radical social work will emerge at the end of the book as a fusion of what can be applied from all this theory in day-to-day social work practice in a manner that will not attract disciplinary action from employers, or feelings of manipulation for political agendas by service users. The emphasis in this chapter will be on the *practical and possible* in everyday settings where social work takes place – typically, public sector offices such as the setting described at the start of this chapter – rather than in idealized workplaces using practice theories that are rarely found. The worth of this book will be in its meaning for workers in such everyday settings and this yardstick will be used throughout the chapters. In that respect, there will be only brief reference to the theoretical debates about modernism, post-modernism and their respective influences on critical and radical perspectives in social work: the book would lose its practical application if it were to divert into what is of interest to academics but, probably, not to practitioners.

Chapter 3 ('Finding Space for Radical Practice') explains, in general terms, where and how discretion might exist. It develops the themes introduced in the Introduction by defining how the contradictions within capitalist societies provide spaces for discretion in a very general sense. It will then go on to examine the notion of the 'streetwise bureaucrat' through a focus on the work of Lipsky and his description of discretion and how that applies in contemporary work settings. These themes will be developed in subsequent chapters around practice areas. The book will critically examine literature surrounding discretion and space for radical practice in managerially-driven environments. The importance of this chapter is in its emphasis on possibilities within workplaces – such as local authority teams, where students on placement and practising social workers are likely to work. Again, its applicability and value has to be judged against its potential application in settings such as the one in which Jamie and I work.

Chapter 4 ('Working with Children and Families') examines the effects of increasing inequality and economic decline on family life. It will look at the main issues facing children and family social workers: drug- and alcohol-abusing parents, domestic violence and the issues of neglect of children's needs that arise from these situations. Feminist-based perspectives will be examined in relation to gender and child protection work. Coverage will be given to issues arising from population movement between countries and regions and the policies that arise from attitudes to immigration and asylum. This chapter will critically examine the risk averse policies and practice that arise from the emphasis on risk described in Chapter 1. Alternative strategies based on human rights-based approaches and European social pedagogical approaches will be outlined, as will the application of material discussed in Chapter 2. This will all be based within a context of research evidence concerning outcomes for children. Some of this will be centred on small areas of practice that can make working with parents and children a genuine partnership, rather than a laboured and forced experience because of statutory considerations and imperatives. It will therefore explore such matters as listening to people, according them dignity and respect, demystifying the work social workers do and looking critically at some aspects of 'professionalism', such as language, dress and the general presentation of frontline staff.

In similar vein, Chapter 5 ('Working with Adults') focuses on the principal strands of work with adults including older people, mental health work and learning disability. The chapter will cover personalization, as this is now a major force in the UK: its background, its attractions and the opportunities it presents. However the chapter will also examine and discuss the threats it might present to service users, their carers, and social care staff. As in Chapter 4, alternative approaches (rather than alternative practice settings) will be discussed based on the radical approaches discussed in Chapter 3.

Chapter 6 ('Community Social Work in the Big Society') will look at the importance of community networks and support in building resilience and finding solutions to the issues facing social workers concerned with social justice. Starting with definitions of community, examination will be given to mainstream models of community-orientated practice, the concept of the 'Big Society' and, finally, to radical possibilities.

Chapter 7 ('Radical Social Work with Individuals and Groups') examines the possibilities that exist for a radical practice in an environment often considered to be straightjacketed by assessment and care management models. It considers these from the viewpoint of the radical fusion of theory outlined in Chapter 2, and will provide a more detailed and general coverage of this theme than would have been possible in Chapters 4 and 5. The chapter will look at narrative approaches, critical psychology and other contemporary models that offer possibilities in mainstream practice settings.

Chapter 8 ('Prospects for Radical Practice: Survival in the Front Line') looks at the organizational forms that social workers require for safety, security and support. Jamie, whom we met earlier, depends on such protective factors. This starts in the workplace in terms of policies that protect staff individually from vulnerability and harm, including support through supervision and effective workload management. The chapter will then go on to explore collective organization including the role of trade unions and professional associations, forums that were fundamental to the radicals of previous generations but which seem to have less attraction to radicals today. Why should social workers bother with such forums and how can they make them better and more responsive? The avoidance of stress and burnout, a theme touched on in earlier chapters, is given a special place here: it is often the trade union activists and those prepared to challenge in the workplace who take the responsibility for such matters. The chapter ends with a summary of the prospects for radical practice.

Each chapter ends with a summary of main points and a list of resources for those who wish to take things further. Chapters will contain case examples, messages from research, as well as some exercises and 'Stop and Think' sections to stimulate debate and discussion. The book uses plain language as accessibility to workers not attracted by academic study is considered crucial. To assist with this process, a glossary is provided which will explain keywords found in the text: such words will be introduced in the main text in *italics*. An Appendix outlines a suggested Manifesto for Radical Practice, which is presented for further discussion.

chapter 1

The Context of Social Work

Overview

The reader looking for a history might want a book written by a historian rather than a social worker. However, the practice-based content that follows in other chapters has to be located in a context created by historical development, and so belongs in these pages. The short historical account (including the place of social work) given in this chapter is one consistent with the radical explanations that underpin this book. It assumes some agreement with the premise that social work service users find themselves the victims of oppression and disadvantage because of their place in society, rather than through individual failing – a theme that will be looked at in more detail in ensuing chapters. This historical overview is followed by some elaboration on the social problems that are generally found in contemporary society in the western democracies, and one of their most extreme negative manifestations – riots and social disorder. There are, of course, alternatives to economies based, like that in the UK, on neoliberal ideas, and these will be touched on very briefly at the end of the chapter.

The state and its functions

Before embarking on a brief history of social work's place in the *welfare states* that characterize western democracies, a basic sociological view of the state and its function is required to provide context for this and following chapters of the book. The notion of 'state' has been much contested over time and a clear agreed definition is difficult to locate beyond the dictionary description of 'an organized community under one government' (*Concise Oxford English Dictionary*).

In his classic 1969 book, Ralph Miliband suggests that there are two principal accounts of the state in advanced *capitalist* countries: a post-war pluralist-democratic account and the *Marxist* view. Miliband describes as post-war pluralist-democratic view as one that suggests that the state is there to reconcile the differences between competing groups and to ensure the needs of all are served. This view assumes that there are no dominant groups in society but that competition between them (for instance, between those who own and manage businesses and those who work in them who might be organized in trade unions) ensures that power is shared and, ultimately, balanced; where elites exist, they lack the cohesion required to dominate and the job of the state and its organs is to ensure that this is the case. Thus, the judges who interpret the law, top-ranking military leaders and civil servants, and others who enjoy executive positions within the state and who are not subject to election are neutral and are there to serve all people, regardless of status and economic influence. This consensual view is the one shared by politicians from the social-democratic parties (such as the UK Labour Party) through to mainstream right-wing parties (such as the UK Conservative Party). This is also the view propagated through school-based education, the mainstream media and the view probably accepted by most of the population.

The Marxist view derives from the nineteenth-century accounts of Marx and Engels, who characterized the state in general terms as an essentially (if not literally) coercive force designed to serve the financial interests of the bourgeoisie (the class who owned the means of production and, therefore, the class with the greatest interest in *capitalism*). Together with their political descendants (including Lenin and Gramsci), Marx and Engels marshalled considerable evidence (although Marx never completed a full study of the state) to show how pre-capitalist societies had a lesser need for the sophisticated state required by capitalism: here, workers had to be educated, looked after to a certain degree and also kept in line by the law, police and judiciary. All this, they calculated, was based on capitalism's requirements as a mode of production, and they traced the historical development of the modern state as a requisite element (see, for example, Engels work *The Origin of the Family, Private Property and the State* (1978 [1884])). As Lenin writes: 'as the social division into classes arose and took firm root, as class society arose, the state also arose and took firm root' (Lenin 1919: 10). Although in outward appearance free and, in its advanced capitalist form, proclaiming universal suffrage, the state's purpose was to hold the lower classes in subjection (*ibid.*: 18). Ultimately, the inner-contradictions of capitalism – including the falling rate of profit, its tendency to go into periodic crisis, and the rising power of workers – would lead to its demise and a revolutionary transition to *socialism* and *communism*.

Critics will be quick to point out that Marx's predictions might seem to have been ill-founded, as capitalism has shown resilience that has kept it buoyant through the nineteenth and twentieth centuries despite recurring crisis and world war. Its defenders (who are diverse in their interpretations of Marx) would argue, in return, that his basic premise remains in place and that his descendants have explained such matters. In particular, they would point to Gramsci's notion of *hegemony* as demonstrating how consciousness is engendered by the class that dominates capitalist society so that even those who are most oppressed will, in most circumstances (but importantly not all circumstances), support the *status quo* (Forgacs 1999). Gramsci's ideas are important for social workers: they demonstrate how personal and private lives are determined by the wider forces in a society that has been socially constructed by the dominant class. They also point to how real freedom to think, act and live might be achieved through the combined efforts of 'intellectuals' able to see through capitalism's trickery (such as suitably equipped social workers) and workers fighting for justice (Garrett 2013). Gramsci updated Marx's thesis, that workers would inevitably combine together to launch a full frontal assault on capitalism (as happened, for instance, in Russia in 1917), to one where class warfare ('the war of manouevre') evolved into a more subtle 'war of position' (Hay 2006). Although these are simplifications of Marxist theory and academic debates surrounding Marx's work and his predictions continue to rage, all that follows in this and later chapters is based on an acceptance of a basic Marxist view of the state, updated by thinkers and idealists such as Gramsci. The Marxist view highlights the state's contradictory nature in advanced capitalist society: the fact that it both oppresses as well as provides benefits for the workers whose labour creates the wealth enjoyed by the ruling classes. Such contradictions are known in Marxist terms as the *dialectic*, and its use in understanding the place of the welfare state in capitalist society and its meaning in regard to the exercise of discretion will also be explored further later in the book.

The emergence, rise and decline of the welfare state

UK and US social services provision has its most direct origins in the charitable organizations of the nineteenth century that were concerned with the worst effects of the industrial revolution on the poor and disadvantaged and their children (Rogowski 2010: 30–6). However, the growth of personal social services as part of broader welfare provision should be seen in the context of the development of the welfare state after World War II. This view sees social work's fortunes as indivisibly linked with that of the welfare state. A discussion about the origins and the rise and fall of the post-war welfare state is therefore an essential starting point for locating the place of social services in contemporary society within the western democracies.

In the late eighteenth century, the wages of rural agricultural labourers in a number of English counties were so low that a top-up was provided from public funds – the 'Speenhamland System' – not unlike the tax credit system of recent times. This, however, proved a disincentive for the movement of people from the countryside to the newly industrializing cities (Esping-Anderson 1990). The result of such tensions was the Poor Law of 1834: effectively, this punished the poor who found themselves without work, by means of the workhouse system characterized in the novels of Charles Dickens. In the House of Lords, Lord Brougham defended the Poor Law in the following words:

> the only evils against which society should protect people are those the prudent man could not forsee; he could forsee old age, illness, unemployment: against those he should make provision. On the other hand society might help him in the case of accidents and violent diseases.
>
> (Hammond and Hammond 1920: 218–19)

His arguments, whilst couched in the values of nineteenth-century England, sound remarkably similar to those neoliberal politicians and theorists of our own time in their characterization of the deserving and undeserving poor: debates surrounding welfare provision have changed little in the past 180 years!

The rise of capitalism in the nineteenth century, with wealth dependent on industrial production and the exploitation of worldwide raw materials and eventual markets for produced goods, rested on the *commodification* of labour. Previously, wealth had typically been created by independent producers, but these now became property-less wage earners. The difference between what those in work could earn and what they and their dependants were considered to require in society at any given time has been the business of welfare, as have the needs of those who, for whatever reason, are workless.

The welfare state that emerged in the wake of World War II ran counter to the nineteenth-century approaches to welfare reform that are echoed today. Whilst some of its roots can be traced back to early twentieth-century Liberal reforms, such as the introduction in the UK of National Insurance and Old Age Pensions, its breadth and scale were the result of powerful social forces and competing ideologies in the wake of the defeat of Nazi Germany in 1945. Total war had necessarily involved total commitment on the part of most of the population. This was achieved through the promise of a brighter future for the ordinary masses who had suffered in the economic depression of the 1930s. In the words of Beveridge, whose 1942 report laid down the foundations of the welfare state: an end to the 'five giant evils that barred the way to progress – Want, Disease, Ignorance, Squalor and Idleness' (Bruce 1961: 72). This would be achieved through a welfare state based on a 'general principal that governments both could and should assume responsibility for maintaining a decent minimum standard of life for all citizens' (Mishra 1990: 18). Wealth redistribution, full employment and the *decommodification* of labour were fundamental to this design (Bruce 1961), leading to *Keynesian* economic policies that continued until the crisis caused by rising oil prices in the early 1970s. Soviet communism, which represented a much more revolutionary vision of wealth redistribution and whose influence had spread through the Red Army's advance to encompass most of Eastern Europe by 1945, was held in check by formal agreement between the allies over post-war spheres of influence (Hobsbawm 1995). This, however, would not necessarily ensure social peace unless a new social order, at least on the surface, could be delivered at home, and this was to be the function of the welfare state (Clarke *et al.* 2001).

Whilst welfare state provision characterized post-war capitalist western Europe, with the UK as the model, bringing with it some state enforced wealth redistribution, this trend did not spread across the Atlantic to the United States. Here, the economy was vibrant and war damage almost non-existent. The onset of the Cold War following World War II ensured that US governments could characterize the welfare state as an alien communist concept and hold it at bay (Pauwels 2002). The post-war settlement in Europe was as much about a temporary resolution of the competing ideologies of capitalism and socialism/communism as it was about military might and conquest. The creation of welfare states and their subsequent fortunes rested on the outcome of that competition. As we shall see, the economic crisis of the 1970s gave impetus to a revival of neoliberal policies; so, too, did the collapse of the Soviet bloc in 1989–90. This meant the victory, as far as the neoliberals were concerned, of anti-collectivist ideas over the collectivist ideas represented by Soviet communism and the main bulwark against their spread: the post-war welfare states in Europe (Hobsbawm 1995). There is some irony in this: trade union strength and influence is associated with welfare state development and extension (Glyn 2006; Brady 2009). At the same time, Marxist historians have remarked that the diversion of trade union energy into disputes around the extent of the welfare state has saved capitalism from more revolutionary solutions that might have been sought had it not been in place in the western European democracies (Braverman 1974). This Marxist critique of the welfare state has influenced activists in the trade unions and the political movements of the left in the UK and elsewhere: that the welfare state is, when all is said and done, a means of social control to enable capitalism to work without the class conflict that characterized western societies in the first third of the twentieth century (*ibid.*). Gough (1979: 44–5), in a UK text aimed at radical social workers that characterizes this position, writes: '[the welfare state is] ... the use of state power to modify the reproduction of labour power and maintain the non-working population in capitalist societies'. In agitational terms, this theme had, for long, been debated within the socialist movement, with no less a revolutionary than Lenin advising that those who argued against support for such reforms were suffering from an 'infantile disorder' (Lenin 1920). Would class conflict, blunted as conditions improved through the birth and growth of the welfare state, now be back on the agenda?

Those on the right of the political spectrum who viewed the birth of these welfare states in 1945 as moments of defeat were back in the ascendancy. Those social democrats who had viewed it in triumphal terms were now in full retreat and, from the 1990s onwards, their efforts were fully concentrated on accepting the main tenets of *neoliberalism* whilst trying to maintain welfare state provision within the newly-developing marketplaces (Cochrane *et al.* 2001). Marxists, as we shall see in relation to social work and state welfare provision within the welfare state, would have to rethink their position.

Social work in the welfare state

We now need to turn back to the post-war period in order to locate social work in the narrative of the welfare state. The framework of provision that emerged in the late 1940s in the UK included provision for personal social services. However, these were peripheral to other major changes, such as the creation of the National Health Service (NHS). Provision to ensure the general welfare of children was located in Local Authority Children's Services, the care of older people and the disabled was located within Local Authority Welfare Departments, and services for learning disability and mental illness were placed under the responsibility of local Medical Officers of Health. Within all three services, a major emphasis was on institutional care, rather than on support within the community. Large areas of provision – including the protection of children; and welfare services for particular groups of the disabled, such as the blind – remained in the voluntary sector, often funded by local authorities. The poor fit of all these services with the giant NHS was, and has remained to this day, a major social policy issue.

By the late 1960s, it had become clear that personal social services had to take a more central position in the still-expanding and developing welfare state. Poverty persisted despite welfare state provision, and the 'problem family' emerged as an issue. In the public eye, homelessness and poverty had been exposed as a national scandal by the left-wing director Ken Loach's 1966 TV Play *Cathy Come Home* and by a series of child abuse scandals (Ferguson 2008). Social work at that time was described by the social scientist Barbara Wootton as having a 'lamentable arrogance of the language ... in which social workers describe their activities ... not generally matched by the work they do ... . The pity is they have to write such nonsense about it' (quoted in Davies 1991: 3). Greater coordination and direction were required to ensure that families in need received appropriate support (Clarke *et al.* 2001). Improved training to a universal standard was also considered fundamental to an emergent social work profession (Younghusband 1964).

The Seebohm Report (1968) for England and Wales and the Kilbrandon Report (1964) for Scotland led to legislative changes that created Social Services Departments (Social Work Departments, in Scotland) in each local authority which brought all the services together in single agencies and, in many cases, created actual generic social work teams. Looking back from the besieged situation of social work today, it is no wonder that this has since been described as the 'high tide' of British social work (Harris 2003: 15). However, at the time, these changes were greeted critically by the radicals in social work: Simkin (1979: 15) describes the increased expectation that social work should fulfil a social policing role with families; the Case Con Manifesto (Bailey and Brake 1975: 145) saw the Seebohm reforms as the main thrust of a process designed to save money, cut specialized services, and 'place the responsibility for welfare on the *family* [original emphasis] not on the state'. Corrigan and Leonard (1978: xi) took a kinder view of what they saw as a Fabian socialist promise behind the reforms, but blamed their ineffectualness on lack of resources, bureaucracy, weak professionalism and resistance to community participation. Whatever the view taken, the years following the implementation of the Seebohm and Kilbrandon reports saw ever-increasing numbers of social workers coming into the new departments and, in broad terms, ever-increasing resources – even if these were never able to match demand (Titmuss 1968; Harris 2008). The left, as we shall examine further in the exploration of the radical social work movement of the 1970s in Chapter 2, was still suspicious of the welfare state.

Social work, by the early 1970s, was seen to occupy an important role in bolstering the family as the main organ of society; services were there to address increasingly visible perceived failures in family functioning (Clarke *et al.* 2001). The main tools were psychodynamic casework theories that placed responsibility for improvement on the individual, although peppered with recognition that social conditions themselves bred problems. On a 'modernist' basis that society is inherently rational, social workers had a role in helping their clients out of the worst aspects of poverty and deprivation through psycho-social and systems theory interventions that were generally believed (but not, as we have just noted, by the Radicals) to have the power to 'problem solve' (McDonald 2006: 31).

Neoliberalism and attempts to dismantle the welfare state

By the mid-1970s, the optimism that had accompanied the years of growth was under threat. The sudden rise in oil prices following the Arab–Israeli conflict in 1973 brought already failing western economies to their knees. Keynsianism was no longer seen to be delivering and the vacuum was taken up by the old school advocates of the free market. The post-war boom had come to an end, giving way to attacks on rising public spending. During the course of the 1970s, the Organisation of Economic Co-operation and Development (OECD) ditched Keynesianism in favour of free markets. This is illustrated by a focus on the UK, but a similar account could be given for many western democracies. In 1976, the Labour government in the UK accepted the recommendations of the International Monetary Fund (IMF) in order to secure a loan to head off inflationary crisis and abandoned full employment as a policy goal. Conservative governments, from 1979, pursued policies of welfare state reduction, lower taxes, privatization and free market economics (Crouch 2011). This was only possible by a vigorous approach to tackling trade union power through a dismantling of its power base. This was achieved by way of wholesale de-industrialization and closures through the course of the 1980s, leading to the destruction and impoverishment of entire communities. However, due to its popularity, plans to reduce the welfare state were not as successful as governments would have wished and a compromise position was arrived at whereby delivery was increasingly contracted out, with new infrastructure built, such as schools and hospitals mortgaged out to private companies through Public Private Partnerships (PPPs) (Mishra 1990; Glyn 2006). Industrial production has almost entirely left the UK, as shown by a balance of payment deficit for manufactured goods in the UK, reported by the Government to be £59.8 billion in 2010 (quoted in Elliott and Atkinson 2012: 210), leaving behind a residue of increasingly squeezed public sector and low-paid service sector jobs. Conversely, as a result of the onset of neoliberalism in the UK, the financial sector has grown disproportionally, and fantastic wealth has been accumulated by a relatively small group of bankers and associated financial specialists.

During the course of the early years of the twenty-first century, the success of UK financial markets rested increasingly on easy credit to poor people. In 2008, the bubble burst when the worst excesses of such practices led to the collapse of a number of financial institutions in the US, swiftly followed by threats to major UK banks, with economic collapse only avoided through part nationalization (financial bailout) of institutions such as the Royal Bank of Scotland and the Northern Rock Building

Society. One might have thought that the collapse of the banks and their bailout by public money would have resulted in a rethink about the trajectory of neoliberalism. However, as Crouch explores in his book *The Strange Non-Death of Neoliberalism* (2011), the opposite has happened, and the fact that the public purse has been depleted to prop up financial institutions that continue to reap huge rewards for those who run them has only served to result in a further attack on the public sector, which is considered more unaffordable than ever. The 2010 general election in the UK was characterized by argument between the major political parties over how much needed to be cut and from where, rather than any suggestion that perhaps the market-led system should be voted on because of its drastic failures. By now, neoliberalism, represented by a dominant theme of 'austerity' as a common interest, had come to represent common sense and could not be questioned. From that time onwards, there has been an almost universal acceptance that cuts, wage freezes and unemployment are necessary in order to revive the economy. The Keynesian solutions of former times, which were almost the opposite in terms of their effect on the poor and disadvantaged, were well and truly out of the picture.

The results of such policies on the welfare state in western democracies have been drastic; at the time of writing, austerity is expected to last until at least 2020. Services that remain are being further marketized, including universal health and education services. Welfare benefits for the poor are being cut and made dependent on willingness to seek work and accept anything going irrespective of skills, choice or absolute unavailability of work because of where the claimant happens to live. The neoliberal consensus in government takes it for granted that the cost of welfare benefits, used by the poorest and most disadvantaged in society, have to be reduced. Ironically, Thatcher's UK governments of the 1980s were so unprepared for the social costs of their de-industrialization policies that access to some welfare benefits – and, in particular, sickness benefits – were used to massage unemployment figures (Jones 2011). In more recent times, ever-increasing controls pressurize those who are dependent on benefits to get into work – *workfare* has replaced welfare (Dominelli 2002; Lymbery 2004; McDonald 2006). This trend has increased as the post-2008 bank collapse crisis has raised unemployment levels. In a particularly vicious twist, UK Conservative Party leaders proposed in 2012 to end all housing benefit (assistance with rent for those out of work or on very low incomes) for those aged under 25 years – a policy that will increase homelessness, misery within already pressured families and inevitably increase social disharmony.

As we shall see later in this chapter, very successful attempts have been made by government in the UK to encourage those on low incomes who are in work to blame those on benefits for the nation's financial deficit.

This can be seen in events over a short period in early 2012: on 23 January, the Government's Welfare Reform Bill (supported, in the main, on its passage through parliament by the Labour opposition) was debated in the House of Lords. The main premise of this legislation was to reduce housing benefit eligibility and cap benefit levels at £26,000, regardless of family or individual circumstances. Critics pointed out that this would result in homelessness and increased disadvantage at a time when jobs were not to be found because of continued recession. The estimated savings this would produce to the state amounted to £300 million, or a loss of £83 per week to the 67,000 families affected (*Herald* 2012). On the same day, coalition Prime Minister Cameron defended the government stance in a well-covered media event where he addressed a group of English workers (presumably earning little more than the minimum wage) who applauded his statement 'Why should families get this much when no one works?' (*BBC News* 2012a). The irony of this coming from a millionaire leading a cabinet of millionaires seemed to have been lost. The poor were being told that the country's problems were the fault of the even poorer, neither group actually having anything to do with the collapse of the banking system in 2008.

At the same time as apparently blaming the poor, the UK government talked of clamping down on the bonuses being paid to certain company chief executives and, in particular, those from banks that had so recently been bailed out with public money. This made it seem as if the rich, too, were being made to pay; however, the comparison was not a convincing one. Those who stood to lose out on enormous bonuses are still very wealthy and able to use every available loophole to avoid contributing through taxes to the welfare state. The cost of tax avoidance was estimated to amount to £120 billion in 2011, whilst the cost of benefit fraud was thought to be £1.5 billion (Public and Commercial Services (PCS) Union 2011), and the savings the Welfare Reform Bill would achieve would amount to £300 million.

The loss will be felt in the poorest communities in the UK, representing not only a loss of spending power to the families concerned, but also less spent in the local economies where they live. Conversely, the rich, who benefit from the bonus culture and widening inequalities, spend their money in the UK's wealthier areas, as well as the world's tax havens. Meanwhile, the average cost of the bank bailout per family in the UK was estimated to be £40,000; this represents a total of over £850 billion that would be taken out of public expenditure on the poor to cover banking losses incurred by the mistakes of the nation's financial elite (Lammy 2011: 221). Some comparative costs to the UK economy are featured in Figure 1.1 (note that the figure relating to savings from the welfare reforms and the figure for estimated benefits fraud are too small to feature in the chart).

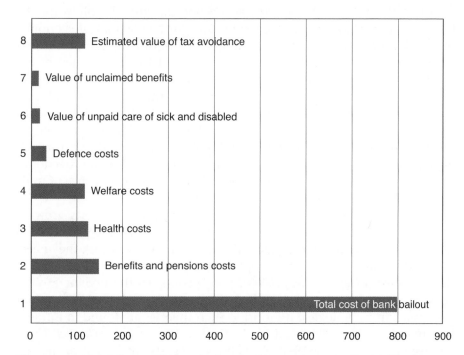

Figure 1.1 UK public spending and related policy comparisons (in £ billion)
Sources: 1 Lammy 2011; 2, 3, 4 and 5 ukpublicspending.co.uk; 6 Carers UK 2012; 7 and 8 PCS 2011.

It would be wrong, despite the realities of neoliberalism described, to consider that the welfare state is inexorably sinking. This is not the desire of most western governments, including the 2010 Conservative led coalition in the UK: leader David Cameron has stated that the welfare state was for 'those who have no other means of support, or who have fallen on hard times' (Prime Minister's Office 2010), a remark similar to that of Lord Brougham in 1834 (see p. 4). The National Health Service remains too popular for such a strategy, as demonstrated by its celebratory place in the Olympic Opening Ceremony in London in August 2012. There are, however, more aggressive neoliberals waiting in the wings, whose intent certainly is to embark on the dismantling of all state welfare provision: they are to be found in the Republican Party in the US, and on the right of the political spectrum elsewhere, including in the Conservative Party in the UK (*Guardian* 2012b).

The consequences of neoliberalism

Neoliberalism is far more than just a means by which to manage the economy. It has its roots in the *laissez-faire* capitalism of the nineteenth century and in the philosophies that justified the class divisions and wealth differences that accompanied economic growth following the industrial revolution. As developed by the Chicago School of economic theorists after World War II, it influenced the right-wing political thinking that emerged from the inflationary crises of the 1970s. One of the chief prophets was Milton Friedman, whose ideas influenced Margaret Thatcher in the UK, and also inspired the anti-collectivist and pro-market right wing military coup in Chile in 1973, that saw thousands murdered, tortured, imprisoned and exiled. However, as we have seen, in most of the world such changes were achieved democratically through exploitation and manipulation of economic crisis, with the 'freedoms' that were introduced through such policies being at the expense of trade union influence and power, and basic state provision.

As the US is the home of neoliberalism, it follows that its growing influence has resulted in the spread and acceptance of US ideas on a range of matters surrounding advertising – what people think they need, the market, mass media, how people see themselves – and, of concern in this chapter, poverty (Brady 2009). Poor people, so the neoliberal view goes, remain poor as a result of bad choices and problematic behaviour that stems from biological inferiority. Such theories are found in influential, popular and widely-read books (in the US) such as *The Bell Curve* (Hernstein and Murray 1994). This book suggests that black people are cognitively inferior to white people (*ibid.*: 315), and has rightly been condemned as racist and unscientific. However, its overall findings conform to the neoliberal view that, if people are poor, it may not be their fault but that there is little the rest of society can do about it and the best plan is to get out there and behave as selfishly as possible: a tradition known as *individualism*. Brady (2009: 17–19) cites a number of reasons why individualist accounts are problematic and inaccurate: they fail to explain the positive effects of widely varying factors such as culture, neighbourhoods, political parties and trade unions; they ignore relations among people and the context of those relations; and, finally, that empirical evidence finds such explanations wanting. Brady cites the fact that, if Sweden has less poverty than the US, it must be because Swedish people have greater intelligence – a premise that is naturally unlikely to be true. Biology, he rightly concludes, does not explain the differences between people. However, despite this, the idea that the welfare state blunts individual enterprise and initiative, and breeds dependency, has found its way into the common currency of government, and the reduction of welfare provision is the consequence.

The drive to put everything into a marketplace and reduce the workings of the state is central to neoliberalism. Supporters argue that, as choice and competition are fundamental, the individual ends up with a more efficient service that they have chosen, rather than services that happen to be available. It is this, arguably positive, aspect of neoliberalism that lies behind the move towards *personalization* in social services discussed in Chapter 5. However, this attack on collective provision has consequences for the way in which services are delivered. In the UK, it used to be commonplace to hear of the 'public sector ethos': a notion that public sector workers gave of their best because they were delivering a public service, rather than one driven by a profit motive. This has been derided in recent years and an opposing view taken: one in which business methods, in fact, increase motivation and improve outputs. Again, the evidence behind this assumption is lacking: commenting on a study of deregulated and privatized bus services in London, Glyn (2006) notes that, as private operators can generally only compete in the marketplace by reducing terms and conditions of staff, this brings a declining sense of employee commitment to the service.

What is true of bus drivers is probably going to be true about home care staff, most of whom now work in the UK for private sector agencies. A US website from a private homecare provider lists signs of poor morale amongst staff and how these might be remedied; suggestions include 'absence of commitment', 'lack of enthusiasm' and 'when low morale becomes a rallying point' (which probably means that trade unions might become involved). Remedies include easing up on deadlines, recognizing good employees, a 'surprise breakfast' for staff, and 'frame a photo from an event, and send it along with a note, to your staff' (Seniors Homecare 2012). The list, of course, did not include improvements to pay and conditions.

To justify their stance, Friedman and other theorists of neoliberalism have argued that reducing state interventions and opening up the free market reduces poverty (for example, Friedman 1962: 169). This is only one of many explanations of how poverty occurs and might be avoided, stretching across to the other side of the spectrum to Marxist accounts that suggest that poverty is an inevitable outcome of capitalist competition. The evidence suggests that poverty occurs and reoccurs in societies that diminish their own responsibility to eradicate it (through such means as collective organization in communist-inspired societies such as the former Soviet bloc, or the welfare state in western countries) and reduces when such responsibilities are taken on again. This was the case in Canada (Brady 2009: 4) and, conversely, poverty is now increasing in countries such as the UK where neoliberal policies are in the ascendancy (Wilkinson and Pickett 2010). It is also the case in eastern European states, such as Poland, that formerly enjoyed a high level of basic health and welfare services (but, of course, lacking basic freedoms), but where the neoliberal project is now well under way (Hardy 2009: 132–3).

The proponents of neoliberalism talk up freedom from state interference as a prime object of their cause (Freidman 1962) and, again, the evidence points in the other direction: poverty and its consequences require a disciplined state with increased resourcing to institutions such as the police, immigration control, the prison system and the military (with bloody foreign interventions to defend such 'freedoms') (Pollack 2010). In neoliberal discussion, freedom is associated with competition and aggression, which are described as natural tendencies in human beings, premises strongly challenged by critics (Crouch 2011: 29).

Neoliberalism has resulted in a concentration of wealth at the top end of society and burgeoning inequality. As with the decline of the welfare state, this is linked with a reduction in trade union power (Wilkinson and Pickett 2010). Inequality has risen steadily in the UK since Thatcher came into government in 1979, and recent estimates show that the richest 20% of the population have seven times as much wealth as the bottom 20% (*ibid.*: 17). This places the UK near the top of the league for inequality amongst the developed countries. The US is at the very top: in Manhattan, New York, the wealthiest 20% of residents earned 52 times more than the bottom 20% in 2000 – a figure that exceeded wealth difference in Namibia, where people regularly starve to death (Dorling 2011: 286). Poverty is, of course, a relative definition determined by the wealth available in a particular society:

> A house may be large or small; as long as the neighbouring houses are likewise small, it satisfies all social requirement for a residence. But let there arise next to the little house a palace, and the little house shrinks to a hut. The little house now makes it clear that its inmate has no social position at all.
>
> (Marx 1847: ch. 6)

This classic quotation explains why inequality creates such social division and social upheaval, and Marx lived long before the days of mass advertising and the deliberate creation and manipulation of consumer demand. Wilkinson and Pickett (2010), in their popular title *The Spirit Level*, list and explain the consequences of inequality: the more unequal a society is, the more likely it is to experience drug misuse, lower life expectancy, health problems, stress and mental health problems, poor eating and obesity, poorer education performance, high prison population, teenage births, murder and poor trust between people. In other words, many of the issues social workers deal with are more likely to be found in the UK than Scandinavia, where inequality is less prevalent.

Social division is such an important trait of neoliberalism that it is worth examining in more detail. Inequality can be justified if those at the bottom of society are looked down on as inferior, and responsible for their own poverty and circumstances. This has occurred throughout history, with the privileged elite justifying their power and wealth, whether through accident of birth, or enterprise, by their social and even biological superiority over others. Within living memory, the extremes of such beliefs resulted in the murder of entire ethnic and disabled groups in the Nazi Holocaust. In the UK, as we saw earlier, the onward march of neoliberalism in the 1980s depended on breaking the power of the trade unions and, in particular, powerful groups of workers who enjoyed a proud heritage such as the mineworkers. Says Owen Jones of this process:

> Margaret Thatcher's assumption of power in 1979 marked the beginning of an all-out assault on the pillars of working class Britain. Its institutions, like trade unions and council housing, were dismantled; its industries, from manufacturing to mining, were trashed; its communities were, in some cases, shattered, never to recover; and its values, like solidarity and collective aspiration, were swept away in favour of rugged individualism.
>
> (Jones 2011: 10)

In a powerful narrative, Jones goes on to explore the difference in media treatment accorded in 2007 and 2008 to the disappearance of two young English children from contrasting backgrounds: Shannon Matthews and Madeleine McCann. One came from a working-class West Yorkshire background (whose family characteristics might be familiar to children and family social workers) and the other from a solidly middle-class background and whose parents were well-respected doctors. On the basis that both girls were each as innocent as the other, whatever the culpability or otherwise of their parents, Jones concludes that journalists conformed to their own class prejudices and stereotyped images of the actors involved and that this affected coverage and, consequently, public perception. This resulted in the vilification of Shannon's mother, Karen Matthews, who was seen to represent an underclass of people beyond understanding and hope, rather than a victim of post-industrialization and lack of requirement for either her or the community in which she lives. On the other hand, Madeleine McCann's parents were treated generally with a deserved dignity and respect. In his book's subtitle, Jones calls this process *The Demonization of the Working Class*. The rest of society is encouraged to blame the victim with a general aspiration to join the middle classes: there is something wrong with us if we are either unwilling or unable to rise above origins of which we might once have been proud.

What is not in doubt is the extent to which hegemony prevails: ideas that, whilst challengeable, are generally believed to be fact, and perpetuated as such through the media, as well as government. Hegemony has other salient aspects that set the victims of neoliberal society against each other. It typically reinforces stereotypes that perpetuate dominant ideas. An example would be the manner in which sexual stereotyping is an undercurrent that, whilst easily ridiculed, is commonly held: examples being that women secretly want to be raped, gays and lesbians are perverts who are dangerous to children, poor people breed like rabbits, black men want to rape white women, disabled and older people have no sexuality. Such ideas reinforce the belief that everyone is inferior and degenerate compared with young, white, bourgeois males (Mullaly 2010).

Whilst working-class deviants such as Karen Matthews are demonized, a different set of rules seems to apply to those at the top of society who disgrace themselves through personal failings, or even outright criminal behaviour. Only two from the many hundreds of Members of Parliament who, through the *Daily Telegraph* investigation in 2009, were found to have defrauded the public, through what were widely regarded as false expenses claims, were actually imprisoned, in contrast to those at the other end of society found guilty of benefit fraud. Since then, the antics of top bankers who continue to receive large bonuses despite the failure of their banks continue to draw widespread criticism, although remaining within the law. As Ferguson points out (2008: 45), the notion of 'personal responsibility' that is so fundamental to neoliberalism sounds hollow when coming from the mouths of many of our politicians.

Exercise 1.1

Challenging media images of people

Think of two contrasting working-class characters known through popular media – they could be fictional (from TV, book or movie), or real life.

What makes one confirm prejudices and stereotypes, and the other challenge them?

Neoliberalism's effects on social work

Neoliberalism has had a very direct effect on the delivery of social work, permeating every agency and workplace; 'austerity' is now the main driving force for reductions in state provision (Jordan and Drakeford 2012). Some of neoliberalism's manifestations are bizarre and extreme: in the UK, a government representative has stated that social work could be undertaken on a voluntary basis by 'retired City bankers and ex insurance brokers' (quoted in Garrett 2013: 2). More seriously, the introduction of a business- and market-based approach to public services brought what has been described as *New Public Management* (NPM) to social services. This incorporated a number of concepts that are now accepted features of any organization: a shift by public sector leaders from policy to management; interest in quantifiable performance measurements and appraisal; the break-up of structures into business units purchasing services from one another; market testing and tendering, rather than automatic in-house service provision; an emphasis on cost-cutting, output targets, rather than input controls; short-term contracts for staff, rather than 'jobs for life'; and the use of regulatory mechanisms, rather than legislation to ensure quality (McDonald 2006: 69). This latter point has been much criticized from within the profession. Soon after the death of Peter Connelly in the UK in 2007 (a child killed by his mother's partner, despite social work and health interventions with the family), following an inspection, the London Borough concerned received a sought-after rating of 'three stars'. This confirmed the view that such target-based scorings were of little value in the real world (Munro 2010). This case later became the subject of huge media attention followed by adverse reaction against particular staff members involved. Other features of NPM include a break-up of fixed salary arrangements in favour of monetary incentives and performance-based pay: these features have yet to come to the UK.

The usual description of the management style associated with NPM is *managerialism*, an influence said, in the Radical Literature, to be all pervasive. The main premise of this book is to demonstrate that all is not yet lost and that practice outside the parameters set by these trends is still possible. One of the features of managerialism is the idea that everything can be broken down into discrete problem categories, allowing the introduction of strict eligibility criteria, with fixed access to assessment and, from there, to costed and care-managed services (for example, the Department of Health report *Modernising Social Services*, 1998). This tends to disregard the complexity of service users' lives and reduce them to compartmentalized problem areas, negating the contribution of the structural causes of their situations such as those by-products of neoliberalism discussed earlier (Harris 2003: 58).

Research Box 1.1

The effects of managerialism

In their study of a remote area where generalist community-orientated practice provided by a generic social worker had been celebrated in previous research, Martinez-Brawley and McKinlay (2012) noted that services had largely gone over to 'top-down markedly bureaucratic structures' with 'silo' provided specialisms. They found 'fatigue and resignation' about changes and cautioned policy-makers to note that these can 'affect the stamina, enthusiasm and ultimately the effectiveness of workers at front line levels' (*ibid.*: 1621).

A constant feature of managerialism is organizational change, as if change could, in itself, address problems arising from ever-increasing need and diminishing resources. In line with this, the combined Seebohm and Kilbrandon social services departments in the UK (see p. 7), have increasingly fragmented into merged departments alongside other local government services, such as education or housing. Within such departments, restructurings occur with regularity, leading to changes in management, flatter structures and short shelf-lives but well-financed retirement packages for senior managers (in contrast, usually, to those available to frontline staff facing redundancy). The managerial framework emphasizes leadership, but this is not about helping empower frontline teams to confront poverty and social dislocation: it is about top-down assurance that government and senior management agendas are being followed, especially those that are associated with 'change' and 'efficiency' – the common euphemisms for cuts and privatization. As we can see in Research Box 1.1, policy-makers and their acolytes tend to view lack of enthusiasm about change as an obstacle requiring removal and are more likely to seek personnel changes than to listen to staff (this is discussed further in Chapter 5).

The structures associated with service delivery are also being affected by neoliberalism in the UK. In a turn towards the market, encouragement is being given to the establishment of social work assessment and care management provision by private companies or groups of independent social workers, funded by local authorities and typically accessed through their call centres. It is a sad sign of the times that the monthly magazine of the British Association of Social Workers (BASW) now has a column devoted to such developments, characterized by lavish praise and the language of welcome 'change', rather than criticism of cuts and privatization of public services. In the US, this is now widespread: a recent and generally excellent standard text on community social work (Hardcastle *et al.* 2011) has an entire chapter devoted to how social workers can apply themselves to the marketplace. In the UK, such business approaches are now the norm in the voluntary sector, a very different situation from that in the past, when they were seen as repositories of good and innovative practice away from the constraints of the state sector.

The practice models preferred within the NPM are associated with evidence-based practice (EBP), a concept borrowed from science and applied widely in medicine. The basis of EBP is that interventions should be based on what works, as typically tested in medicine in random control trials (RCTs), offering value for money and predictable outcomes. Such neat formulae rarely fit in social work settings, where human beings and the relationship-based nature of social work produce so many variables (Frost 2000). Whilst there is an attraction in the idea that interventions should be soundly based, increasing client wellbeing and professional accountability, there is a danger that a focus on outcomes can lead to an unreasonable method of evaluating the individual performance of staff (MacDonald 2006). However, despite criticism based on the notion that EBP often fails its own criteria for consideration as an effective tool (Gray *et al.* 2009), it is probably here to stay in one form or another: constructive ways of incorporating such approaches will be touched on in subsequent chapters.

Linked with EBP as an important feature of managerialism and the NPM, is the emphasis within social work on managing risk, rather than addressing social problems and their causes (Stanford 2010). In fact, the change in the direction of the welfare state from one of universal provision to that of minimizing risk is seen as fundamental to neoliberal ideas (McDonald 2006). The concept of risk implies that, with the right tools, risk can always be assessed and then managed, and that, if something goes wrong, then it is the individual practitioner who must be at fault. This lies at the heart of formal child protection inquiries such as those that have followed well-publicized tragedies such as Victoria Climbie – a child from the Ivory Coast killed through neglect and violence by the aunt and partner she had been sent to for a better life – and Peter Connelly (p. 17) in the UK in recent years. Such events are usually followed by disciplinary measures against staff perceived as having failed to protect the child concerned through poor assessment of risk, or other misapplication of procedure. An acknowledged expert in this field, Eileen Munro, remarks that this emphasis encourages organizations to 'transfer or dissipate blame by means other than reducing harm to children, namely seeking to reduce institutional risk without reducing societal risk' (Munro 2010: 1146). The defensive culture that arises from NPM inevitably results in the establishment of more rules and procedures in an effort to identify risks and manage them, rather than the exercise of discretionary early judgement about whether such a process is required (*ibid.*: 1147). What is needed, the critics of the NPM-based approaches argue, is a greater emphasis on supervision, reflection and education (UNISON 2009a; Broadhurst *et al.* 2010). This theme will be returned to in Chapter 8.

The means by which senior managers of social services organizations impart the ideas that stem from the NPM have produced a whole new language that is sometimes bewildering to listen to and, in general terms, is only understood clearly by those who subscribe to it (the military language that has become the norm in everyday social work will be touched on in Chapter 2). The rest of us, however, are forced to endure it in our daily working lives. The following is not untypical of the content of mission statements, strategy papers, directors' blogs or any of the other means by which social work's leaders wrestle publically with the problems of the world:

 The strategic vision of this Council is to provide efficient and modern services that fit with what our residents tell us they want and require. To provide this, we will embrace change and promote a culture of best practice within a right-sized workforce and a local marketplace. This will enable us properly to target delivery of service from within a vibrant and mixed local economy. Within our Social Services, we will facilitate the empowerment and choice of our users through a vigorous transformation of current service-led and fixed provision to one of personalization.

Roughly translated, this means:

We, as your Council, have decided that service delivery as presently provided is unaffordable and we expect our staff to believe that this is the case. On the basis of the cheaper services that we have convinced some of you that you really require, rather than those most of you have come to expect, we intend making cuts. This will involve loss of jobs and privatization, so that private business can make profit from our difficulties. Within Social Services we intend to pass responsibility for the organization of support for the most vulnerable people from us to them, and we will close our day centres and other associated directly-provided services.

These are hypothetical statements but I do not feel the first is untypical of output from the jargon-infested world inhabited by many senior managers and top council officials. What is increasingly clear is that candidates for top jobs in local authorities and voluntary organizations are required to speak in these terms if they want to stay in the club and get on with their careers. Commonly understood concepts such as 'meetings', 'money' and 'people affected' are replaced with 'symposium', 'revenue stream' and 'stakeholders'. This, of course, results in the creation of a self-perpetuating and unreal world that is far removed from the lives of service users, or the pressures of those tasked with supporting them. Within this world, acceptance of 'change' can render (as we saw earlier: p. 18) very short shelf-lives for such managers: within the logic that accompanies this notion, loyalty, service and experience count for little. This increases the *alienation* of employees who neither recognize, nor are recognized, as individuals by the senior managers who oversee their activity (apart from the odd one picked out for a special mention or award). Ironically, it is common for expensively paid-off redundant senior managers to reappear within the Councils that no longer required them as external and well-paid 'consultants' offering advice on further 'change'.

The NPM has also introduced business methods to social work practice that have become part of the everyday managerial approach to issues. A common example is the use of SMARRT (Specific, Measurable,

Acceptable, Realistic, Results-Orientated and Time Specific) criteria to assess the value of interventions. This, as we shall see in Chapter 7, can be adapted as a tool for progressive practice (Hardcastle *et al.* 2011).

It is questionable, however, whether uncritical acceptance of mainstream ideology and the language used to try to persuade of its normality and good sense, fits with the values that social workers train for and regard as fundamental to practice. In the UK, the main professional association, the BASW, include in their code of ethics the principle that:

> Social workers, individually, collectively and with others have a duty to challenge social conditions that contribute to social exclusion, stigmatization or subjugation, and work towards an inclusive society.

(BASW 2012a)

This notion is central to the Radical Literature. It needs to be spelled out in very clear terms that the principal welfare agenda concerns cuts in public spending, pay restraint and attacks on welfare benefits and pensions. All are means by which the vast majority of people in the UK that are dependent on low and modest incomes are being made to pay for an economic crisis that was caused by the actions of those who control the financial markets, most of whom continue to reap huge rewards for what might, in a more enlightened society, be regarded as criminality. This is not just my view, or even that of the authors of the Radical Literature – it is shared in part by the present Governor of the Bank of England, Mervyn King (*BBC News* 2011). The new language and managerial discourse discussed above helps organizations gloss over realities that might have been more openly addressed and challenged in the past.

We need to note at this point that attitudes engendered by neoliberalism have reached a stage in its heartland, the US, where 'The decay of social work skills and commitment has accompanied the erosion of community spirit and social commitment … . It is reflective of the "me-ism", the libertarian, self-centered philosophy currently rampant, and the social isolation and fragmentation of contemporary America' (Hardcastle *et al.* 2011: 10–12). This should be a warning to us all, and suggest that more enlightened forms of practice – radical approaches – are more important than ever, if social work is to survive as a value-based profession.

The 2011 riots: myth and reality

In highlighting the effect of neoliberalism on social division, this chapter has made reference to two popular contemporary commentaries on the state of UK society (Wilkinson and Pickett 2010; Jones 2011). Wilkinson and Pickett describe the toxic effect of growing inequality, and Jones describes how the working class has been socially and economically marginalized since Thatcher's defeat of the trade unions in the 1980s. These factors collided dramatically in the summer of 2011, with a scale of rioting not seen in the developed world since the race disturbances in US cities in the late 1960s. Fear and loathing of the 'underclasses' are nothing new, and it has always suited ruling elites to characterize poor people as a threat to the values and norms of the rest of society: the social violence and damage inflicted on the poor by very unequal societies will always result eventually in mindless anti-authority violence and riot (Jones and Novak 1999). This is, indeed, what happened with the English riots of 2011, with a response that confirmed the fear that such damage to property represented for those who control society.

Karen Matthews, the vilified mother of Shannon Matthews referred to on page 15, and working-class people in general, are required as consumers and customers to buy goods to maintain the economy even though they may no longer, post-2008 credit crunch, be required to borrow money from the banks to the extent they had been. The neoliberal society in which we live overwhelms us with advertising that is designed to make us feel inadequate and failing unless we keep consuming. In his widely-read examination of the problems of contemporary UK society *Injustice: Why Social Inequality Persists* (2011: 279), Daniel Dorling calls this process 'fostering acquisitive individualism'. Children and young people typically spend twice as much time in front of a TV screen as they do in the classroom, where they are 'schooled by marketing consultants to believe their worth is determined by what they wear – that they "need" the new trainers or the platinum chain to keep up' (Lammy 2011: 32). Low pay, reducing benefit levels, joblessness and all the other features of poverty make these must-have items somewhat inaccessible to those at the lower end of society; and these are the people most likely to be exposed to uncritical consumerist advertising. The middle classes are more likely to benefit from an educated scepticism towards consumerism encouraged by the Church and other moderating civic influences in society. This is the real impact of inequality, as outlined earlier from Wilkinson and Pickett's studies, and as noted by Marx (p. 14) in 1847.

The spark to the English riots of 2011 was the shooting dead in London of Mark Duggan, on 4 August, by police officers belonging to a unit dedicated to combating gun crime in the black community. Within hours, his home area of Tottenham, the scene of a previous riot following police action in 1985, was rife with rumour that had spilled out into an impromptu protest march on the police station. The march was orderly and, by all accounts, a legitimate action with peaceful intentions organized by his family and friends. However, its aftermath saw disorder by large numbers of young people that involved the looting of shops in the area. The next night, similar disorder had spread to various areas of London and, over the next few days, to Manchester, Salford, Liverpool and Nottingham. Disorder on a lesser scale was also reported in Kent, Thames Valley, Bristol, Leeds, Huddersfield and Gloucester. Initially, the police and authorities were taken by surprise, and seemed powerless to protect property and prevent the violence associated with the disorder. However, national coordination was put in place involving the deployment of police from as far away as Aberdeen in Scotland and, within five days, the riots had come to an end.

The immediate response from government and establishment was to condemn the rioters: statements from ministers described them as 'feral' and representing an 'underclass' (Lammy 2011: 55). Prime Minister Cameron talked of Britain's 'broken' and 'sick' society (*ibid.*: 54) and observed that the rioters represented 'criminality pure and simple' (Klein 2012: 133). The sentences that have followed on those convicted of crimes associated with the riots (2000 people, by October 2011) have reflected these views: a mother of two who took no part in the disorder, but accepted a pair of looted shoes from a friend, received a six-month prison sentence, as did a young man who took a bottle of water from a smashed up Lidl store (*Guardian* 2011a).

The rioters themselves came predominantly from the poorest parts of the country (*Guardian*/LSE 2011). Respondents to research into who had taken part saw themselves as reacting to (in declining order): poverty (86%), policing policies (85%), government policy (80%), unemployment (79%), the shooting of Mark Duggan (75%) and other issues (*ibid.*: 11). When asked about whether they felt integrated into British society, only 51% agreed, as against 92% of the population as a whole (*ibid.*: 24). The targets of the rioters were the same all over the country: predominantly, the businesses that retail sought-after consumer goods that accord status, such as mobile phones and trainers (*ibid.*: 28). It is also worth noting that the riots followed a winter of social disorder in the UK (and elsewhere worldwide) involving students and anti-cuts protests, in which these same dispossessed youth were on the edge, if not directly involved (Mason 2012). These were linked to the Arab Spring, which saw Middle-Eastern dictatorships that had been considered secure toppled by popular uprising (*ibid.*).

The riots were an indirect reaction to the inequalities brought about by neoliberalism and, as such, are likely to reoccur (81% of the 237 participants who took part in the *Guardian*/LSE survey thought this). They represented an individualized reaction that saw people coming together for the common purpose of 'shopping for free' (*ibid.*), rather than an organized and planned social/political protest. Winlow and Hall (2012) argue that the problems that result from inequality experienced by working-class people in the UK are now individualized and not subject to a common political reaction that might, in the past, have been provided by the labour and trade union movement, with whom there was mutual identification. For these commentators 'consumerism acted as a perverse default position that achieves its primacy only in the absence of more appealing or progressive alternatives' (Winlow and Hall 2012: 162). Elsewhere in the world, the effects of neoliberalism are being met with a more unified and politicized response, as seen in anti-global protests and the reactions on the street to austerity policies in Greece and Spain in 2011/12. Socially progressive forces have a responsibility to assist the channelling of anti-authority feeling into effective protest. This may be a tall order for individual social workers, but these could be legitimate aspirations for the organizations of which they are members (their professional associations and trade unions), as we shall see in Chapter 8.

Exercise 1.2

Confronting popular myths

Someone in your work or study setting announces that the cause of social problems in modern society is widespread drug misuse.

Should this be challenged and, if so, why?
What approach could such a challenge take?
What arguments might be used to promote your case?

This exercise might be best conducted in a group setting.

Alternative strategies

This is a book about social work, so it is not appropriate to lay out detailed stalls for all the alternatives to neoliberalism. It just needs to be emphasized that there are alternatives. These range from those represented by previous generations of social democrats and expressed through the Keynesian policies that, as we saw earlier in this chapter, characterized the welfare state up until the 1970s (which are those still promoted by the trade unions in the UK and elsewhere in Europe, where austerity policies are biting hard), through green politics to the more fundamental changes in society promoted by Marxist-inspired socialists. Common to these ideas is an earnest belief that the natural resources of the world are running out quickly, climate change issues are pressing, and that the market-based policies of neoliberalism are doing nothing serious to address these crucial issues. We live in a global economic system where a large proportion of power lies not with nation states but, rather, with worldwide corporations who care little for national borders or democracy. Alternative political and economic systems are not an option, but a necessity. Social workers have a unique insight into neoliberalism's consequences and so have a civic duty, as well as a right, to participate in legitimate political change processes.

It is no longer 'radical' to write off the welfare state as a method of saving capitalism from class conflict. That argument might have had a resonance during the boom years after World War II but, in a situation of recurring economic crisis characterizing most global economies since the 1970s, the welfare state has to be viewed as an essential cushion for the majority in societies across the world who are not benefiting from the present economic order – its extension is a legitimate agitational demand. The need to defend the welfare state from the onslaught of neoliberalism is the theme of a book largely authored by two of the Radical Literature writers, Ferguson and Lavalette (Ferguson *et al.* 2002). Whatever one's vision might be of a future where the resources of the world are shared more equally, we live in the here and now: it is out of the struggles of the present that the future will be shaped, a message emphasized by these writers. The contention of this chapter, in line with the radical mission of the book, is that the welfare state, as an institution, has to be promoted and defended as the best guarantee that inequalities are reduced and that basic welfare provision is laid on for people that includes good social services.

stop and think

- Some newly-qualified social workers express disappointment that they do not find the value base for social work they learned on their courses amongst colleagues and managers when starting out in practice. Why might this be?
- Organizational theory considers that those who resist change are barriers that have to be overcome through a series of methods ranging from education and participation to coercion and manipulation (Hughes and Wearing 2007). How might you respond to organizational methods to reduce resistance to change if this involved cuts in essential services?
- Is it the business of social workers to involve themselves in politics? Think of arguments that you might use to counter suggestions that social workers should not concern themselves with political issues.

- Modern social services development in the UK and the western democracies is linked with the rise and decline of the welfare state as an institution.

- The decline of the welfare state (and the threat to social services) is associated with the rise of neoliberalism and its universal acceptance as the only available method of economic and social organization of society.

- Neoliberalism has, itself, introduced widening inequality and a long list of societal disorders that arise from such inequality, ranging from individual health deficiencies to riots.

- Whilst multiple oppressions exist, their presence still links to fundamental power differentials in society that relate to class position and division.

- The marketization of social services associated with neoliberalism has brought about a decline in the quality of social services camouflaged by the language and ethos of organizations.

- Neoliberalism has been achieved through a rise of individualism and at the cost of social organizations such as left-wing political parties and trade unions that might have provided a collective resistance and alternative.

- Problems of resource scarcity and climate change mean that alternatives to neoliberalism are a necessity and that this remains the greatest contemporary challenge for mankind.

taking it further

- Brady, D. (2009) *Rich Democracies, Poor People: How Politics Explain Poverty*, New York, Oxford University Press. Written from a progressive social democratic US standpoint, using research this book highlights the importance of welfare states and their place in reducing poverty, and promoting fairness and justice.
- Crouch, C. (2011) *The Strange Non-Death of Neoliberalism*, Cambridge, Polity Press. This book provides a useful account of the history, growth and consolidation of neoliberal ideas from a mainly UK perspective.
- Dorling, D. (2011) *Injustice: Why Social Inequality Persists*, Bristol, Policy Press. A popular and very readable account of why inequalities are perpetuated and why we seem to allow this.
- Jones, O. (2011) *Chavs: The Demonization of the Working Class*, London, Verso. This is an angry book that correctly places the reduced state of the working class in the UK, and how the contempt

associated with the 'Chav' stereotype serves the interests of those who benefit from rising inequalities.

- Jordan, B. and Drakeford, M. (2012) *Social Work and Social Policy Under Austerity*, Basingstoke, Palgrave Macmillan. A detailed account of the impact of austerity on social policy and its implications for social workers.
- Wilkinson, R. and Pickett, K. (2010) *The Spirit Level: Why Equality is Better for Everyone*, London, Penguin. Absolutely essential reading for understanding how inequality adversely affects the whole population.

2 Radical Theory

Overview

The first chapter explained the growing presence of inequalities between the rich and poor in society, and their consequences in the UK and western democracies. This chapter will look at the theories that help to inform how social workers who understand and accept such explanations deal with their role in society in terms of a radical practice. That role, as indicated in Chapter 1, is primarily about managing risk within a managerially-driven environment. Anti-oppressive practice (AOP), its antecedents and its offshoots provide a basis for forms that challenge managerially-driven social work and so are discussed here. Ideas surrounding community social work practice, social pedagogy and other theories that also facilitate radical approaches, will be covered in ensuing chapters. Chapter 1 also explained the rise of social work in the welfare state up until the 1980s, and the critiques of the radical social workers of that time. This will be the starting point of this chapter, before we embark on a journey through the progressive theories that have emerged in the years since. These will be described chronologically as they became influential, but each section will also bring them up to date as far as their contribution to a contemporary practice is concerned. The coverage of and emphases within these ideas will reflect a view on their applicability in the real world of social work, especially in state or state-sponsored settings (rather than idealized ones). This will culminate in a radical synthesis of theory that will be demonstrated in the practice-based chapters to come. The chapter will end with a summary of the positional point we will have reached.

A word about theory ...

There can be a tendency amongst practitioners to dismiss theory as something studied during professional training, which is replaced by practice knowledge once the real world of work is entered. Whilst this book rests on its own use and applicability in real-life practice, it is not dismissive of theory. Workers are often required to justify their actions in terms of theory (as well as in terms of evidence base – a concept that will be touched on later in this chapter), and this can apply to work required for a legal setting, or simply whenever it might be challenged. Howe (1987) suggested that the tendency to place practice knowledge above theory was wrong because theory is part of everyday life, and that theoretical ignorance was an excuse for poor and dishonest practice. Garrett (2013) makes a similar point, stating that even those who claim that common sense and experience are driving factors are, in essence, stating a theory about such matters. Even 'radical non-intervention' (doing nothing at all), is, as will be seen in this chapter, based on a theory. Theories can predict what might happen in a given situation and so explain matters to us and help us plan what we do. What we do may seem instinctive but it is generally based on a theory, even if that theory has been forgotten, or was never known to us in the first place, because it is simply what we have been told to do if we come across a particular set of circumstances. So, in social work, theories explain why we choose (or are pointed towards) a particular method or model. The able social work practitioner should be aware of what they are doing and why they are doing it, and not simply follow a set of procedures or instructions as if they were fixing a mechanical object (theories to do with human beings and social conditions should not claim to be universal in the same way as, for instance, the law of gravity).

In social work, there is a body of theory that is based on a view that the way society is organized is beyond the scope of the profession, and that practice is about maintaining people within the economic and social system; such theories are to be found in psycho-social models and approaches and might be described as mainstream, traditional, conventional or contemporary. They generally follow a course that seeks to change the individual within their environment, or within the immediate environment that the person occupies (for example their home, or their family) so that they cope better. Typifying anti-oppressive criticism of mainstream approaches, Dominelli writes: 'enabling people to adapt to the status quo in more purposeful ways is a major preoccupation' (2002: 61). In similar vein, McDonald comments that such theories 'deny categories of class, race and gender that continue to represent virulent social divisions ... and destabilize[s] the emancipatory and progressive intent of social work' (2006: 91).

Whilst these explanations are required here to explain how progressive approaches are necessarily different from mainstream ones, there are differences with the former that also require noting. I might have preferred keeping debates between *post-modernism* and *modernism* out of this book (I have never met a social worker with any real interest in them) but, if a way forward to a truly aspirational radical practice is to be found, this, too, has to be given some coverage in this chapter on theory.

At this stage, it is also worth postulating on the interaction between theory and practice. This matter is influenced by the context of work, and Chapter 1 discussed the challenges associated with employment in declining public service settings within states whose policies are determined by neoliberal agendas. Schon (1983) describes a cycle of reflection and action that is generally accepted as useful within social work literature. Charles and Butler (2004) develop this to demonstrate how reflection-in-action, which brings theory into meaningful and confident practice, can be used to develop transactions with service users that defy managerial prescription: 'even when workers consciously use theories or practice models, they remain dependant on the fusion of judgement, performance and intuition … such reflection-in-action is the antithesis of the rigid application of mechanistic procedures and techniques' (*ibid.*: 65). The artistry, skill and use in relationships this necessarily involves will be discussed more fully in Chapter 7. Praxis, to use the term employed by the Marxist philosopher Gramsci, describes how any theory can only be said to be true when it is applicable and useful in practice – theory and practice are related to one another and indivisible (Gramsci 1982).

Social justice and oppression

Before looking at theory and its application, some explanation is required for the term *social justice*. This will be found throughout this book and within any social work literature that has critical, radical or emancipatory intentions and pretensions.

Social justice is a contested term and not one that can be assumed to enjoy acceptance as an aspiration for social work (Davis and Garrett 2004). It implies that not all citizens are equal, and that social workers and those concerned with social policy issues should concern themselves with reducing material inequalities and with wealth distribution issues (Mullaly 2010). This is enshrined in professional association codes (such as that of the BASW in the UK and the National Association of Social Workers (NASW) in the US) that reflect the IFSW statement on social justice:

> Social workers have a responsibility to promote social justice, in relation to society generally, and in relation to the people with whom they work. This means:
>
> 1 *Challenging negative discrimination* – Social workers have a responsibility to challenge negative discrimination on the basis of characteristics such as ability, age, culture, gender or sex, marital status, socio-economic status, political opinions, skin colour, racial or other physical characteristics, sexual

orientation, or spiritual beliefs. *In some countries the term 'discrimination' would be used instead of 'negative discrimination'. The word negative is used here because in some countries the term 'positive discrimination' is also used. Positive discrimination is also known as 'affirmative action'. Positive discrimination or affirmative action means positive steps taken to redress the effects of historical discrimination against the groups named in clause 4.2.1 above.

2 *Recognising diversity* – Social workers should recognise and respect the ethnic and cultural diversity of the societies in which they practise, taking account of individual, family, group and community differences.

3 *Distributing resources equitably* – Social workers should ensure that resources at their disposal are distributed fairly, according to need.

4 *Challenging unjust policies and practices* – Social workers have a duty to bring to the attention of their employers, policy makers, politicians and the general public situations where resources are inadequate or where distribution of resources, policies and practices are oppressive, unfair or harmful.

5 *Working in solidarity* – Social workers have an obligation to challenge social conditions that contribute to social exclusion, stigmatisation or subjugation, and to work towards an inclusive society.

(IFSW 2012a)

The reality, of course, is that these matters are not something that many social workers would recognize and not ones discussed in mainstream literature. In fact, so alienated are most workers in contemporary state systems from an ability to put these (and the other ethical considerations contained in the IFSW and associated codes) that one commentator (perhaps influenced by the radical pessimism that will be discussed in Chapter 3) has likened these codes to being 'as useful as a chocolate teapot' (Petrie 2009). I am registered with the Scottish Social Services Council and their code of practice, which dictates the principles to which my employer and I are supposed to adhere, makes no mention of 'social justice' (SSSC 2009). However, it is basic to this book that social justice should be the concern of social workers who believe that their service users are not responsible for their place in an unequal society and for the consequences that flow from this. In this sense, we should remind ourselves constantly of the principles of the IFSW and use them as a basis to use social work to promote social justice, however difficult that may be. This is one of the premises of this and any other book on radical social work and its possibilities.

'Oppression' is linked with social justice and is also a term found throughout the book. A discussion of its meaning will be found in the section in this chapter that considers anti-oppressive practice.

The difference between Critical practice and Radical practice

Social workers interested in the theory underpinning progressive practice will draw on two broad traditions that have similarities and overlaps, but which arguably point in different directions: Critical practice and Radical practice (Ferguson 2008). Their similarities lie in broad agreement that service users are not the architects of their own misfortune but that other forces are responsible for oppression and division in society. Both are transformative in a broad sense. Where they disagree is exactly what those oppressive forces are that require change and how they should be tackled. Unfortunately, because these theories ultimately pull in different directions, it is difficult to find common ground between them in terms of their contribution to changing the sources of oppression. In crude terms, the pursuant of Radical theory will take an essentially Marxist view that the problem with society is its economic class base and that this requires challenge, if the problems and issues of clients are to be resolved. The adherent of Critical theory is more likely to see oppression as being caused by various forces that might include those who exploit for economic reasons, but will also look for oppression caused by identity, whether as a woman, a person from an ethnic minority, or a person's sexual preference or other difference. This will target anyone considered to benefit from whatever oppression is under scrutiny: this might be men if the oppression is that suffered by women, or white people if the oppression is that suffered by people of colour. The major difference, therefore, is in where they lead and the emphasis given: Radical approaches assume that society requires fundamental socialist change (but would not ignore identity-based oppression); Critical approaches require that the target oppression is addressed in some way (but they also might not ignore structural causes).

Whilst Marxist-based Radical theory is considered *modernist*, in that its roots lie in the nineteenth-century Enlightenment that saw all things as contributing to a whole, Critical theory is considered *post-modernist*, in that it rests on a belief that there are no overarching explanations: we all construct our own reality and there are therefore no global solutions to the world's problems. Webb (2010) concludes that post-modernist approaches tend to diminish the politics of redistribution in favour of the politics of recognition (or identity politics) and that this adversely influences social work approaches to their detriment. Post-modernist belief is partly born out of the pessimism that has accompanied developments in society in recent decades, with the growth of individualism and the lack of any serious challenge to global capitalism. It is interesting to note that recent challenges to global capitalism (evidenced by the Arab Spring of 2011 and the worldwide anti-capitalist student movement of the same year that saw the London headquarters of the ruling Conservative Party trashed by demonstrators) are seen by one commentator to mark the end of post-modernism as a viable concept and a return to class-based social change as a possibility (Mason 2012).

Critical (post-modern) practice seems to be most to the fore in Canada (as exemplified by Mullaly (for example, 1997) and Leonard (for example, 1997) who was previously associated with the 1970s UK radical social work movement. In Australia, critical or post-modernist practice is associated with Fook (for example, 2002) and Healy (for example, 2000). In the UK, it is best exemplified by Parton and O'Byrne (2000). Critical social work with a capital 'C' should not be confused with 'critical social work': in the UK, this latter term is used to describe reflective practice that asks social workers to be critical of themselves and what they do (Webb (2010) describes this difference). The UK definition can be found in Adams *et al.* (2002), where critically reflective practice is described in various settings, and a children and family example of the genre would be H. Ferguson (2011). These critical approaches are compatible with both types of transformative practice debated here but, in themselves, do not extend to resistance to structural oppression (Webb 2010).

Mullaly (1997) believes that the use of the *dialectic* method (see Chapter 3) allows the strength of the Marxist approach to be used alongside the aspects of post-modernism that allow us to look at the various oppressions that impact differently on individuals. He argues that to opt for either Marxism or post-modernism because of the arguments that are summarized above results in potential contributions from either being omitted, with consequent disservice to the oppressed. This is an argument that is both cogent and persuasive, and one that forms a premise to this chapter so long as primacy is given to Marxist notions of class and attention to the base (the requirement for fundamental change in the way society is organized): in other words, a Radical Social Work and method that is informed by post-modernism, rather than a Critical Social Work informed by Marxism. Ultimately, this book is about practice and, if theory helps us take forward transformative practice, it should not be disregarded because of its origins or associations. This is Mullaly's proposition and it is echoed in Dalrymple and Burke (2006); it is not so far from Marx's view when he famously stated that, whilst philosophers had interpreted the world, the point was change it (Marx 1845).

Having given an overview of these differences, explanation is now required as to the emergence of the different progressive traditions and their contribution to a contemporary radical practice.

The radical social work movement of the 1970s

Radical approaches based on a belief that the conditions from which social issues arise require change have a long history in social work. In the 1930s, some social workers in the US aligned themselves with movements of workers providing militant opposition to the effects of the depression (Ferguson 2008). In general, the radical movement in the US has suffered from the virulent anti-communism that has pervaded US politics since the 1950s but writers such as Galper (1980) and Burghardt (1996, 2010) have attempted to maintain the tradition. In Canada, the development of training around 'structural' theory – for example, Moreau (1979) – was influential from the late 1970s onwards. This attempted to provide an umbrella taking in Marxist radical approaches and the emerging politics of identity around *feminism* and anti-racism (Mullaly 1997) and, in this sense, tries to combine Critical and Radical approaches. These perspectives have continued through the work of Baines (2007) and Mullaly (2010). In Australia, Throssell (1975) embodies the 1970s tradition of Marxist influenced theory, whilst Fook (1993, 2002) demonstrates its diversion into Critical Practice.

Radical roots in the UK can be traced in social work back to the nineteenth century (Lavalette and Ferguson 2007). In the 1970s, UK radicals came together in the *Case Con Collective*. This loose grouping held conferences and put out a quarterly magazine, *Case Con*, between 1970 and 1977. Their background can be traced through the general militancy of the period and the aspirations that rose in the late 1960s through the anti-Vietnam war movement and the anti-establishment events in Europe (especially France) in the summer of 1968. Case Con involved a number of left-leaning practising social workers and academics who were disillusioned with the failures of their agencies and the mainstream ideas of social work to address the inequity and poverty associated with capitalist society in the UK (Weinstein 2011). Case Con spawned the text edited by Bailey and Brake, *Radical Social Work*, in 1975, Corrigan and Leonard's *Social Work Practice under Capitalism* in 1978 and Simkin's *Trapped Within Welfare* in 1979. Statham's *Radicals in Social Work* (1978) takes a less strident tone and, instead, asks important questions of aspiring radicals; it ends with a cautionary note that the radicals of one generation are turned into liberals by the next as the impossible for one becomes possible for another. That accurately predicted how some of the aspirations of the 1970s generation, such as anti-racism, have become mainstreamed, whilst some of 1970s radicals went on to become senior managers in agencies or leading academics in universities. However, as we saw in Chapter 1, little might actually have changed for the better out in the world inhabited by the poor and disadvantaged.

These 1970s texts share a Marxist-based class approach to the problems experienced by social work clients, and all urged readers to engage in activities at work to battle the effects of capitalism and, in the words of the Case Con Manifesto (Bailey and Brake 1975: 144–7), to 'join the struggle for a workers' state'. Corrigan and Leonard urged readers (in the words of champion boxer and anti-establishment figure Mohammed Ali) to work within the bureaucracy but 'float like a butterfly and sting like a bee' (1978: 155). Differences in emphasis reflect the politics of the authors/editors: Bailey and Brake were non-aligned socialists influenced by far-left and libertarian (anarchist) politics, and their contributors were from similar and mostly academic backgrounds; Corrigan and Leonard were from a Communist Party background, so their emphasis, with its lengthy Marxist explanations, critically reflects a view that was sympathetic to societies in the Eastern bloc of Soviet Russian dominated states; Simkin, like several of the Radical Literature authors of today, was a member of the Socialist Workers Party (whose International Socialist forebears had been instrumental in setting up Case Con), and his book reflects their analysis of the prospects for socialists at that time.

The emergence of the radicals in the 1970s occurred at a particular phase in the history of social work within the welfare state in the UK. Social work was expanding: its educational base, heavily influenced by the emerging academic discipline of sociology, was inviting students to look critically at capitalist society (Jones 2011) and the trade union movement was at its membership peak and power. Whilst Case Con disappeared, the influence of radical social workers in the white-collar trade union NALGO continued and grew, resulting in strikes across the country for pay re-grading for social workers in 1978/79, and for residential social workers in 1983. Neither was totally successful and, by the mid-1980s, with the defeat of the miners, trade union power was in retreat with the onslaught of neoliberalism (as we saw in Chapter 1). Radical social work was down, but not out.

The influence of Marxism as the basis for approaches to social work issues did not disappear and continued to be found in Canadian structural theory and some of the other critical methods discussed in this chapter.

Radical non-intervention theory

It used to be fairly common to hear social workers, whose failure to see a service user for a long period had not led to bad outcomes and perhaps even the opposite, state humorously that they had been practising 'radical non-intervention'. Few probably realized where this had come from, and its origins have been largely forgotten. The practice theory concerned was not just an excuse but, rather, an important radical position, developed by the US sociologist Schur in the 1970s (Schur 1973). The theory holds that most young offenders appearing before the US courts were not very different from their non-offending peers, except that they were predominantly working-class and had been caught. Schur held that many would embark on offending careers because of the labelling process engendered by their presence in the Court system, as this would now be what was expected of them by parents and teachers, effectively spoiling their life chances. Their peers who had been involved in similar behaviour but had not been caught were, meanwhile, allowed to grow out of such behaviours and move on with their lives. Schur contended that as many young people as possible should be kept out of the system and their issues dealt with in more imaginative ways – hence radical non-intervention. He also argued for the de-criminalization of minor offences that were only crimes because of the age of the young person.

The current experience of black youth in Britain's inner cities would suggest that differences in policing policies at local level still exist and that these continue to criminalize certain groups of young people in the way suggested by Schur. In more general terms, his idea that longer-term outcomes for interventions should be assessed when addressing immediate issues and that, in some cases, this might bring into question whether such interventions should take place at all, holds true in many areas of social work. Whilst this 1970s contribution to theory was of its time and much has thankfully moved on in youth justice, it still has some relevance to a critical view of social policy and social work practice.

Anti-racist practice

The decline of the radical movement in the 1980s and the onset of neoliberalism saw those activists who wanted to look beyond mainstream psycho-dynamic and individual explanations for the plight of their clients seek explanations elsewhere. Marxist class-based theory was criticized for its alleged inability to recognize oppressions other than the one that concerns the ruling elite and the workers they oppress (Dominelli 2002). The idea that the *status quo* needed to be altered because of its systemic inequality was replaced for many with the notion that it needed to be transformed because of its inherent racism, sexism or homophobia (Trainor 1996). Langan explains: 'The collectivist outlook of the earlier radical movements was undermined by a new emphasis on difference and rights' (1998: 213). A number of social work academics launched their writing careers on the basis of the ensuing interest (and key place in social work education) of these notions of anti-racism and feminism. The place of identity politics in social work practice has since been debated hotly, as noted earlier in this chapter (see Williams 2011).

Anti-racist practice developed in the UK in the 1980s from models first theorized in the US – in particular, the notion that 'racism equals prejudice plus power' (quoted in Langan 1998: 213). One of the particular forms that such practice took was the assumption by some exponents that, unless you were black, you were racist, and that this had to be acknowledged and then eradicated through 'Race Awareness Training' (Dominelli 1988). This was taken on by agencies and often delivered in a top-down and confrontational fashion that sometimes humiliated and belittled participants. Vigorous anti-racism training was, of course, much easier to address than structural issues of poverty. A further problem with such an emphasis was that it made racism seem a problem to do with the attitudes of individual white people, ignoring the institutional racism that, for example, affected police attitudes to the murder of Stephen Lawrence in 1993. Although supported by progressive elements within social work at the time, this approach is now looked back on with some embarrassment and in its 'cruder forms has been largely abandoned' (Langan 1998: 213).

The fact that it took until 2012 to bring to justice the murderers of Stephen Lawrence, a young black person killed in London by a racist gang in 1993, underlines the continued importance of anti-racist approaches to public service delivery, including social work. Black and ethnic minority populations tend to inhabit the inner cities and are always amongst the poorest in society. The experience of their members is often of a society dominated by institutions that are led by an ethnic majority (white people) that is ignorant and unsympathetic to their situations and experiences, and sometimes racist. Reaction to such prejudice in urban areas with concentrations of such populations resulted in the inner city riots of the 1980s and contributed to the riots of 2011 (Lammy 2011).

It is also now recognized that anti-racist practice must extend beyond skin colour and the issues of black and Asian people: probably the most misunderstood of minority groups in Britain (and the subjects of widespread discrimination) are indigenous Gypsy travellers. Their right to be regarded as a minority ethnic group recognized in law has only been accepted in recent times (Cemlyn *et al.* 2009; Turbett 2010). In the 2000s, there has also been a focus on the situation of asylum seekers and refugees. All these groups are the target of far-right extremists (in the UK, the British National Party and English Defence League), and anti-immigrant attitudes are in the mainstream of politics throughout Europe.

Anti-racism therefore involves a variety of potential approaches in social work. The emphasis, however, is on challenging racism and racist views, and using laws and policies to promote anti-racism (Bhatti-Sinclair

2011). In social work, there is also an emphasis on avoiding racial stereotyping that might affect service delivery. An example of this might be an assumption that families of South Asian origin always look after their own older people, which might lead to a diversion of resources away from support to an older person being assessed. Questions of cultural relativism (basing practice interventions/non-interventions on ideas about difference in cultural norms) will be explored in the Human Rights section of this chapter.

Feminist practice in social work

As with anti-racist approaches, *feminism* as a particularized social work approach came to prominence with the decline of class-based radical approaches in the 1980s, and criticism of radical practice as being 'gender blind' (Day 1992: 12). In some of its forms, feminist practice represented a diversion from the structural causes of oppression in a way that was also the case with anti-racist practice. Bricker-Jenkins describes feminist practice as aspiring to go 'beyond a non-sexist or women's issues orientation, and beyond a grafting of feminist perspectives onto a humanistic core' (1992: 272). It would be difficult to gloss over the reality and effects of the oppression of women: whether through their role as unpaid 'housewives' central to the notion of the family in capitalist societies, their predominance in low-status and low-paid work (including employment in the care sector), their exploitation by the state as unpaid carers of the sick and disabled, or their place as the victims of domestic violence and sexual abuse perpetrated by men.

All these symptoms of women's oppression have a daily interface with social work, both for women as clients and as social services staff members. One of the early feminist criticisms of women in social work was that they failed to work in a women-centred way, and that they reinforced gender stereotypes and even pathologized women who came into contact with agencies (Orme 1998). However, the reaction from feminists was to develop narrow forms of practice that centred on consciousness-raising, self-recognition and separateness, exemplified by the practice of referring women to groups that had no other purpose or function. These methods were seen by socialist feminists to offer little of use to women, especially working-class women, in the daily reality of their lives. This was not to deny the appropriateness of challenges to male power and hegemony in society, as represented by gender-specific language that reinforced such power (chairman, fireman and so on), or the absence of women in particular occupations or the boardroom.

Socialist feminists, contrastingly, linked the oppression of women to capitalism. They were therefore able to analyse that replacing men with women in positions of power did not threaten the system in whose interest they were kept in the home and/or low-paid employment. Socialist feminists recognized that 'To tell a woman user she is oppressed is no more liberating than labelling her as depressed, unless there are ways of changing the situation' (Orme 1998: 225). Their analysis moved away from the notion that feminist practice was about women working with women about women's issues and also enabled some focus on work with men as both perpetrators and victims of women's oppression.

The theory of *patriarchy* is an essential one for social workers, accounting for the dysfunction often seen in family life, and the absence of economic power and influence by women over what happens both in their lives and those of their children. As we shall see in Chapter 4, awareness of patriarchy will help practitioners avoid holding women entirely responsible for the welfare of their children when the men in the household are invisible to staff who try and engage with them. The socialist feminist position recognized that women's experiences of 'the sexual division of labour are mediated by their class position' (Day 1992: 13), which explains why working-class women are the most powerless to deal with male patriarchy. Feminism has been criticized by Marxists for its weakness in recognizing men as also oppressed, in situations where they might be oppressing women through, for instance, domestic violence. This is not to condone male violence or dominant power, but to acknowledge its roots in a society which encourages masculinity but then denies its expression to poor males at the bottom of society (Ferguson and Lavalette 2004).

White (1999) brings together feminist views that consider that pure feminist practice in statutory settings is an impossibility because of constraints on practice. This pre-supposes that feminist practice has to be based on equal relationships and common and unique goals based on a mutual sharing of women's experience – a situation that might only be found in alternative women's services. However, a place for anti-discriminatory practice that takes account of feminist analysis and theory is considered important in state settings (White *ibid.*; Penketh 2011). What might this mean in practice on a day-to-day level? Women fill roles in society that are often determined by their gender, and this can predetermine their need for welfare and protective services: mothers of children who require support through child protection services, as carers demanding services, or as older people in need through ill health and the ageing process. Practice has to challenge views that see such women as having 'individualistic or moral character deficiencies' (*ibid.*: 45). It has to understand that, as most such women are likely to be poor, their situation is the result of the neoliberal policies defined in Chapter 1, which have reduced the welfare state, overseen economic collapse, raised unemployment and poverty, and increased inequality. These are issues that will be returned to in Chapter 4, which is practice-based and concerns children and families, and Chapter 5, which concerns adults.

Anti-discriminatory practice

The 1960s and 1970s saw the introduction of anti-discriminatory legislation to the UK some considerable time after the 1948 United Nations Universal Declaration of Human Rights had declared that:

> All human beings are born free and equal in dignity and rights. They are endowed with reason and conscience and should act towards one another in a spirit of brotherhood.
>
> (Article 1, quoted in Ife 2008: 230)

This started with Race Relations Acts, which attempted to deal with racial and religious discrimination in 1965 and 1968; the Sexual Offences (Homosexual Reform) Act of 1967, which legalized homosexuality (lesbian relationships had never been outlawed); an Equal Pay Act in 1970 and the Sex Discrimination Act in 1976, both of which tried to tackle discrimination on gender grounds. The other important liberalizing legislation of this era was the 1967 Abortion Act, which legalized abortion under certain circumstances and gave women some limited control over their bodies. In 1995 came the Disability Discrimination Act, which sought to outlaw discrimination against people on the basis of disability in terms of employment, or the provision of goods and services. This, and much of the earlier legislation, was subsumed into the Equality Act of 2010, which also effectively outlawed ageism. However, just like the United Nations Declaration of 1948, these pieces of legislation seemed, then and since, difficult to enforce and easily ignored, even by public bodies, and none could be said to have completely addressed the problems they set out to tackle. Gender inequality, equal pay issues, lack of opportunity for disabled people, homophobia and age discrimination all continue. The responsibility for issuing guidance and enforcing equal rights legislation was taken over by the Equality and Human Rights Commission (EHRC) in 2007, but they, too, have found the task of implementing civil (rather than criminal) law difficult. Similar slow progress is recorded in other western democracies as evidenced by ongoing policy debate concerning gay marriage.

Anti-discriminatory practice has its roots in the social work radical movement of the 1970s. Just like anti-racist and feminist practice, it also represented a watering-down of aspirations. Additionally, it represented a realization that legislation could not tackle attitudes, and that this required a proactive approach. Its most passionate advocate in the UK has been Neil Thompson, and he has argued that its purpose is to ensure everyday practice takes account of the multiple oppressions experienced by disadvantaged groups (Thompson 2001). Some critics extol anti-oppressive practice as a more robust alternative because it is based on a notion that challenges the roots of discrimination, rather than just its symptoms. They suggest that, as anti-discriminatory practice is largely based on pursuing the legislative requirements outlined above, it is limited in its scope to challenge the sources of oppression (Dalrymple and Burke 2006). This is denied by Thompson with the defence that, as discrimination leads to oppression, you have to tackle the one before you can address the other (*ibid.*: x).

Anti-discrimination should be defined through an understanding of the concept of citizenship because it implies that not all members of society should be dealt with equally. Citizenship was considered important by Beveridge when he drew up plans for the welfare state (Dalrymple and Burke 2006) because it describes how the relationship between the state and the individual is mediated by public institutions such as the police and the law. The welfare state would provide the institutions that would ensure that citizens were able to contribute fully by addressing the 'five giants' (poverty, poor housing, unemployment, poor education and disease) that impeded personal growth. However, citizenship has always been a contested concept and, whilst it has connotations of membership, rights and empowerment, it also describes notions of obligation, duty and exclusion (*ibid.*: 78). Those asylum seekers and others who live in the UK who have been granted visas to stay and who want UK citizenship now have to pass an examination that the vast majority of UK born 'citizens' would fail. Citizenship does not imply equal access: that, as we saw in Chapter 1, is determined by class and place in society.

Citizenship as a notion that seemed to spell out basic rights was much propagated by the governing Conservative Party of John Major in the early 1990s. Through the almost forgotten 'Citizen's Charter', the citizen was seen as a consumer with rights to redress if he or she felt they had cause for complaint. However, the reality was that concepts of citizenship were 'familialist and normalising' and that the typical citizen was a white, middle-class male (Dominelli 2002: 29) – the 'Mr Angry' of phone-in radio shows and newspaper letters pages. The aim of citizenship-type charters often seemed to ensure that road cones were not placed unnecessarily on motorways, or that bins were emptied efficiently by councils. What does remain from this period are the complaints procedures now required of every organization: these uphold the consumer's right to complain and outline response times (for the complaint) if a delivered service fails to meet expectations. However, they cannot address services that no longer exist, or have never existed, and so are narrow and consumerist in their scope. Such charters and procedures fit perfectly with the neoliberal agenda and its aim of replacing inefficient public services with privatized ones (Dominelli 1998; Dalrymple and Burke 2006). The notion of individual freedoms and associated rights to such freedoms, are basic to neoliberalism and its mistrust of complex state provision (the 'nanny state' which encourages dependency). However, there are charters that uphold the rights of minority and oppressed groups and these can be of use as tools of social work practice (Dominelli 1998). Examples in the UK range from the officially sponsored Charter of Rights for People with Dementia in Scotland (Scottish Government 2011a) to the Charter of Rights for Women Seeking Asylum, a campaigning tool aimed at making the UK Government treat women asylum seekers with fairness, dignity and respect (Asylum Aid 2008). In 2012, UNISON, the principal trade union for social workers and social care staff in the UK, launched an Ethical Care Charter aimed at tackling the worsening of standards accompanying the widespread practice of outsourcing care at home services to the private sector (UNISON 2012a).

The welfare consumerist vision of the neoliberals contrasts strongly with the call made in the same era for user empowerment through collective action for change (Mullender and Ward 1991). Whereas the former were calling 'for the right to buy choice and expect certain standards in a mixed economy of care, the user movements and its advocates were calling for control over the design and delivery of services' (Mullender and Hague 2005). These two contrasting models have become much blurred in the subsequent discussion about 'user participation' and 'user involvement' to the extent that this process has become a tokenistic aspect of managerialist control within social work and the public sector generally. Many public sector workers and community activists can quote examples of 'consultations' that were anything but: I recall a Health consultation where I live about changes to Primary Care service delivery; about twenty people turned up to the local public hall for an advertised presentation and question/comment session. After an hour or so of criticism from almost the entire audience, the senior manager present announced that the changes would almost certainly go ahead anyway as only a tiny proportion of the population affected had turned out!

At the same time as promoting citizenship, the Tories in the UK exploited concern about the spread of HIV and AIDS in order to outlaw the 'promotion of homosexuality' in schools through an amendment to the Local Government Act (section 28) in 1988. This grossly homophobic legislation was not repealed until Labour's second term in office in 2003 (Miles 2011). More recently, Conservative-inspired attempts to roll back the nanny state – with its rules and regulations governing every walk of life and its obsessions (from their point of view) with 'political

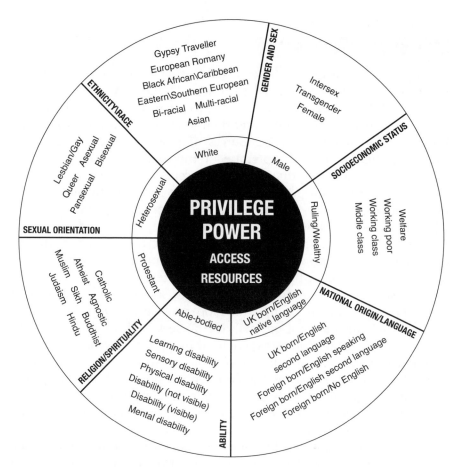

Figure 2.1 The web of oppression

Source: Mullaly, B., *Challenging Oppression and Confronting Privilege*, 2009.

correctness' – have been limited. They concern a largely unsuccessful attempt to curb the health and safety laws that try to keep people safe at work and the relaxation of planning laws to allow middle-class house-owners to extend their houses by eight metres without Council planning permission. Laws underpinning anti-discrimination remain largely intact. It would be hard to argue that anyone signed up to the regulatory social work codes of conduct should not take an interest in and try to tackle the discrimination experienced, for example, by lesbian, gay, bisexual and transexual people (LGBT), or disabled people – in fact, anyone who is outside the central circle described in the Web of Oppression that features in Figure 2.1. However, it is difficult to see how this differs significantly from the all-embracing anti-oppressive practice that will be described next.

Anti-oppressive practice

Anti-oppressive practice (AOP) emerged in the 1990s from the developments of the previous two decades (Dominelli 1998). In order to begin to understand AOP's breadth and complexity, it seems reasonable to start by trying to define oppression, and then to locate oppressed groups and how they interrelate with the sources of power in society. As stated earlier in this chapter, the premise of this book is to base such an account on an analysis that sees this, essentially, in class terms. The neoliberalism that now pervades most western societies still accounts for fundamental differences of interest between those with power and those without. In Marxist terms, the ruling class of capitalists and their allies differ from those who produce the wealth and create profit, or who are excluded from the process by dint of disadvantage. The latter groups include the oppressed who appear in this chapter.

Oppression is a multi-dimensional and socially-constructed term (Dalrymple and Burke 2006) which operates and reinforces itself at various levels in society. Dominelli (2002) sees it as a continuum: this stretches from oppression as experienced by particular groups and their individual members, through accommodation and acceptance of subjugated status, to resistance and then on to non-oppression, where egalitarian relationships are based on acceptance and celebration of difference.

Figure 2.1 explains oppression in UK society, and how it links to power and influence. With slight differences, a similar diagram could be made for any western democracy. In general terms, power and wealth (through access to resources) are found at the centre of the circle and, the further you are from that position, the more likely you are to lack these things and to experience oppression. An individual might encounter oppression for more than one reason – they might be gay, physically disabled and also be black. This combination accentuates oppression but it will be the one (or more) that denies wealth which could be regarded as most dominant. According to Mullaly (2010), from whom this model is borrowed, it is important to recognize that oppressions exist as a total system within this web, and not in only one dimension. The web does not rule out the possibility that an individual might be in a position, through wealth, to negate an aspect of oppression that would otherwise push them out of the central ring. In general terms, a place in the centre will not be possible unless one has wealth and, even there, security of position will depend on presence in two or more aspects of the inner circle central domains within the model. Thus, the individual who is gay, black and disabled might enjoy privilege and access to resources through wealth, but their situation will be precarious and they are still likely to suffer oppression: the further the reason for the oppression encountered is from the centre of the diagram, the less likely it is that wealth will offset that oppression.

The model also requires us to take account of the impact of oppression on the individual: again, the further one is from power and wealth at the centre the more profoundly this will be experienced. Our understanding of this notion is helped by the work of Frantz Fanon, an Algerian psychiatrist who took part in the struggle against French colonial power in the 1950s. He saw and studied the impact that colonization had on the indigenous population: their culture was suppressed by the domination of European values in much the same way (but far more profoundly) that Jones describes the effects of neoliberalism on working-class people in the UK (see Chapter 1). Many took on the values and views of the dominant power, forgetting their own heritage, values and cultural traditions. Over time, many moved beyond such compromise and accommodation either to take flight, or to fight back (Fanon 1967).

The Canadian writer Donna Baines defines anti-oppressive practice as 'An umbrella term for a number of social justice orientated approaches to social work, including feminist, Marxist, post-modernist, Indigenous, post-structuralist, critical constructionist, anti-colonial and anti-racist' (2007: 4). This is an extensive list based on North American developments in radical thinking and not all will be covered in this chapter. It covers recognition of the place of First Nation peoples in approaches to practice, a consideration that applies also to Australia and other nations colonized by Europeans in the eighteenth, nineteenth and twentieth centuries.

AOP also critiques and questions the role of professionalism in defining the social work task: how workers see themselves and wish to be seen. The managerial developments arising from neoliberal accommodations have been accompanied by a shift away from 'indeterminate' areas requiring exercise of professional judgement, to 'technical' roles prescribed by rules and procedures, weakening claims to professional status (Lymbery 2004: 52–3). Managers are now the dominant voice, and are often keen to display this authority and importance by particular dress codes and other refinements that remove them even further from the world inhabited by service users. In an antidote to this, Mullaly (2010: 120), in the manner of Alcoholics Anonymous, suggests a 'ten-step plan' to help wean social workers away from damaging professionalism – which he suggests is conservative, self-interested and orientated towards the *status quo*. The ten steps include 'I admit to believing that I had no useful skills unless I called myself a professional', 'I admit to calling myself a professional in an attempt to cover up my insecurities and self-doubts' and 'I came to convince myself that wearing expensive clothes and driving a fancy car did not separate me from my resource-poor service users'. Pinkerton (2002: 98) suggests that ideologies are expressed in many ways, including the way in which a social worker dresses, and that this is as important as the ideas discussed in a case conference.

Similarly, AOP also questions the use of language common in social work because of hidden underlying assumptions that can influence attitude. Ife (2008) examines the use of military metaphors in common usage (especially in community work), including the following: 'strategy', 'tactics', 'target', 'outflanking', 'engagement', 'alliance', 'operational plan' and 'guerrilla tactics'. 'Frontline' is also a word with military connotations, and perhaps its common and accepted use challenges Ife's concerns. If the 'war' is against poverty (and all its causes) and social work's purpose is to defend those who are suffering the consequences, then 'frontline' accurately describes the position in which many social workers find themselves; I would argue that the team I work in is in a very exposed position far out in the frontline. Ife's line has definite credibility if the 'war' is against service users and care has to be taken that this is not what is meant. Ife might prefer the words of the late Fred Edwards, who, when Director of Social Work in the Strathclyde Region in Scotland in the 1980s, described his staff as working at 'the frontiers of human experience'.

Ife also questions the application of the widely-used word 'intervention' as this, too, implies that all the power and ability to bring about change lie with the social worker (*ibid.*). Bricker-Jenkins (1992: 284) questions the common use of other terms such as 'treatment and therapy' (suggestive of pathology), 'mediation' (ignores power imbalances) and even 'provision of social services' (suggests a disempowering and active-to-passive approach). Some of this might seem pedantic, but language is an important concept in oppression theory. Without such an emphasis, care would not be commonplace (since the rise of the feminist movement in the 1970s) in relation to gendered language. However, Hawkins *et al.* (2001) suggest, from research in Australia, that social workers do not commonly use the language associated with social justice (words such as 'disadvantaged', 'equality', 'discriminatory', 'empowerment', 'oppression', 'feminist'), so there would seem to be an issue here for radical practitioners.

The web of oppression model helps us understand how human characteristics arising from an accident of place or birth account for differences that are experienced as oppression. Therefore, as an aid to anti-oppressive practice, it takes us beyond the narrower forms that were seen with anti-racist and feminist approaches, and the anti-discriminatory practice that developed from them. It therefore incorporates the structural sources of oppression found in neoliberal capitalist societies.

If one accepts that welfare organizations, and especially state organizations within a welfare state setting, have functions within society that are related to social control and mediation, then the possibility of AOP becomes problematic. Dominelli argues that social workers working within agencies not signed up to AOP are in a precarious position (2002: 33). Even in agencies that are signed up, Dominelli argues, their isolation in a society based on inequality renders growth unlikely, and she considers the goals of AOP unrealizable in the short term (*ibid.*). However, as we saw in the section on anti-discriminatory practice, the legal framework provides possibilities for exploring such approaches and ensuring that such considerations are included in social work agendas involving individuals. It is unlikely that agencies will promote such activities through their procedures (even if they are given credence in their policies): that will fall to the practice of individual workers who, as well as seeking support for their position from agency policies and legal avenues, might find professional codes of practice useful: social work, after all, is supposed to promote social justice. The space for such discretionary practice will be explored further in Chapter 3.

Also on a positive note, on the basis that AOP is an approach, rather than a theoretical model for prescriptive application, Mullaly (2010: 226) looks at how a worker might approach an oppressed service user. This involves a checklist of questions the worker should ask themselves which include:

- Has the person been able or invited to tell their story of injustice?
- What awareness do they have of the impact of oppression?
- What beliefs do they have about their capabilities and about the possibility of escape from their plight?
- Do they blame themselves or blame social inequity?
- How can they be empowered to take action?
- With whom could they collaborate?
- How could services be more sensitive to their special needs?
- How could their potential and strength be released so that they can challenge unfairness and meet their needs?

Predicators for such approaches are that the service user is the agent of their own change (that it is not imposed on them), that power is managed so that they are empowered and, finally, that oppression is not reproduced through attempts to practise AOP through the use of critical reflection (Mullaly 2010; Schon 1983). These principles should also inform approaches to assessment in most circumstances (Dalrymple and Burke 2006), especially those conducted for inter-agency purposes such as community care, mental health and child protection (this might not be possible for some closely prescribed report formats such as those for a Court setting). AOP principles also underpin the practice of sharing written reports and records with service users.

Dalrymple and Burke (2006: 95–6) offer the following list (summarized here) of anti-oppressive possibilities for practice that takes account of the constraints determined by legislative frameworks that most of us have to work within in the real world:

- Focus on the experienced reality of people on the end of draconian and punitive legislation
- Work from a basis that is well-informed about legislation and its implications for service users and workers
- Use opportunities provided by supervision, team discussions, training and conference attendance to engage in critical reflection and discussion
- Critically analyse research evidence, policies and practices from an AOP perspective
- Work collectively with others committed to an AOP perspective
- Use legislation as a tool to combat oppression
- Engage in campaigns against legislation and policy that is oppressive
- Engage in dialogue across agency boundaries
- Actively engage with service user forums
- Become involved in groups within organizations you work for that might be able to influence policy and practice.

Empowerment and advocacy

These terms are given separate heading and brief discussion in this section because they crop up so regularly in the literature and will feature in subsequent chapters of this book.

Empowerment is considered a central concept to anti-oppressive practice and is described as 'a process through which oppressed people reduce their alienation and sense of powerlessness and gain greater control over all aspects of their lives and their social environments' (Mullaly 2010: 237). However, it is a term that is perhaps overused and features as much in the managerial speak of mainstream social work as it does in the progressive and radical literature (Smale *et al.* 2000). Cooke and Ellis (2004) describe empowerment as a ladder on which users are allotted differing degrees of power: at the bottom they might be given information about services, whilst at the very top they will be given authority to take decisions. This description usefully delineates the more tokenistic use of the term from truly empowering practice that might challenge neoliberal agendas concerning resource allocation and justice.

2.1 A collective response to service reduction

In Glasgow, Scotland, in 2012, an alliance was formed between learning disabled service users, their carers and trade unions representing the staff that provide their day care services. This was to resist the council's plans to close three out of five day centres in the city in order to promote 'choice' within a personalization agenda. The new strategy would also save money demanded by government-imposed spending limits. The previous year, a high-profile campaign had started to prevent the council closing a highly-valued centre whose site was required for the Commonwealth Games in 2014. These experiences drew large numbers of previously acquiescent and individualized service users and carers into meetings and discussion about the services they needed and wanted. From a truly empowering perspective, the alliance was a more positive experience than the council's proposal to axe services, although both would claim the term (UNISON 2012b).

Campaigning

Why and how might social workers involve themselves in campaigns around issues related to poverty and inequality? Think about local and national campaigning bodies and list some examples. Now, consider whether involvement in these campaigns is passive (for example, by financial donation) or active (actual personal involvement in campaigning activity), and which is more consistent with radical approaches.

Empowerment is fundamental to the work of Paulo Freire, the Latin American educationalist and revolutionary (Freire 1996). He proposes education for oppressed adults (the poor and dispossessed) that opens up their critical consciousness and enables them to see the world through new eyes. This will empower them to take on their oppressors and challenge power structures. Freire will be considered further in Chapter 7.

Advocacy is often related to empowerment. It rests on the idea that empowerment requires access to information and a voice in using it to exercise choice and control. Often, information is a privilege restricted to professionals, or those such as the small selected groups of individuals invited in by organizations for 'consultation' purposes. Social workers concerned with empowering their service users will share information so that individuals can self-advocate, or, in simple terms, articulate their own issues for themselves (Smale *et al.* 2000). Advocacy services can usefully help give a voice to those who might otherwise have difficulty; examples would be children or adults with communication problems. Social workers also act as advocates when they and their managers argue for increased resources or changes in policy. Trade unions act as advocates when they give collective voice to staff in organizations. These themes will emerge again in later chapters.

Human rights-based practice

Human rights practice (HRP) deserves discussion in its own right, although it might be considered to come under the AOP umbrella. This is due to its important place in the radical armoury, sometimes having a credibility that other methods might not hold in the real world of social work practice because of roots in internationally agreed declarations and charters. The latter also link with professional codes of ethics and practice discussed earlier in this chapter. The basis of HRP is the Universal Declaration of Human Rights agreed by the United Nations General Assembly in 1948. Its 30 Articles include principles that underpin legislation within individual nation states and which can be used as a benchmark for examining human rights within them (Johns 2011). In the years since 1948, numerous other international declarations and agreements have consolidated these basic principles. Amongst the most important of these in a UK and European context is the European Convention on Human Rights, originally drawn up in 1950 (but not recognized in the UK until 1965). This includes a number of articles that affect social work and its legislation, including Article 5 (which guarantees a right to liberty and security) and Article 8 (which guarantees a right to family life). Adherence to the principles within such declarations was enshrined in the UK in the 1997 Human Rights Act. All this sounds very top-down (flowing from legislative prescription, rather than a practice base): however, the Australian writer Ife (2008), whose work on this issue is internationally important, contends that human rights-based practice should be based on critiques applied within local contexts. Reisch (2013) suggests that such approaches will avoid simply reaffirming dominant orders.

Knowledge of human rights declarations can be useful when advocating and campaigning on behalf of some of the most marginalized groups in society, such as asylum seekers and Gypsy travellers. This is because national law is either ambiguous or, as in the case of incarcerating asylum-seeking children in Australia, against the spirit of international declarations. HRP is also important in considering civil liberties and their erosion in response to the 'war on terror'.

HRP can also help us when looking at issues surrounding cultural relativism. This concept concerns differences in cultural norms between community, ethnic or religious groups that might be used to explain or excuse customs and practices that are not the norm within white European or North American-based cultures. Examples would include women wearing a burka in certain Muslim cultures, or arranged marriages without consent in other cultures. More extreme examples would involve the practice of young female circumcision, or the honour killings of women who are thought to have brought shame to families. Reichert (2007: 10) suggests that a human rights approach to such issues would involve examination of the history of the practice, and who establishes and enforces the cultural norm, and then examining it against contemporary human rights standards. This is a difficult area requiring a sensitive approach based on sound principle, cultural sensitivity and religious tolerance. Right-wing inspired developments have resulted in the banning of the burka in France. In the UK, intolerance fuelled by Islamophobia, partly arising from interventionist wars in Afghanistan and elsewhere, has inspired the growth of the far-right English Defence League (and its Welsh and Scottish equivalents) who attack Muslims on the partial basis of a spurious defence of women's rights.

Human Rights should not be taken for granted, even in advanced capitalist countries. In the UK, the Conservative Party is committed in its manifesto to the repeal of the Human Rights Act 1997, should they hold power outright in a future government (in 2010, they failed to win such a majority and went into a coalition government with the Liberal Democrats).

Small-scale resistance: deviant social work and anarchist influences

Whilst HRP could be described as progressive but within the mainstream, 'deviant' social work (Carey and Foster 2011) is descended directly from the radical practice of the 1970s and based, like them, on left-socialist and anarchist critiques of society. Such approaches have also been described in the UK as social work 'guerrilla warfare' (Ferguson and Woodward 2009) and in Canada as 'resistance' and 'stealth' practices (Smith 2007).

From an academic viewpoint based on research amongst frontline social work staff, Carey and Foster (2011) criticize the Radical Literature. This is because such works have 'maintained a general incapacity to offer practitioners tangible pragmatic or sustainable ways by which to meet the pressing, local, crisis-orientated yet relatively small-scale or *micro* needs of service users and informal carers' (*ibid.*: 577). This is a cogent criticism and one which forms a basic premise of this book. They go on to discuss small-scale attempts by individual social workers to obtain the best for service users. These might involve economies of truth, or an emphasis on putting forward particular types of information in order to negotiate eligibility criteria. The workers undertaking such practice typically do so individually; are cynical in their attitudes towards their agencies and their managers; have little interest in the ideas of those who make grandiose claims to empower service users and fight oppression and so on; and have little interest in career advancement and realize that they have to be careful if they want to avoid disciplinary action. This is not unlike some of the responses found in the focus groups organized by Ferguson and Woodward (2009) when they tried to locate a radical practice. The fact that they did so rather gives the lie to Carey and Foster's notion that the Radical Literature agenda is often about career advancement or 'ego or other power centred drives' (Carey and Foster 2011: 590).

In their findings, Carey and Foster describe such small-scale resistance as not collectivized. Its adherents only express their anti-establishment attitudes publically when it comes to organized actions through trade unions around wider disputes; by Carey and Foster's account, they will not themselves take responsibility for such collective action but restrict themselves to 'surreptitious or hidden activities (and sometimes values) that contrast with any priority given to more conspicuous collective or class-based struggles emphasized by radical social work' (*ibid.*: 590).

Although they do not make the link, with their emphasis on individualism, Carey and Foster's examples of deviant practice are not dissimilar to accounts given in *Anarchists in Social Work* (Gilbert *et al.* 2004). This UK book offers diverse and very personal first-hand frontline experiences and opinions, mostly from the 1970s and 1980s, and tries to offer some pointers to a libertarian practice. These include:

- *Power-shedding* – trying to minimize power differential with service users through attention to dress, language, self-direction, self-awareness
- *Accessibility* – being flexible and unencumbered by management superstructures
- *Accountability* – being accountable to clients and being seen as a community resource, rather than being accountable to elected members and those managers who do their bidding without question
- *Professional responsibility* – to resist authoritarianism and the influence of the managerial elite.

These are useful ideas and quite in keeping with broad radical approaches; however, some are at least as hard to deliver in practice as much other progressive theory.

Carey and Foster's notions surrounding deviant social work practice are feasible and deliverable but involve hidden practices that are therefore not transforming. They also carry the risk, due to their inherent dishonesty and lack of transparency, of breaching employer's codes of conduct and professional codes. Although probably satisfying to the individual, deviant or guerrilla practice cannot be recommended as a coherent radical approach. Unless its practice was so widespread because the rules being breached were in general disrepute (perhaps in a situation of general social upheaval), the individual practitioner might be easily picked off and neutralized: radical practitioners are too valuable a resource to lose so easily.

Twenty-first-century radical social work

The Radical Literature of recent years has brought Marxist approaches out of the sidelines to which they had been condemned with the onset of the 1980s and the emergence of social work practice based on identity politics. However, as Mullaly argues (2010), and as suggested earlier in this chapter, the various strands of anti-oppressive practice, including those that stem from post-modernism, can usefully inform a twenty-first-century radical practice. Marxism, however, should not be dispensed with, as suggested by purist post-modernist thinking, but, as we shall see also in Chapter 3, is of importance for locating the original source of oppressions located in Figure 2.1.

Ferguson (2011: 129), in a chapter titled 'Why Class (Still) Matters', suggests that Marxism 'provides a coherent and convincing explanation for the development of the unprecedented levels of inequality' and a 'framework for understanding the specific ways in which the neoliberal agenda has reshaped social work and social welfare'. In accentuating notions of class and linking them with evidence of inequality and poor life chances for the majority of the population, Ferguson was only too aware of how unpopular such theory is in the western democracies where the neoliberal project has advanced. Although most people still describe themselves as working-class, there is a generally ascribed aspiration for us all to be middle-class and to enjoy a stake in a society associated with secure incomes, home-ownership, and access to the material comforts and consumer products we are constantly asked to believe we need. This concept was discussed in Chapter 1. A Marxist class-based analysis assumes that workers have a collective interest and that the exercise of this necessarily threatens the ruling classes in society, whose own interests are served through continued austerity, social division and general compliance with neoliberal values.

Twenty-first-century Marxist approaches have had to deal with criticisms that, by placing emphasis on class, they fail to deal with diversity and difference and the oppressions that arise from them. These could be from being a woman, being LGBT, having a physical or learning disability, suffering from mental illness, being an older person, being of non-white colour or having minority ethnic status. This, however, is very contentious: socialists have been prominent supporters of most of the campaigns and user movements associated with diversity and difference (Ferguson 2011: 97). What makes Marxist approaches different is the notion that an emphasis on identity politics is divisive and inhibits the solidarity between oppressed groups that, as we saw above, is considered an essential for radical practice. It is on this basis that we can draw positives from the various anti-oppressive strands.

Basic Marxism holds that the common base of all oppression is the requirement in capitalist society for profit. Labour is required at the lowest possible cost and this needs a uniform and disciplined workforce who are kept in their place through a belief that they are better than others who are obviously different, and from one another. This is the basis of all social division and, as we saw in Chapter 1, promoted through neoliberalism. It explains racism and nationalistic jingoism, homophobia, misogyny and the failure of society to make proper adjustment for those whose abilities are different from the norm. Marx described this process as resulting from the alienation that arises within the capitalist mode of production, where workers have little say over what they produce and receive minimum return: this alienates workers from the productive process, and from one another. As a theory, it is of interest to social workers not just because it explains social division, but also because it explains how they themselves feel disempowered within the bureaucratized and managerial organizations most work in (Ferguson and Lavalatte 2004). It also underpins Fanon's ideas about the effects of oppression on the individual discussed in the AOP section in this chapter. Radical social workers from the Marxist tradition therefore support the self-organization of minority and marginalized groups, just as they support the release of women from traditional family and low-paid caring roles. Difference and diversity are only problematic issues in a society that is inherently divided on a class basis: they would not be issues in a truly egalitarian society.

A Marxist approach to social work is therefore an emancipatory one, in that it seeks to provide people with the tools to free themselves from the oppressive circumstances capitalism has defined for them. In the words of McDonald (2006: 91): 'How ... can social work exist if it denies its emancipatory purposes?' In chapters to follow, discussion will focus on how this might be done in practice. Marxism also help us understand the growth of social welfare as described in Chapter 1 and its place in contemporary society; it is from here that we can see the potential for social work. The US social work academic Steve Burghardt describes it thus:

> Marxism helps social workers understand that social welfare (and the social work welfare state itself), rather than standing outside of existing class and social forces, is an active part of them. Workers have the potential to function not simply as simple agents of social control but as individuals utilizing the contradictory functions of the state to open up avenues of potential gain for workers and their families.
>
> (Burghardt 1996: 420)

This theme of opportunity and discretion will be developed in Chapter 3.

The choice for social workers is essentially a simple one: do they work defensively, going by the book defined by their employers, and do their duty as prescribed, or do they operate reflectively, which means recognizing conflicts, contradictions and the effect of power structures in society (Banks 2012). Such critical reflection is a good starting point, but radical activism and practice require more.

Putting the 'doing' into radical practice

Whilst this is very much the theme of the rest of this book, it is worthwhile at this stage looking at some case examples from the point of view of the main perspectives described in this chapter: Mainstream Psychosocial, Critical and Radical. The following exercise asks you to take account of what you have learned from this chapter and your own reflected experience in relation to some case scenarios.

2.2 Assessing initial information: Lara and her children, Nico and Donald

Malcolm (3 years) and Whitney (4 years) have been referred to Social Services for assessment after a series of recent domestic violence incidents in the home between their mother, Lara (20 years) and a boyfriend she describes as 'casual not serious'. As a consequence of her own mother's alcohol and drug issues, Lara spent her teens in the care system, resident in a small Children's Unit where she met the father of the children from whom she is now separated after other repeated domestic incidents. He was an unstable individual, very damaged by his childhood experiences, and is currently in prison for various offences, including breach of bail conditions preventing him from visiting Lara's home. Her recent boyfriend, aged 23 years, enjoyed a reputation for extreme violence associated with local drug dealing. She met him through her mother, who has been involved in a relationship with his father. Lara gained little from her formal school education and left when pregnant with Whitney; she has never worked or studied. She is described by a social worker from the team who knows her well as 'very intelligent' and a good parent, in terms of providing and homemaking. She has no known drug or alcohol issues.

Nico is a six-year old child from a Romanian Roma family. He has been found by the police during the day apparently begging in a city centre street. His mother was nearby and seems to speak little English. They are all now in a police station awaiting the arrival of Social Services.

Donald, who is 67 years old, lives alone on a permanent caravan site on the outskirts of a large Scottish town. He has been reported to Social Services by a local shopkeeper concerned at his personal presentation and poor hygiene, constant drunkenness and the nuisance he causes to other customers.

From mainstream to radical assessments

Look at each of the vignettes in practice example 2.2 in turn. From the point of view of Mainstream Psychosocial, Critical Anti-Oppressive and, finally, Radical Marxist perspectives (all of which have been discussed in this chapter), consider the following:

How might you approach assessment? What considerations would you take into account (for all three, think about agency expectations and requirements, as well as other *macro* and micro issues).

What would be the aim of your interventions?

To help you on your way, consider the following points that help characterize (perhaps rather stereotypically) the three streams. These are themes that will also be developed in practice-based chapters to follow.

Traditional mainstream approaches might emphasize managerial agendas to do with risk management and cost; initial assessments might focus on individual weakness and risk factors.

Critical anti-oppressive approaches might focus on strength and resilience, identity and the oppressive factors that might arise from this.

A *radical approach* might take the anti-oppressive features on board but might look beyond to locate the individual's place in a class-based and unequal society, and might look to linking the individual's issues with wider social and political campaigning.

main points

■ Theories are vital tools to understand situations and their component parts so that we can predict what might happen and work out what we should do. Practice-based knowledge or wisdom are important but they are not substitutes for theory. The human situation is subject to many variables and so cannot be predicted with absolute accuracy – unlike theory in relation to physical objects which can be predicted through universal laws.

- Feminist practice, anti-discriminatory practice, human rights-based practice and other strands of anti-oppressive (or progressive, emancipatory, empowering or transformational) practice, all contribute, together with past radical Marxist-based approaches, to a radical practice perspective for the twenty-first century.

- All such approaches hold in common that society contains deep inequalities and various oppressions that arise from them. These should be taken into account when approaching most of the issues that social workers face in their daily work.

taking it further

It goes without saying that the Radical Literature referred to in the Introduction comprises essential texts for further exploration. In addition, the following are to be recommended:

- Baines, D. (ed.) (2007) *Doing Anti-Oppressive Practice: Building Transformative Politicized Social Work*, Nova Scotia, Fernwood. This Canadian book, with contributions from radical academics, makes a useful effort to bridge the gap between theory and practice.
- Dominelli, L. (2002) *Anti-Oppressive Social Work: Theory and Practice*, Basingstoke, Palgrave Macmillan. A basic text that should be on every student social worker's bookshelf.
- Garrett, J.M. (2013) *Social Work and Social Theory*, Bristol, Policy Press. Students and practitioners wanting to find out more about the theoretical base of critical and radical social work will find this text by an Irish author very useful.
- Ife, J. (2008) *Human Rights and Social Work: Towards Rights-Based Practice* (2nd edn), Port Melbourne, Cambridge University Press. Given neoliberal intrusions on basic rights and liberties, this book from an Australian author has all the right information to use this perspective when required.
- McDonald, C. (2006) *Challenging Social Work: The Context of Practice*, Bristol, Policy Press. From an Australian author, this is a thought-provoking text that looks in depth at the implications of neoliberalism for social work practice.
- Mullaly, B. (2010) *Challenging Oppression and Confronting Privilege* (2nd edn), Ontario, Oxford University Press. This superb Canadian book is packed with ideas, examples and information on a wide variety of anti-oppressive themes. Some of its suggestions are also laced with humour, which makes it very readable.

- Social Work Action Network http://www.socialworkfuture.org/ An online resource with links to various features and articles associated with the activity of the network and its promotion of a radical critique and practice in the UK.

As this book was being completed, a new journal has commenced publication titled *Critical and Radical Social Work* to be issued twice a year in March and September. Its co-editors, Michael Lavalette and Iain Ferguson, are associated with the Radical Literature. The journal aims to include a 'Voices from the Frontline' section which will address 'the experience of frontline workers and services users'. Details at www.policypress.co.uk/journals.

chapter 3

Finding Space for Radical Practice

Overview

This chapter looks at the spaces and opportunities for radical practice that arise from discretion still available to social workers, with a particular focus on statutory settings. This is based on Marxist explanations of the state that were introduced in Chapter 1 and on the work of a non-Marxist but cogent commentator, the US sociologist Lipsky. This chapter, as Chapter 2, will focus on theory. There would be little point in pursuing this argument (which is a basic assumption of the book) unless evidence can be located that supports it as a proposition. Such a focus will also have to address the arguments of the critics who suggest, on the one hand, that Lipsky's ideas are not relevant to social work, or who regard the managerialist project in social work to be so complete that discretion, however explained or previously demonstrated, has been curtailed. This chapter will therefore look at how spaces might be found within the agendas set by state organizations concerned primarily with risk management and evidence-based practice.

The origins and conclusions of radical pessimism

Radical practice cannot take place if its opportunity is denied by a managerial framework: this fear is to the fore in much of the Radical Literature. In the early 1970s, the government established a number of community development projects (CDPs) in areas of the UK that were suffering intense deprivation. These projects were closed when it became apparent that workers were aligning with community members to challenge the very basis of social structures and discrimination. This has been much quoted since to demonstrate that pure radical practice in state-sponsored settings is an extremely unlikely possibility. If anything, the effects of neoliberal policies since the 1970s and the rise of managerialism have reduced possibilities even further, and there should be no doubt about this. Following the CDP experience, many social workers who wanted a practice more in tune with the basic values of social work turned to the voluntary sector (Howe 1991; Ferguson and Woodward 2009). However, reduced public spending has put a squeeze on such settings and most voluntary organizations now project a business model in efforts to win contracts from the public sector for particular pieces of work. Their staff are, as a consequence, insecure, with work tied to service delivery models prescribed by local authorities and provided as cheaply as possible in order to win contracts. Whilst some organizations, such as Women's Aid, might still provide some opportunity for particularized forms of anti-oppressive practice, opportunities will not be as great as they seemed in the 1990s with the upsurge in voluntary sector growth promoted by the then Conservative government and its neoliberal vision of a mixed economy of care (Ferguson and Woodward 2009).

With the voluntary sector and not-for-profit sector apparently offering little opportunity, the Radical Literature has become very pessimistic, considering the managerial project to be so advanced that opportunity for its practice in statutory settings is well-nigh impossible (Ferguson and Woodward 2009; Langan 2011; Ferguson and Lavalatte 2013; Woodward 2013). The alternative that is proffered concerns support for social movements (such as mental health clubhouse initiatives, or disability users movements) that are self-organized and politicized, and linking these with national, Europe-wide and international social movement forums. Such forums as the World Social Forum (WSF) are organized annually and bring together social movements from across the world, as well as anti-capitalist and anti-global organizations. This neat tie-up between radical practice and radical politics unfortunately has little resonance beyond those whose sympathies lie with such trends anyway, and has made little or no impact in workplaces. These writers also suggested that resistance to managerialism was beginning to extend beyond left-wing radicals to a wider social work base because traditional relationship-based work was under attack: they did not, however, provide examples. The Radical Literature authors have also spread their message in the UK through the Social Work Action Network (SWAN), which organizes regular, well-attended conferences; however, without a message that impacts on day-to-day practice, their influence is inevitably limited (details were provided at the end of Chapter 2).

It might be that, because they are not rooted in everyday practice, the Radical Literature authors do not see the opportunities that exist, perhaps because these will not change the world. This is intended as very fraternal criticism, as their pessimism also seems oddly at variance with the intention of some of their own writings: Ferguson *et al.* (2002) placed a Bertolt Brecht poem 'A Bed for the Night' at the start of their book on the welfare state: this brilliantly illustrates how small and good deeds show the way to a better world. How the spaces are created for such 'small and good deeds' now follows.

The Marxist dialectic and the welfare state

It is hoped that this heading will not prove an immediate turn-off to the reader more interested in practice than complex theory. The general need for theory was explained at the beginning of Chapter 2 and, if we are to understand why and how opportunities exist to practice in ways unintended by policy-makers – and even individual employers – we need to see where this comes from. Classical Marxists viewed the state in structural terms and every aspect of the state machine was subordinate to its function as a means to ensure the propagation of wealth accumulation within capitalism. Post-war Marxists such as Miliband (quoted in Chapter 1) debated the relationship between structure (the capitalist state itself) and agency (the various organs of the state that regulate and manage its functions within individual nation states). From this evolved the notion that, at any one time, their colliding forces and different interests determine levels of class struggle and how the state organizes itself to achieve survival (Hay 2006).

The *dialectic* is the scientific explanation given by Marxists for the interdependency of all things within the universe: everything that happens is the result of the cause and effect of the intermingling of natural objects. Thus, culture and consciousness within human beings are all the product of the endless change and motion of natural forces. The dialectic also explains that within each object is its opposite, so all natural forces and creations (including human institutions) contain internal contradictions. It is from these that change and progression occurs, and the Marxist formulations of *Dialectical and Historical Materialism* explain the impact of such natural laws on the economic order within societies throughout human history (for full explanation, see Collier 2004). Unlike his predecessors, who recognized the dialectic in history, Marx and his followers were clear that human consciousness does not determine the environment but, rather, that social existence determines consciousness and this is established by the mode of production in his famous expression:

> Men make their own history, but they do not make it as they please; they do not make it under self-selected circumstances, but under circumstances existing already, given and transmitted from the past.
>
> (Marx and Engels 1848)

This can also help us understand how social change occurs. Dramatic transformation has happened periodically since humankind first walked the Earth, and its force and potency is not always predictable to even expert observers. An example would be the Arab Spring in 2011. The Tunisian revolution that came first started with the self-immolation of an unknown street vendor upset by the local corruption of officials that destroyed his business. Within months, a sequence of events took place that saw successful revolutions in Tunisia, Libya and Egypt, together with major eruptions in Syria, Bahrain and elsewhere. These came out of nowhere and toppled dictatorships often supported by the major world powers who had considered these states secure (Mason 2012). Clearly, the power of workers, long thought spent, was still a potent force capable of major change. The influence and use of social media through the Internet apparently more than made up for the sophistication and brutality of the oppressive regimes concerned. This all proves that nothing stays the same and the dialectic of history lends no stability to states, societies, regimes and institutions riven by contradictions and faced by human determination and imagination, amongst other variables.

The point of summarizing these rather complex concepts is to introduce the scientific notion that contradictions within capitalist society create opportunities for promoting change on a large scale (as with the Arab Spring) as well as creating opportunities for small changes, such as we might discover in social work. Such contradictions arise, for instance, between the needs of capitalist society to create the opportunity for the exploitation of workers in order to produce wealth and the need for these workers to be looked after, educated and kept in a reasonable state of contentedness – the basis of the welfare state. The welfare state becomes not just a tool for the ruling class, but also improvement in its capacity and provision becomes an objective for the working class. Within the workings of the welfare state lie further contradictions that throw up opportunities because the state functionaries (including social workers) who provide services are themselves workers with, ultimately, the same interests as the exploited classes at the lower ends of society (Ferguson *et al.* 2002). Solidarity between workers against the state might be considered more likely in a period of austerity and threat to public service jobs and security (such as that existing more or less permanently since the 1970s, as we saw in Chapter 1).

Lipsky and discretion in the public sector

Whilst Marxism provides an explanation for the contradictions in society that both divide and unify those with similar class interests, another theory helps focus more precisely on opportunities to practice the radical and transformative theories sampled in Chapter 2. This is based on the work of Michael Lipsky, who wrote about US public sector bureaucracies in the 1970s and 1980s (Lipsky 1980). Lipsky was especially concerned with frontline public employees such as police officers, teachers and social workers, whom he termed 'street level bureaucrats' because of their role in translating the policies of their employers into realistic and meaningful practice at frontline level. His descriptions were of public sector agencies under huge pressure to reduce budgets, and so are similar to social services organizations today. Whilst Lipsky took account of the tendency of some workers to distort policy and subvert rules in order to minimize work for themselves (observing that clients fared badly because of this), he also recognized that many workers wanted to do a good job and make the lives of their clients better, but could only do so if they applied their own rules. Not to do so would only result in them becoming overwhelmed by paperwork, client referrals, client and/or agency expectations, over-complexity, under-resourcing, alienation from the work task and those dependent on it, insufficient time and other pressures. It was clear from his studies that agencies and their managers relied on street-level bureaucrats to ration services and resources. Lipsky considered that workers managed all these pressures and dilemmas through exploiting areas of discretion that were an essential survival technique. He considered that some degree of autonomy from organizational authority would always exist because:

- Human services often involve complex tasks that cannot always be fully covered by agency guidelines, rules and procedures.
- Workers often need to respond to the human dimensions of a situation, requiring observation, judgement and individual assessment.
- The interactions of workers with clients involve relationship-building, which is in the interest of both parties, so that a balance is found between compassion and flexibility on the one hand, and impartiality and the rigid application of rules on the other.

Lipsky considered how workers cope when they do not share the objectives of their superiors or agencies. He found that they devised an array of strategies – from negative ones (such as absenteeism and work avoidance) to collective strategies (such as trade union organization) – that he considered only compounded such differences. He also considered more subtle methods, such as enhancing expertise in order to become indispensable to the organization, or performing in such a way that discredit is brought on the supervisor for, perhaps, failing to deliver performance targets. They can also 'work to rule', deferring to supervisors for decisions that they might be expected to make themselves even though delegated authority might not be formalized. If used successfully, such strategies could enhance discretion through either explicit or implicit agreement of managers. These are not suggested here as a methodology for radical social workers but, rather, as examples of the dynamics of the street-level bureaucracies where street-level bureaucrats are located.

Lipsky also found that his subjects could determine their decisions on the basis of their knowledge of likely outcomes, rather than the rules of the agency. This, he suggested, could involve them in 'redefining their jobs' (Lipsky 1980: 150) so that their role is being exercised in the longer-term interests of the client, rather than the immediate demands of the agency. The examples he uses concern lower court judges who avoid imprisoning offenders who they feel might be damaged by such an experience, or housing officials who try to divert particular families towards better housing. In both cases, the bureaucracy might react by imposing more rigid rules to ensure the implementation of their policies. The dilemmas for street-level bureaucrats working with scarce and reducing resources remained.

Lipsky's suggestions for how bureaucracies might deal with workers whose exercise of discretion militates against their attempts to standardize procedures, increase accountability (to the agency) and reduce spending contain all the features we saw in Chapter 1 that characterize managerialism: clear expectations of objectives and processes, work measurements, mechanisms to compare the performance of workers and incentives alongside sanctions to keep workers focused on the agency's agenda; the latter will outweigh other rewards and sanctions that might be operating unofficially. However, he recognized that street-level bureaucrats will always have to operate flexibly and with an aptitude for fresh thinking, and this has to be recognized by their agencies. Accountability can never simply be to the organization, as there must also be accountability to clients. Workers can deal with their agencies' demands for performance-related information by tailoring what they provide about themselves, especially as much of their engagement with clients takes place in private spaces. Lipsky also reminds us that attempts to over-proceduralize and reduce individual initiative can backfire, achieving a poorer quality service that is less responsive. Agency objectives can also be ambiguous, reflecting different levels of societal expectation: schools, for example, are expected to teach children how to read and write, but they are also expected to teach responsibility and citizenship.

Lipsky concluded his work with the proposal that discretion will always be required and will always be exercised in bureaucracies that reflect the uncertainties and ambiguities of the societies within which they operate. He felt that, in a society of 'protected interests' (*ibid.*: 211) – for him, that meant US capitalist society – things would only really change when humane concerns came to the fore of social policy. If and when this happens, people will demand respect for themselves and support for the workers who serve them, who are doing their best under adverse circumstances. Lipsky was clearly not a revolutionary seeking fundamental change in society but his social-democratic sympathies with public sector workers provide a cogent analysis of opportunity for the exercise of discretion and are quite compatible with Marxist theory. Indeed, Marx's dialectic suggests that the opportunity for different practice can arise through unpredictable circumstances. An example follows in the next section in relation to a weather-based emergency.

Applying Lipsky's ideas to twenty-first-century social work

The starting point for any discussion of Lipsky's ideas has to be a belief that social work is not inherently oppressive. As we saw in Chapter 2, radicals have been divided on this matter in the past but, if we believe that people enter into social work because they want to make a positive difference to people's lives (Ferguson and Woodward 2009), then we can assume that there is at least this potential. If social work, as an agent of state social control, carries aspects of oppression, then this must be because of the laws, procedural guidance, customs and everyday common practices that govern what most of us do. Lipsky tells us that these are all open to interpretation and individual influence, and that no amount of prescription can remove this. Historically, within totalitarian states, workers in human services such as education, health and social work have been able to carve out individual practice that can be celebrated as heroic: in Nazi-occupied Poland, social worker Irena Sendler was able to save Jewish children in the Warsaw Ghetto from certain death (Brophy Down 2012). In the field of literature, social workers are never described as state automatons lacking autonomy: Konrad (1975), Lewycka (2010) and Ungar (2011) provide varied examples from 1970s Hungary, the UK and contemporary Canada which suggest that this is not a common perception.

It seems disingenuous to describe the advance of managerialism as having removed all possibilities for discretion. Indeed, it has been argued that the more rules there are, then the greater is the pressure on individual workers to avoid goal conflicts by using their interpretive powers, or even through manipulation (although this might not necessarily be in the service user's interests) (Evans and Harris 2004; Ostberg 2012).

Lipsky's mainstream critics have suggested that his work is of little relevance to social work. One of the most clearly articulated examples is that of Howe (1991). He argues that social work practice is prescribed by matters such as law and statute, procedures, rules, guidelines, resources and managerial command. It is therefore accurate to describe state practice as defined very much by welfare organizations and their managers, and not by individual practitioners (Howe 1991: 204). He concedes that there are spaces for individually defined practice but that these tend to be those of least consequence for managers in terms of risk and resource implications. As soon as such matters are paramount, procedures kick into place and discretion is effectively removed.

In an excellent paper, Evans and Harris (2004) discuss these debates. Their starting point is the three areas of analysis outlined by Lipsky: that street-level bureaucrats operate human services that aim to meet unpredictable and variable needs; that they are often required to translate ambiguous policy into practice; that they create spaces in order to advance their own values, interests and needs (Evans and Harris 2004: 883–4). They conclude that it is a mistaken assumption to see discretion as associated only with strong professional autonomy and self-regulated practice as experienced by doctors and lawyers (*ibid.*: 892). Laws, rules and guidance can never be fixed determinants in human services, as all will require an interpretation to fit the circumstances in which they require to be applied. Social work is riven with ambiguities that underlie its position as a mediator between state agendas and the desire to control social problems on the one hand, and the social worker's trained response to exercise compassion and outcomes that favour the individual service user, on the other (Roose *et al.* 2011).

3.1 A collective response to a weather emergency

practice example

An abnormally heavy snow storm in March brought me unexpectedly back to the island location where I still live but no longer work: out of child protection and back into general community welfare – but with a difference. Cut off entirely for several days and without power for over a week. The health and welfare of a population numbering hundreds was in danger and a coordinated emergency response was required from the Police, local authority services, Mountain Rescue, Coastguard, Fire and Rescue Service and others. Social work's role from the start was to ensure that vulnerable community members were quickly identified and, as best as possible, looked after. Unable to get home, I spent an initial period in the incident HQ led by emergency planning 'experts', but managed to leave in one of the 4x4 vehicles allowed to cross the island to a remote and relatively isolated local centre nearer my home where a small group of local health workers, social work staff and volunteers were providing care and support to a scattered rural community. This was also the area where the worst weather and prolonged power loss was experienced.

Health and social work staff spontaneously dropped their agency differences and worked together in a spirit of cooperation not bound by protocols or rules, or prescribed by government 'integration' agendas. Bureaucratic considerations were set aside and real partnerships forged with community members to address need. Decisions were made collectively and, when support or resources were required from outside –

for instance, to obtain an emergency generator for someone particularly vulnerable who could not be moved, or to take someone into a care situation – this was done as effectively and quickly as circumstances would allow utilizing whatever means seemed best, rather than normal organizational protocols. Some very vulnerable people experienced a level of support that had unintended but positive outcomes – very isolated individuals began to come out of themselves and feel part of their community.

Because of our isolation, events determined who were the natural (rather than externally-appointed) leaders, and who the staff and community members were who would take initiatives and act reliably. Senior managers and chief officials largely left us to get on with it – our only visitation was from the commanding police officer who ceremoniously helped bring in a delivery of food before disappearing without having spoken to anyone.

Exercise 3.1

Seizing opportunities

Think about how unusual and unexpected situations can be used to promote alternative approaches. Can you think of other examples? How does this compare with the mainstream theory of crisis intervention?

Space in risk assessment

In Chapter 1, risk was identified as a major preoccupation of social workers in managerially-driven state settings: effective risk assessments rely on the information input by the assessor, as well as their predictors concerning possible outcomes. This can never be a pure science but the robustness, effectiveness and credibility of risk assessments depend on the individual skill of the worker involved. In this sense, they involve a notion of professional status that Evans (2011) considers is downplayed in Lipsky's original 1980 analysis of street-level bureaucrats. However, the negative and potentially oppressive aspects of street-level bureaucracy might include individual, or even unofficial, local practices designed to protect the worker from blame, litigation or job loss (Hughes and Wearing 2007). If this is to the fore with management agendas, it would be surprising if risk-averse cultures and practice did not extend unofficially to practitioner level.

Conversely, a radically inspired risk assessment can be used to highlight the risks to an individual of intrusive actions that might accompany risk-averse and safe practice. Such radical assessments can be used to enhance social justice and human rights agendas. Stanford (2011) describes this process as constructing 'moral responses' to risk. She suggests that using theory surrounding oppression and injustice (such as that discussed in Chapter 1) can be used to challenge 'at risk identities' (*ibid.*: 1528). This is based on 'resilience, hopefulness and optimism as staple resources that support a strong sense of social worker's professional identity ... [which] enable[s] them to resist invitations into the moral conservatism engendered by neo-liberal risk society' (*ibid.*: 1517). The message here is that the process of risk assessment can be used to promote practice based on notions of social justice.

Payne (2011) is concerned that traditional risk assessments tend to focus on factors that present risk, rather than protective factors that offer security. He suggests that risk assessments should focus on the factors that counter risk, as these can correct the balance in favour of positive interventions to bolster security. Payne also suggests that a focus on risk creates a false confidence in the efficacy of risk assessments and the increase of surveillance of peoples lives that then arises. He believes that it is 'better to enhance security, dignity and resilience' on the basis that these factors are associated with equality and fair treatment (*ibid.*: 199). Because risk assessments have the power to reduce individual rights and freedoms as well as to protect them, it is important to recognize when involved in such work that they are not seen as a mechanistic exercise, but that they take full account of issues of empowerment, the right to independence, and to citizenship (Kemshall and Pritchard 2005). Risk assessments are now a part of everyday practice but their operation will always involve discretion about their application and a radical practice here has a clear place.

Knowledge, research and evidence-based practice

Evidence-based practice (EBP) was also identified in Chapter 1 as being a central tenet of the managerial environment occupied by workers in state settings. According to its critics, however, it is more talked about than actually undertaken because of the difference between the aspirations of policy-makers and the actualities of frontline practice (Gray *et al.* 2009) – which is, of course, one of the themes that underlies this chapter. An Internet search for working examples of EBP in the UK will provide little evidence of its use in practice, despite an emphasis by the government-funded Social Care Institute for Excellence (SCIE) on developing this concept in social work in order to give it equal status to health care (for example, Marsh and Fisher 2005).

Whilst criticism of EBP as a concept because of its questionable application in human services (rather than a science-based practice, such as health and medicine) seems justified, the need, whenever possible, to base practice on research findings is another matter and has a long history in social work. The crucial question here is what constitutes evidence, with a belief that positivist research findings based on random control trials (RCTs) and *quantitative* evidence (the basis of EBP) have little application in social work. *Qualitative* findings, on the other hand, are based on practitioner knowledge, longitudinal research or other methods that have a better fit. An example would be the recent findings of Farmer and Wijedasa that concern outcomes for looked-after children who are returned to their parents (2011): this is not aimed at prescribing interventions but it can certainly guide decision-making. Such research looks at issues including poverty, its impact on particular families and what resilience factors are found to alleviate the effects for children, including interventions or non-interventions by social workers.

This leads us to agree that 'Decision making in social work will always entail a complex mix of life experience, professional judgement, heuristics, political expediency and research knowledge' (Gray *et al.* 2009). Good defensible practice should therefore be based on whatever research is available, and the radical worker will try to keep abreast of trends so that they are seen as professionally proficient (Mullaly 2010). It should be noted that some commentators are now suggesting that the concept of evidence-based practice should be replaced with one of evidence *informed* practice, to 'Indicate that evidence is only one of the considerations to inform practice rather than being the basis, and it should be used critically and with understanding' (Forrester and Harwin 2011: 171). EBP is, by definition, prescriptive: if, for instance, workers are told by their employing agency to base early intervention on a solution-focused approach, then they may have no discretion in the matter. However, there is little evidence that this actually happens and, whilst this is the case, spaces for the discretionary use of knowledge that fit with the reality of a client's situation will be available.

stop and think

- Do you think that social workers should simply get on with the tasks that managers expect of them, such as those associated with assessment and care management, or do they have other responsibilities?
- Is it right to practise as a 'street-level bureaucrat', or is this dishonest?

Figure 3.1 shows how a radical practice helps us to see over the obstacles created by a neoliberal society.

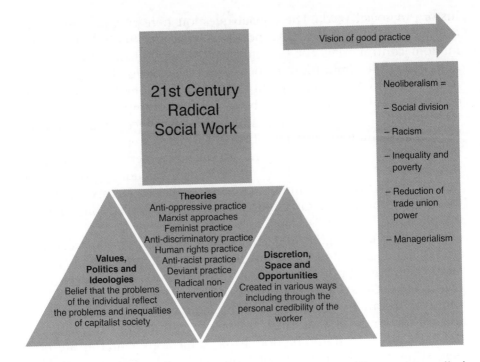

Figure 3.1 The building blocks of radical practice in twenty-first century radical social work

Influence on policy-making

In addition to finding spaces for small-scale practice with individuals that might make a difference, social workers can also attempt to make inroads into policy decisions that enhance values of social justice on a broader scale, even if these may not impact widely. According to Marston and McDonald (2012), this might be achieved through activity that breaks down stereotypes that reinforce oppression. This might involve the promotion of sporting events across cultural boundaries (they give an example from Australia involving asylum-seekers), or being involved in policy formulation or practitioner research that challenges prevailing views.

Influence on policy matters can also be achieved through involvement beyond that with individual service users. At a local level, workers might be offered opportunities to become involved with forums, focus groups or working groups. Whilst a cynical view can be taken of such activities, in that they might be operating to agendas set by management for their own purposes, this cannot be assumed. Perhaps more discreetly given managerial prescriptions, workers might be in a position to promote service user involvement in pressure and campaigning groups around common issues at local, or even national, level.

Lara and her children, Nico and Donald: looking for spaces for good practice

In the exercises in Chapter 2, we met Lara and her children, Malcolm and Whitney, whose lives are affected by domestic violence; Nico, the Roma child who is in a police station with his mother after being found begging; and Donald the Scottish Gypsy traveller with alcohol issues.

Look back to these examples and, on the basis of your knowledge of likely agency procedures, first, list the non-negotiable procedure that would determine your approach to these people and their situations. Then list the areas of discretion that might be available to you. Include big and small matters. Compare the lists and consider how important a factor is the discretion available to you as a worker.

- Radical approaches require space and opportunity for the exercise of discretion. Possibilities might be small-scale but will, nonetheless, be worthwhile.

- Despite limitations such spaces can be found within statutory settings as well as voluntary specialized ones. Indeed, in the latter the enforcement of business models and competition for funding is rapidly closing off some of the opportunities that existed in the past.

- Concerns about risk are now fundamental to managerially-driven practice, with risk management and assessment required in every setting. There are approaches to risk that embody social justice objectives and these can be embodied in radical approaches.

- The managerial drive for prescribed types of evidence-based practice is more of an aspiration than a reality actually present in most work settings. However, knowledge from research can play a very positive role in radical practice and practitioners' credibility will be enhanced if they can demonstrate this in their work.

■ Evans, T. and Harris. J. (2004) Street-Level Bureaucracy, Social Work and the (Exaggerated) Death of Discretion, *British Journal of Social Work* **34**(6): 871–95. A paper that gives good coverage to the debates surrounding the application of Lipsky's ideas to social work.

■ Gray, M., Plath, D. and Webb, S. (2009) *Evidence Based Social Work: A Critical Stance*, Abingdon, Routledge. This book critiques and counters the trend for EBP, explaining its rise and non-emergence. It also talks up the genuine need for knowledge-based practice that cuts with the needs of service users and their workers.

■ Lipsky, M. (1980) *Street Level Bureaucracy – Dilemmas of the Individual in Public Services*, New York, Russell Sage Foundation. This book has recently been republished on its thirtieth anniversary and is still of huge relevance to social workers in state settings.

■ Marx and the Dialectic – Marx's works are not especially accessible to the twenty-first-century reader but, if an attempt is to be made, *The German Ideology* written in 1845 provides a good starting point to his ideas on historical development. This and many of his other works can be accessed online: http://www.marxists.org/archive/marx/works/

There are also a number of shorter explanatory guides including: Collier, A. (2004) *Marx: A Beginner's Guide*, Oxford, One World.

4 Working with Children and Families

chapter

Overview

This chapter moves the book on to discussion surrounding practice. It will begin by looking at how theories of child development influence approaches in work settings and will then move on to look at practice itself, with a focus around child protection. As population movement from poor to rich countries continues, the economic recession creates tensions in the latter, leading to the popularization of policies limiting immigration and asylum. This impacts particularly on children, and so will be given coverage in this chapter. Finally, social pedagogy will be discussed as a possibility for a creative style that has the needs of service users at its heart. Because this section is practice-focused, there is little attention to either explanation or critique of mainstream approaches but there will be critical comment if this underpins explanation of alternative approaches consistent with radical practice.

Child development, poverty, class and social justice

Children and family social workers commonly use child development theory to make sense of what they do, sometimes to explain complex situations and sometimes in an effort to provide assessments that will be seen to be robust and professional when presented to other agencies within legal or multi-agency settings. Child protection and safeguarding is an area of social work most open to public scrutiny as a consequence of high-profile public inquiries that follow child deaths, such as those of Victoria Climbie or Peter Connelly in the UK, and it should be no surprise that social workers are generally keen to prove that their practice is knowledge-based. It is important from a radical perspective to ensure that such theories do not confirm the inequalities that, as we saw in Chapter 1, create the social situations in which the majority of our clients find themselves.

The average social worker would probably accept that outcomes and life chances for children are determined by numerous factors ranging from those that occur pre-birth and affect the foetus, to those that arise from the economic circumstances of their parents. The emphasis in how these are presented can make a difference to the manner in which we plan interventions and the way Social Services and their partners make people feel about services. Sometimes, theory is picked from a menu because it seems to provide a key to understanding a particular situation; sometimes a theory is used because the worker is familiar with it, or it may be that it is one favoured or acknowledged within the worker's agency or a partner agency that is considering the worker's view. Attachment theory is familiar to most children and family workers: its focus on the emotional development of the child and the conditions that enable or disable this are important factors when considering the family environments where children are at risk of harm (see, for example, Howe *et al.* 1999; Howe 2005). With chaotic families, it can explain why children's behaviour is challenging even when their situations seem to be improved through placement in alternative family settings where there are parents able to offer the consistent care and love believed to have been missing in their birth homes.

However, for every theory there are others that can offer an equally coherent explanation and we need to give prominence to those that challenge stereotypes and the oppressions that follow on from them. Take, for example, the fact that it is now recognized that foetal alcohol syndrome (FAS) accounts for permanent brain damage affecting the behaviour and presentation of an unknown, but probably very large, number of children (Morleo *et al.* 2011). Knowledge of risky neo-natal behaviour by working-class women is likely to be picked up more readily than it might otherwise be if the parents are middle-class, articulate and presenting well. Working-class parents are more likely to be referred for pre-birth child protection investigation and social work scrutiny, especially if they have a history of illegal drug misuse. However, increased alcohol use is prevalent across all social classes and, indeed, rising amongst 'professional' and 'managerial' groups (NHS 2012). This is encouraged by a politically and economically powerful drink industry whose influence might be considered out of balance with the devastation caused by alcohol's widespread misuse. As a result of possibly unconscious risky neo-natal behaviour by middle-class women, alcohol misuse may well be causing a generation of children whose behaviours are not the subject of social work interventions. Instead, these children are likely to be referred to general practitioners (GPs) and Child and Adolescent Mental Health Services (CAMHS) with eventual diagnosis of autistic spectrum disorders or attention deficit hyperactive disorder (ADHD). Brier-Thomson, an adoption specialist in the US, has put together a list of characteristics and diagnoses relating to a number of mental health conditions experienced by adults: FAS has the most with 40, 12 of which overlap with ADHD and 20 of which overlap with autism (such as *over or under responsive to stimuli and often interrupts or intrudes*) (Brier-Thompson 2006).

ADHD itself is socially-constructed with vested interests, such as pharmaceutical companies, benefiting from diagnosis and medicalized treatment. Schools also benefit from settled children and parents' own responsibility in terms of matters such as dietary control (avoidance of sugary foods) (Rogowski 2013). It is not therefore surprising that diagnosis will differ when symptoms are apparently so similar. The examples suggest that use of theory is leading to surveillance and interventions in the lives of working-class women and their children, when similar behaviour by middle-class women results in different medically-led approaches in the child's life that might be less socially stigmatizing.

FAS and ADHD are raised as examples of how class, and even the operations of the marketplace in capitalist society, reflect differences in perception of child development issues. Whilst the working-class person in this hypothesis will be made to feel individually responsible for the risk to their child's health, the middle-class parent is unlikely to be made to experience the same level of shame and guilt. Instead, they will be reassured by a medical explanation and perhaps a treatment for their child through medication. Radical social workers should approach their assessments with a critical view of theory offered to explain matters and with an eye to the inclusion or exclusion of structural explanations for an individual's reaction to their circumstances. Reports, assessments and meetings such as case conferences are all forums where inclusion of considerations that go beyond individual description can be ensured. This is not new and many workers do this anyway: like so many examples of radical practice in action, good critical practice challenges stereotypes.

Another example of how attitude to social issues shapes responses concerns the approach taken in social policy to perceptions of poor parenting. In western societies, the role of parents, especially mothers, is considered crucial for good life opportunities for children. This, like many ideas about children and their growth, is a social construction that has changed in history and is viewed differently across different types of society (Smidt 2006). The fact that neoliberalism (which wants child care to be a private and not a state concern) is so dominant should not blind us to this fact; such considerations do not deny the basic rights of children enshrined in United Nations and other human rights declarations concerning children. The majority of children in the world grow up with norms and expectations that do not involve the ideal nuclear family of stay-at-home mother, working-provider father and economic security along with a warm, comfortable and spacious home. Governments in the UK have promoted parenting programmes as the answer to what they see as family dysfunction (that is, families who fail to cope with adverse circumstances). These are aimed at poor families who are told that middle-class parenting styles must be better because middle-class children do so much better at school and in life generally (*ibid.*). Referrals involve working-class mothers who are not coping with poverty and inequality, although most do manage surprisingly well (Welbourne 2012). The notion that their children's life opportunities will improve if parents engage in such activities as talking and reading to them seems, on reflection, bizarre (Smidt 2006; Langan 2011). Such programmes are, of course, a cheaper option than those that might really address poverty and its causes. This is not to dismiss the very real benefits that can accrue from group and individual support for parents experiencing adversity: such approaches might help them cope better with their situations, and this theme is exemplified later in this chapter and will also be returned to in Chapter 7 when looking at groupwork. The difference here is that 'parenting programmes' typically concern the failure of a parent to match up to the ideals perpetrated by a society whose values are constructed by the marketplace, based on the practices of a social group who do not have to pass the test of dealing with the economic and emotional consequences of poverty (Welbourne 2012, Rogowski 2013). In contrast, support from peers and those who understand the real meaning of adversity and its causes can be very helpful in building resilience and helping families with children survive.

The key message for practice here is that theories used should support the location of causes, symptoms and effects concerning the real issues in the lives of children and their families. They should not be used to pathologize parents with blame when they fail to cope with problems that are related to economic circumstances beyond their control. Because we must recognize that some areas of the country have been blighted by industrial decline for several generations, there are now children whose parents – and their parents before them – have known nothing but such adversity. Drug misuse in some areas of the country goes back three or more generations to the onset of economic decline. Under such circumstances, despair and hopelessness are handed down from one generation to the next. Victims should be treated with all the dignity and respect society accords to people affected by sudden disaster. Although everyone makes choices and social workers help parents make those that are better for them and their children, our starting point should be that the majority of service users should not be treated as if they were the architects of their own misfortunes.

4.1 Lara and her children: anti-oppressive responses

We met Lara, Whitney and Malcolm in Chapter 2. Lara had spent life from her early teens onwards in a Children's Residential Unit. She had grown up in the area in which she now has a council tenancy – a post-industrial town with high levels of unemployment, drug and alcohol misuse, and domestic violence. Lara's mother was a chaotic drug user who failed to provide her with routines or boundaries as she grew up. She was admitted to local authority care because she was increasingly beyond control, involved in drug and alcohol experimentation and showing no interest in education despite very obvious potential. Soon after her sixteenth birthday she was pregnant with Malcolm and, by the time she was eighteen, she was living in her own tenancy with Elliott, the father of the children. By this time, she had settled down in terms of her own lifestyle and was generally considered to be a good mum, quickly developing the skills to budget on a low-benefit income and managing her home. Her life was fraught, however, because of ongoing relationship problems with Elliot. He was repeatedly involved in offending behaviour and drug abuse, but eventually left the home for good and life for the mother and children became more stable.

Within six months, the children had been referred back to Social Services because of domestic and violent incidents in the home featuring Lara's new boyfriend. A serious offence involved his arrest and bail conditions preventing contact with Lara or her home. She was happy with this as she described the relationship as casual and was pleased to end it. A case conference considered the high level of exposure to violence the children had encountered and made them the subjects of Child Protection Plans. The social worker, with the support of her supervisor, decided on a different type of approach to securing the children's long-term safety and centred the children's plans on empowering Lara to raise her aspirations and improve her personal situation. At the case conference, she had stated that all the young men in her home area were like the partners she had known, but she listened and reflected when this was challenged. It was agreed from this that help and support should focus not on her parenting, which was excellent, but, rather, on her self-esteem, education and future prospects. Lara, who had been initially resistant, helped set her own goals and objectives. From this point on, the social worker introduced her to a self-help programme: this included the establishment of a small group involving Lara and others like her, with a life coach, and encouragement of reading which she anyway enjoyed (emphasis was placed on novels with strong and independent female characters ranging from Steig Larsson to Charlotte Bronte). The social worker herself was from a working-class background and her own career was built on a similar (but not as starkly disadvantaged) experience.

Thinking about parenting programmes

Parenting programmes are popular responses to the issues presented by young parents that bring them into social work processes including those of child protection. Thinking about Lara and her children, what might have been the outcome had she been referred to a 'parenting programme': list positive and negative features of approaches that focus on parenting and the situations where they might be appropriate.

Positive approaches to child protection and safeguarding

Child protection can involve social workers as blunt instruments of the state working in partnership with the police in a role that can seem to both service user and worker as inherently intrusive and oppressive. However, it does not have to be like that. The protection of children from harm is also a role that many new entrants to social work relish and look forward to, not because they want to emulate police officers or exercise power over people, but because they care about children and their wellbeing. Whilst this was an area of social work that was the choice of few not many years ago (Ferguson and Woodward 2009), developments in adult work and community care have, as we shall see in Chapter 5, served to change this to the extent that most workers coming into children and family work in the UK do so because they really want to. Such workers are likely to care about parents and not view them as always responsible for their own failings and the ways in which they fail their children. On the basis that much of what social workers do in child protection involves interaction with these parents, this can be the starting point for an anti-oppressive practice that is based on:

- An acknowledgement of power differentials
- Openness and honesty
- Reliability
- Minimization of 'professional distance' and the use of clear language transmitted in a friendly and respectful manner
- An ability to listen to parents and see them as capable of change
- Involvement of parents in assessments
- Sharing of information, plans and goals and, where possible, agreement about them.

In Canada, such anti-oppressive child welfare practice has been described as 'mutual involvement', in that social worker and parent work together to identify plans and goals (Strega 2007: 77). The components of such practice are now described in further detail.

Acknowledging power differentials is about recognizing that the relationship between the service user and the child protection worker is not an equal one, and that this is the case for both child and adult service users. For the adults, the intervention of social workers can be threatening, given that family life might be the only area of their lives over which they feel they have any control. It is rare for workers following up a child protection investigation to be greeted with understanding and support from parents who are coming under scrutiny. This can be achieved but only by being honest from the start about the process and the authority held by the worker, including the steps that could be taken to protect children, including their removal from the home. The rights of parents and the options available to exercise such rights should be explained clearly and, if possible, provided in written form. All this should be discussed in a manner that is non-threatening and fashioned towards partnership-building. Inquiry reports and research suggest that social workers have to be vigilant to superficial compliance and that cooperation in itself is not an indicator of willingness to engage in change (Turney *et al.* 2012: 203). Confident practitioners who believe that service users should not be under any illusions regarding a practitioner's authority will make it clear from the outset that they will require to see areas of the home not normally entered by visitors: bedrooms, kitchens and bathrooms. Once this has been dealt with, it will be easier to raise again and parents need not feel that they have been given false assurances or understandings by workers. Practitioners who try to tread around such sensibilities out of a false respect, or even out of fear of the parent, are effectively handing over power to define the boundaries of the working relationship. The use of such authority by the worker may sound incongruent within a radical perspective but this is not so if one believes that child protection – and, indeed, social work as a whole – has a positive function. Our experience is that good working relationships with parents only occur and develop if such matters are clarified early.

For children, loss of control over the consequences of a disclosure can be as traumatic as the abuse or neglect they may have experienced. Skill is required to reassure children that the worker's power and authority will be used in their best interests and the worker, too, has to believe that this is the case.

Acknowledgement of the power differential works alongside *openness and honesty*. This is basic to good practice and must accompany any intervention including, wherever possible, with children. Workers will also be judged on their *reliability*: keeping appointments, or notifying if they will be late, will help people feel that they are being treated respectfully. The building of trust is an essential feature of any social work relationship and its absence will impede information gathering required for assessment purposes and any hope of achieving change. Assessment is mentioned here because, as we saw in Chapter 2, risk assessment and management are seen as primary social work functions within western managerial frameworks. Again, it must be stressed that this is not about manipulating individuals for organizational purposes but, rather, for effectively seeing through processes that end in good outcomes for children and families. Attention to the breaking down of barriers created by *professional distance* is also important here, as we also saw in Chapter 2: the worker who erects barriers by arriving in an expensive car wearing designer clothes and who uses phrases and jargon alien to the parents is unlikely to win confidence or trust. Similarly, office-based meetings should only be used when necessary and dialogue should usually take place in an environment where the parent feels comfortable. Communication with parents should always be conducted in a friendly way and with due respect for their feelings; their accounts and narratives should be *listened* to carefully and their capacity for change never underestimated. However, the worker will always balance what they are told with verifiable history and evidence from other sources. Assessments and their conclusions should never be undertaken over the heads of parents, but should always *involve* them as much as possible. In this respect, *the sharing of information, plans and goals* should never be left to formal meetings; effort to prepare parents will always pay dividends in building the trust and good working relationship that can lead to the desired possibility of *shared plans and goals*.

Research Box 4.1

What parents want from social workers:

- Approachability
- Honesty
- Time to Listen
- Understanding
- Reliability
- Helpfulness.

Statham *et al.* (2006)

All this sounds like simple good practice but is emphasized here because the radical practitioner will adopt such a stance through principle. The practitioner who sees the client as to blame for their circumstances may struggle with these matters and may fail to build a relationship that is in the interests of children and their parents (Mullaly 2010). Most parents will know when workers have empathy and respect for them, and will also know when this is lacking. Workers need to increase their skills to use relationships positively, a trait pointed out in the Radical Literature (Ferguson and Woodward 2009: 155). Such skills were also recognized as leading to good outcomes in an Aotearoa (New

Zealand) study of a group of workers in a child protection agency (Keddell 2011). These social workers tried not to characterize the parents as culpable; they saw them as in need of support but were, nonetheless, able successfully to balance a caring approach with their power and their responsibility to manage risk and, if necessary, remove children. Turney *et al.* (2012: 111), in their study of what constitutes good assessment skills in workers, also emphasize the quality of building good relationships. Munro (2011), in her influential UK review of child protection, juxtaposes the 'rational-technical' approach associated with managerialism (tight procedures, formulized information gathering and planning leading to the idea that most social work is done on a computer) with the work done through the building of good working relationships with children and their families (*ibid.*: 87).

Research Box 4.2

Working with resistance

Forrester and Harwin (2011: 153–67) studied how social workers worked with resistance amongst parents who misused drugs and alcohol. They found that it was workers who were best able to show empathy who met with positive responses. This involved two main aspects: obtaining the parent's point of view and demonstrating understanding of that point of view.

Resistance is commonly encountered in child protection work. This is hardly surprising, given the potentially oppressive factors involved, some of which have already been mentioned in this chapter. To those already listed, we might add: dented pride, humiliation, fear of public criticism and even reprisal. Whilst this reaction might be understandable, factors concerning resistance as a family or client trait and resistance as a product of the interaction between the worker and the client should be added as additional types that require consideration (Forrester and Harwin 2011: 146). It has been suggested that interventions that reduce anxiety through use of the characteristics associated with good practice covered above are likely to be most successful in reducing resistance: in other words, it can be affected simply 'by the way we talk to clients' (*ibid.*: 150). Harry Ferguson discusses the use by workers of 'good authority', which comes from belief and confidence in their role, empathy and also from the respect and manner in which they are treated in their employing agencies (H. Ferguson 2011: 172). This last point will be discussed further in Chapter 8. Building on strengths, rather than always focusing on deficits, results in better relationships and therefore common understanding, better cooperation and improved outcomes (Pinkerton 2002; Turney *et al.* 2012). This is fundamental to a radical approach based on empathetic understanding of the pressures in neoliberal society that create alcohol problems, drug misuse, and the despair and hopelessness that contribute to the neglect of children's emotional and physical needs.

As we saw in Chapter 1, our experiences should tell us that these matters are usually associated with poverty, which has been described as the 'forgotten' side of the assessment triangle (the child's characteristics, the parent's characteristics and wider environmental factors) familiar to children and family social workers in the UK (Welbourne 2012: 114). Service users will often have suffered misfortunes that workers may never experience, so humility – an underrated quality in social work – is always important.

practice example

4.2 Liam moves on

Liam's early years were spent with his mother in circumstances affected by her poor health. When Liam was aged four, his mother died as a result of the issues she had failed to address for much of her life. Liam went to stay with his pensioner grandfather and two adult uncles, one of whom had mental health problems and the other of whom was unemployed. Their home was frequented by other adult members of the family who were prone to take from, rather than contribute to, household resources. Liam seemed happy when he started school but was behind in most areas of his development. He was poorly turned-out but adequately clothed, features not unusual as far as the school was concerned, given levels of poverty experienced generally in the area. However, a caller to the home was concerned at the chaos and poverty found in the home, and asked the Children and Family Team to assess further. This resulted in Liam being made subject of a Child Protection Plan. An intensive support package involving several agencies was put in place to improve his home situation, as it was clear that the family were all devoted to Liam.

After several months, it was clear that the support plan was failing: the grandfather was constantly distracted from his duty to Liam by the demands of the needy adult members of his family. Whilst there was sympathy with this, and earnest attempts were made to help him care for himself and Liam and leave the care of his grown-up dependants to others, this was not happening. The home was deteriorating in standards. The home continued to be frequented by all these adults and a choice had to be made about whether or not this was good enough for Liam. Meetings and dialogue took place with all the family so that they could reach their own conclusion as to what was in Liam's best long-term interests. This eventually resulted in him being matched with a long-term foster carer in the area who was committed to facilitating his ongoing contact with his natural family, especially his grandfather. By the time he moved to the carer's home, the family had accepted that this would be best for Liam and this helped him move on.

Removing children from their families

Think about Liam's situation and what he needs from those around him. Was the approach taken by his social worker in keeping with radical practice, even though it resulted in placement away from his family? What questions does this case raise for you?

stop and think

66 I want social workers to be more assertive with dysfunctional parents, courts to be less indulgent of poor parents and the care system to expand to deal with the consequences.

(Michael Gove, UK, Tory/Coalition Minister with responsibility for children, quoted in *Guardian* 2012c).

Does this statement challenge or justify the basis of radical social work?

Gender and child and family social work

In the discussion on theory in Chapter 2, feminist views that consider the effect of the oppression of women were considered. This has particular application in children and family work, where practice tends to focus on women as parents and protectors of children. Almost without being conscious of what they are doing, social workers regard women who are mothers as being primarily responsible for the wellbeing of their children, whilst men who are fathers or partners are either written off as useless and incompetent, or regarded as dangerous (Scourfield 2003; Strega 2007). Men can become almost invisible, slipping in and out of family life and responsibility without being called to account unless they commit domestic violence, or perpetrate abuse towards children directly. This was the case in the UK with Peter Connelly, whose death in 2007 brought criticism on social workers for failing to take account of the dangerous males in the lives of Peter and his mother (Department for Education 2012b). This, like so much in social work in western societies, is a class issue: this typology of 'dangerous' or 'useless' men is usually accompanied by a characterization of them that resembles Jones' descriptions of 'chavs' or an 'underclass' discussed in Chapter 1 (Jones 2011). Such men are typically perceived as: involved in criminal activity; heavy alcohol users and/or illicit drug users; unemployed or employed illegally; having a propensity for violence and little in the way of loyalty to their partners or children, whom they view as possessions over whom power is exercised (Scourfield 2003). They may project a 'hard man' image characterized by the keeping of dangerous dogs or being heavily tattooed. This stereotyping of men (based, possibly, on real but not generalized experience) is sometimes used to avoid having to deal with them when, in fact, many are not dangerous and may hold the key to positive change within a family (Strega 2007, H. Ferguson 2011).

Unsurprisingly, social work interventions are often aimed at freeing women and children from the control and influence of violent and abusive males: this has led to increased police activity around domestic violence based on 'zero tolerance' approaches that sometimes, at best, criminalize men in order to try to protect their female victims. This, of course, has to be welcomed when seen in the context of past police and agency views of domestic violence as being a private matter that is only of concern and the subject of intervention if it becomes extreme. However, although conforming to a type of feminist-inspired practice, it is hardly progressive if it simply blames men for their behaviour and, consequently, sees solutions only in their exclusion. Whilst such exclusion should always be an option for the victimized women, we know that many would prefer it if their families could stay together. Also, as those of us who work in child protection know, those same men are likely to re-emerge as similarly problematic in new relationships and as parents or step-parents of other children. Their behaviour will not have been corrected but their experience of social workers and partner agencies is likely to further their invisibility. Avoidance of aggressive men is naturally an understandable response for workers who take their own personal safety seriously, but women victims report that social workers prepared to visit homes and stand up to such males elicit respect and confidence (Welbourne 2012: 161).

Practice that recognizes that men might also be the victims of a society that, as we saw in Chapter 2, encourages masculinity but then denies positive expression for this to poor working-class men is important to radical approaches when working with domestic violence. Masculinity (like femininity) is a social construct and not a biological imperative, and its inner contradictions can result in dysfunction. The Canadian author David Trantor (2005) writes about the following aspects requiring attention by social workers seeking change in male perpetrators of violence:

- *Discrepancy strain* – the difference between what a man should be and how he perceives himself
- *Dysfunction strain* – the notion that traditional masculinity can result in social problems such as domestic violence
- *Trauma strain* – the imperative for men to be emotionally independent results in the traumatizing negation of vulnerable and hurtful emotions – especially in childhood

■ *Denial of emotional expression* – symptomized by fear of intimacy, inability to empathize and difficulty with grieving.

The Australian author Raewyn Connell (2005) is acknowledged internationally for work on 'masculinity' and its causes and consequences, contending that neoliberalism with its emphasis on entrepreneurialism and individualism (traditional masculine qualities) has no interest in social justice and equal opportunity, and so pushes back the position of women. The new masculinity, Connell adds, that is associated with business success, can do without older 'bourgeois' patriarchal associations such as religious commitment, marital loyalty and personal probity. It has also accentuated the role of competitive sport and reconfirmed a commitment to military confrontation as a way to resolve conflict with states that threaten economic interests (such as the 'war on terror', and the Iraq conflicts) (*ibid.*). It should not surprise us that men who are denied any pride in themselves according to conventional societal values will sometimes retreat into violent patterns within the only areas of their lives in which control might still be available – the home and family.

'Father-inclusive practice' (H. Ferguson 2011: 163) is helpful in all families where men have a presence. Models, however, are hard to find. In Scotland, a government-sponsored programme (the Caledonian System) is being rolled out to help men who have been convicted of domestic violence crimes address their behaviour through a two-year programme ordered by a Court (Scottish Government 2011b). This has to be an improvement on traditional punitive models of dealing with crimes of violence in the home. Whilst it is not immediately preventive, it does have the potential, in extreme cases, to stop male violence being passed down between generations from father to son. The Caledonian system involves three dimensions: direct work on a cognitive behavioural basis with convicted male abusers, work with the women who are direct victims of their violence and work with the children affected. There is no reason why earlier interventions involving direct work with males along similar lines cannot take place less formally, and this would be both creative and progressive. There is evidence that suggests that, when robustly followed, such programmes can have a transforming effect on men: 'The (groupwork) skill lies in challenging directly and facilitating meaningful discussion, so as to draw men into confronting one another's denial, minimisation and projection (blaming others)' (Mullender 2002: 70).

Social work with families that focuses only on the mother and children reinforces societal views on gender roles and avoids important issues that can help poor families cope better with adversity. Radical practitioners should always ensure that men are receiving adequate attention and, wherever possible, are seen as agents of change included in children's individual plans. There will be exceptions involving especially high-risk behaviours such as paedophilic tendencies.

It remains a fact that, in advanced capitalist countries, mostly male-perpetrated domestic violence continues to blight the lives of large numbers of women and children. Notwithstanding the remarks made about challenging male responsibility referred to earlier, there is evidence that, at a very basic level, women victims feel that they are unsafe and unbelieved (Mullender 2002). A basic principle of good practice is that women and girls should be protected and empowered, and that this is the most effective way to protect children from harm (Dalrymple and Burke 2006). This requires attention to matters such as economic dependency, housing and the effective use of legal frameworks, all of which are basic to a progressive practice.

It is important to acknowledge that gendered oppression is reinforced by marketing methods that play on idealized images of how men and women are supposed to behave and look. These reinforce notions of submission, dependency, caring and the homemaker role on the part of girls and women; they also reinforce physical strength, technical superiority, dominance and out-of-home identity on the part of boys and men (Dominelli 2002). Whilst these subtler forms of gender difference are perpetuated by means such as those listed, in advanced capitalist societies, they are reinforced by religious and legal frameworks in other societies that cast women in a commoditized role from the moment of birth. Given the mobility of people from repressive regimes and poorer regions of the world towards the richer north, such matters become issues for social workers. In Glasgow, Scotland, the Royston social work children and family teams deal with a population who speak 12 primary and 53 different languages. Here, genital mutilation is a live issue, as are forced marriage and people trafficking, especially in girls and women for prostitution purposes.

Alcohol and drugs

It is estimated that between 1 in 10 and 1 in 14 children in the UK live in families affected by alcohol and drug misuse (Forrester and Harwin 2011). The problem is a massive one, with significant cost implications for government agencies, particularly Health and Social Services. As we have already seen in this chapter, social policy is influenced by economic imperatives such as the power of the drinks industry. It is also affected by global considerations: in particular, the alliance of post-war UK governments with the US and its commitment to a 'war on drugs' that is widely believed to be failing. The war on drugs is considered by many critics to be out of control and actually fuelling organized crime on a global scale (*Observer* 2011). In addition to this, the criminalization of drugs use has contributed to the creation of the 'underclass' in society described in Chapter 1, and so also to social division. It is important from a critical and radical point of view that we see the bigger picture when we look at the implications for children of their parent's misuse of alcohol and drugs, and when we consider strategies to help them avoid being caught up in the same cycle as they grow up. As with so much else in radical practice, this starts from a position of understanding and empathy, rather than blame and punishment. This can help avoid the break-up of families and the criminalization of parents, even though both might, in some cases, be unavoidable in the real world of child protection practice.

The fact that practice with parents who abuse alcohol and substances is no different to any other aspect of social work with people who are essentially poor and disadvantaged needs to be highlighted. There are currents in contemporary thinking that have been so swept along by the social and economic costs of these issues, especially in relation to drugs misuse, that solutions are being proffered that deny basic human rights. One of the advocates of such changes in policy is Professor Neil McKeganey of Glasgow University, who has the ear of populist politicians in the UK (*Telegraph* 2004). He suggests that the growth in the scope and power of the international drugs economy is as great a threat to western democracies as climate change, or global terrorism (McKeganey 2011). He therefore proposes drastic solutions that take the emphasis away from a present focus on harm reduction to:

- a stigmatization of drug misusers based on societal moral reprehension of their activities
- tougher anti-drugs enforcement policies aimed at increased criminalization and abstinence, rather than tolerance of users and harm reduction (for example, an end to the methadone programme).

In relation to the activities of social workers charged with mopping up the consequences of parental drug misuse for the child victims, McKeganey suggests:

- parents should be given, perhaps, 18 months to resolve their issues and, if they fail to do so, their children will be removed from their care
- female drug users should be offered financial incentives to use long-term contraception
- when we know that children are at risk of exposure to drug misuse within their homes, closed circuit television should be installed to ensure that the children's interests are protected.

There are a lot of problems with McKeganey's ideas that radical social workers should not stay silent about because of their potential impact on practice, but there is only space to touch on these briefly. Social policy can often be criticized for tackling symptoms, rather than causes, but

McKeganey's solutions to drug problems in society are punitive and socially divisive. His rather alarmist predictor of the future breakdown of law and order is premised on the UK becoming like Mexico, Brazil or other Latin American nations that have experienced recent dictatorship together with severe levels of poverty and economic dislocation. There is nothing inevitable about this and, whilst it could happen, the premise of Chapter 1 of this book suggests that a society that cares about its citizens, provides work opportunity and reduces inequality can reduce social division and problems such as crime and drug misuse.

McKeganey's idea that drug abusing parents should not be given chance after chance to fail their children is already, in effect, policy at local level and backed by guidance from national government in the UK. This is evidenced by increasing numbers of children coming into care with 'family dysfunction' and 'family in acute distress' as the two highest presenting causes (drug and alcohol misuse were not categorized) (Department for Education 2012a). This should, as it is now, be a matter for professionals to decide on a case-by-case basis. His views that CCTV cameras be installed in user's homes takes intrusion to previously unheard of levels and runs counter to such basic human rights as the right to family life, as do his ideas about incentivizing contraception (some of his supporters take this further and suggest Nazi Germany-style compulsory sterilization). Finally, his suggestion that harm reduction be overturned in favour of criminalization and intolerance is unlikely, in itself, to reduce drug misuse. The methadone programme requires intense (and almost certainly increased) resourcing to ensure that those who are involved get every opportunity to reduce and end their addiction. Were the programme to end, crime levels would rise dramatically, together with the influence of drug dealers. That would increase the misery of children affected by drug misusing parents and possibly overwhelm social work agencies. McKeganey's views are deliberately controversial in order to stimulate debate, but they should be viewed for what they are: right-wing ideas that see policing the consequences of society's inequalities as more important than curing them.

4.3 David enters the world

practice example

David's parents are both long-term drug users in their late twenties who are being treated on the methadone programme. His mother was referred for pre-birth child protection assessment, which resulted in a case conference. At that time, risk factors for the unborn child were identified as the father's criminal record and alleged activity in drug dealing, his continued drug misuse and the couple's lack of a suitable home for the baby (their privately-rented basement flat was considered a poor environment for a baby). The unborn child was made subject of a Child Protection Plan. A month prior to the expected birth, concerns increased when Health and Social Workers visiting the home noticed the repeated presence of other known drug users leading to suspicions that drug dealing activity was continuing. Further dialogue took place with the couple: it was made clear that the baby would not be able to return to their care following birth, and that they would have to change their lifestyle and associations if they seriously wanted to be given a chance to be parents with responsibility for their child. There was considerable debate about exactly what was expected, with the social worker and team leader spending time listening to the parents and trying to enter into a positive dialogue, as both wanted to be active parents and keep their child. This included a great deal of discussion about the local drug culture and such matters as the couple's aspirations for the future. Agreement was reached that a legal order to remove the child would not be taken and that the baby would go, when ready for discharge from hospital, to the father's mother's home. The parents would initially be given supervised contact under the direction of Social Services.

This is what happened when David, who was fit and well on birth, arrived a few weeks later. The couple were keen to prove that they could change and agreed to engage with services. Agreement was reached that the couple would give up their private let and move into the paternal grandmother's home with David. However, initially they would not be allowed to look after David themselves without the grandmother being present. Within a few weeks, this was reviewed in the light of very good progress with the parents and they were allowed to take David out on their own. Now, several months on, they are still living with the grandmother and awaiting allocation of their own council tenancy. The father is considered to be doing very well through his engagement with addiction services and both parents are proving to be capable and loving parents. David is thriving. The plan is that the couple will move themselves into their new tenancy and then demonstrate that they can be responsible in terms of their personal lives and their gatekeeping. They have established a trusting relationship with social work staff and all this has, so far, been achieved entirely voluntarily.

Drug-using parents

Should David's parents have been given a chance to prove their worth as carers? How should this be assessed, and how might the approach of a practitioner who takes a radical perspective differ from that of any other worker?

Refugees and asylum-seekers: social justice, population movement and children

The movement of peoples from one part of the planet to another because of climate change or problems created by humankind, such as war or economic hardship, is as old as history itself. We are all the products of such change and movement. Over the past five hundred years, the economic plundering by northern peoples of southern peoples through slavery, imperialism and colonization have accentuated difference and inequality, making the former rich in relation to the latter. Not unnaturally, as communications have improved poor people who want to improve their lives have sought to move northwards. Other population movements across Europe – or, in the past, from Europe to North America and elsewhere – have occurred for similar reasons and have been accompanied by their own issues: their cultures, however, have been better absorbed (with the notable exceptions of Jews, at times in history, and of Romany peoples).

Population movements, even in times of recession, serve someone's economic interest. In Europe and North America, there are literal attempts to reinforce borders through 'Fortress Europe' policies, or the policing of the border between the US and Mexico. However, those who get through illegally provide a source of cheap unregulated labour in agricultural production and the service industries. It is only when disaster strikes that most of us become aware of their presence: Woody Guthrie, the US folk singer and radical, sang of the 1948 plane crash that resulted in the deaths of 28 migrant farmworkers who were being returned from California to Mexico as deportees ('Deportee – Plane Wreck at Los Gatos'); similarly, in our own time, the Irish folk singer Christy Moore sings as hauntingly of the death of 21 Chinese cocklepickers in the UK in 2004 ('On Morecombe Bay').

When it has suited, such migrations have been encouraged to bolster the economy: the immigration of the colonial descendants of slaves from the West Indies to the UK in the 1940s and 1950s to fill low-paid jobs in the health and transport sectors; the recruitment direct from the Punjab of Indian workers for Glasgow's public transport in the 1950s.

Social workers with values of social justice who can see beyond the rhetoric of politicians should determine no difference between the Polish family who have moved to the UK as the result of the extension of the EU in 2004, the Albanian whose presence is illegal, or the Chinese teenage girl trafficked across borders to work as a prostitute.

The law, however, provides an extremely hostile framework for non-discriminatory practice, even with children who should enjoy protection under Article 22 of the UN Convention on the Rights of the Child. Social work is expected to police this aspect of social policy as a result of the drift to the right of immigration policy in the UK since the 1990s. Although openly fascist political parties continually fail to gain a foothold in electoral politics (there are European countries, such as Hungary, providing worrying exceptions), right-wing parties, such as UKIP in the UK, are pushing the centre-right parties on immigration policy: sadly, rather than facing them down, centre-left parties, such as the Labour Party in the UK, are echoing this drift to the right. Unsurprisingly, such attitudes are reflected in the way asylum seekers are treated by government bodies across Europe: in the UK in 2010, a UK Border Agency worker in Cardiff exposed how officials who granted refugee status were labelled 'grant monkeys', and that it was common for asylum seekers to be 'mistreated, tricked and humiliated' (Webber 2012: 35).

I am indebted to Steve Rogowski (2013) for his discussion on the issues this policy context raises for UK social workers wanting to pursue a critical and socially just practice with asylum-seeking children. He examines the areas of discretion created by the legislative requirement to assess 'children in need'. In England and Wales, he argues, the Framework for Assessment also provides opportunity to exploit the difference between the aims of the UK National Asylum Support Service (NASS) (essentially, a deterrent service) and the preventative and welfare aspirations of UK child care legislation. Such assessments can highlight the disadvantages faced by asylum-seeking families and their children in terms of such issues as isolation, economic hardship, personal safety, past trauma and other adversity. Here, too, there is scope for the quiet challenges of deviant practice discussed in Chapter 2.

Rogowski (2013: 120) provides an example of a Libyan family who have applied for asylum in the UK after years of harassment and persecution in their home country. Both parents have severe health problems and the six-year-old daughter seems traumatized by her experiences; she and her four-year-old sister enjoy school, but have attendance issues owing to their parents' health needs. NASS have placed them in an English town where they are isolated and the subjects of racist abuse; apart from providing the family with financial assistance and accommodation, NASS seem unconcerned about the family. Rogowski points out that the typical response is that, unless there are serious child protection issues, local authority services refer such families looking for support back to NASS, which is often non-productive. However, a social work assessment brought the issues affecting the children into a broader perspective and led to further multi-agency consideration about how needs were being met by education, police and health agencies. It also led to pressure on NASS to ensure that the private landlord was fulfilling their responsibilities. Children's Services, too, were made to consider what financial assistance they might have to provide under legislation to meet assessed need.

Radical social work approaches might also take account of the considerable opportunity for collective and community responses through campaigning organizations. To look at some examples from Scotland: in Glasgow, the charity 'Positive Action on Housing' has been involved in a great deal of support activity for asylum seekers. In the same city, the 'Glasgow Campaign to Welcome Refugees' has organized mass resistance to efforts by the authorities to deport those whose applications for refugee status have been turned down. Such campaigns have the potential to become popular: seven schoolgirl students from Drumchapel High School in Glasgow started a movement in 2005 to prevent the deportation of a friend that caught public imagination and highlighted the plight of other pupils facing similar treatment from the same school. In 2013, their achievements were celebrated in a musical show that has toured the UK. UNISON, the trade union representing social workers, together with the professional association BASW, took up the issue of social work assessment of asylum seekers with the Scottish government in 2006 and published guidance for members (UNISON Scotland 2006). Such activities in general will be discussed further in Chapters 7 and 8.

Alternative directions for working with children: social pedagogy

The idea that relationship building is a key to good work has already been indicated in this chapter. Notions of social pedagogy which are very influential in Europe can help guide a radical practice that facilitates work with children and young people. Social pedagogy describes a positive approach that is not focused on deficit (as is much of social work practice) but, rather, on seeing all children as requiring educational support to reach their potential and to all have capacity, given such support, to develop themselves further (Lorenz 2008). Social pedagogy is a development of theory from a number of sources, from German social democratic ideas about education developed in the nineteenth century (and subsequently perverted by the Nazis in the 1930s) to other thinkers such as William Morris, Rousseau, John Dewey, Pestalozzi and Montessori, all of whom shared an idealistic vision that child development and education had to be see holistically and depended on the investment of the adults around them (*ibid.*). Another leading influence was the Russian psychologist Vygotsky, whose work took place in the context of the idealistic early years of the post-revolutionary era in Russia. His particular contribution was to see children's development as influenced by the culture around them and the skills of the teacher who was able to use the space that existed between the child's level of achievement and their actual potential: what he described as the 'zone of proximal development' (Smidt 2006). The UK psychologist Bruner developed this further to describe the concept that children require 'scaffolding' to be erected around them by adults, through which they learn and achieve independence of thought as they grow into adulthood (*ibid.*). The common thread is that children do not develop of their own accord, or through rote styles of learning that are outcome-focused; rather, they require nurturing through a conscious use of relationships with the adults who are responsible for their growth within a culture where this is promoted (Coussee *et al.* 2010).

Research Box 4.3

What children want from their social workers:

- Be reliable and keep promises
- Give practical help and support
- Have time to listen and respond
- Talk about all aspects of life and not just the problem areas.

Statham *et al.* (2006)

Such ideas have been put into practice in child education in the Northern Italian City of Reggio Emilia. This came out of a background of a Communist-dominated municipal authority that was keen to develop policy based on the principles of equality and emancipation that are fundamental to social pedagogy. Schools, particularly in early years education, have been using such approaches since the 1960s. Classrooms, which are designed to give physical space to development, include atelieristas (artists who are there to encourage and stimulate the children's use of imagination and creativity) and pedagogistas who work with teachers to enhance understanding of learning processes; two teachers are provided per classroom (Cameron and Moss 2011; Moss 2011). Emphasis is placed on 'continuity' to ensure that, when children move from one phase of early years education to the next, they are prepared for the event with the active participation of parents, past and future teachers, and the use of materials that they will take with them (Rinaldi

2006). These ideas have been spread within education to influence provision throughout Europe, including parts of the UK.

> ### Research Box 4.4
>
> *Children's understanding of child protection*
>
> Fern (2012) undertook some action research in Iceland to study an initiative in which social workers sought to use relationships with children involved in child protection processes to help them better understand and influence processes. This was in contrast to normal models that largely exclude children because they are seen as vulnerable victims for whom adults have to make decisions. The results showed that children felt better about interventions.

Social pedagogy has relevance to social work. This is certainly the case for residential workers: social pedagogy is fundamental to the care of looked-after and accommodated children in Denmark and Germany, where there is evidence that they enjoy better outcomes than their peers in the UK (this must be treated with some caution due to differences within the broader structures of these countries) (Cousee *et al.* 2010). Social workers also can find, within social pedagogy, an antidote to the managerial trajectory that would make them do little more for the children and young people they work with than 'assess' and 'care manage'.

All these factors are compatible with a pedagogical approach based on the conscious use of relationships. However, it will not happen without belief on the part of the worker that they can make a difference: the radical social worker needs to retain enthusiasm as well as commitment – what has been described as a 'professional heart' (Boddy 2011). Constant career moves to further personal prospects work against social pedagogy: success is based on trusting professional relationships that see children and young people through crisis and then on to develop their lives in new directions. The social pedagogically-inspired worker needs to engage with the child or young person through activity and shared experience, and not just through words in routine meetings, or crisis-driven interventions (*ibid.*). They must be vigilant to criticism that their efforts are symptomatic of over-involvement and always ensure that professional boundaries are maintained; they are then in a strong position to argue for space to sustain such work so that children can benefit from the scaffolding that the worker helps build.

- Radical practice with children and families is, above all, good practice: respectful of people, inclusive of their views and therefore robust when it comes to the difficult decisions that sometimes have to be made to safeguard children.

- Theoretical approaches and programmes based on them that seem neutral should never be taken at face value, but must be viewed critically to see whether they reinforce inequalities and class structures, or challenge them.

- Authentic engagement with parents and children is based on recognition of the real roots of social issues, and a realization that poor and disadvantaged people should not be assumed to be responsible for their problems.

- Such engagement includes acknowledgement of power differentials; honesty; clear communication; willingness to listen; a belief in capacity for change; humility; and, wherever possible, agreement about goals and means of achieving them.

- Gender is an issue in children and family work that requires positive attention as a component of radical practice.

- Drug and alcohol issues are also symptomatic of an unequal and market-based society. Addressing issues requires a vision that extends beyond the symptoms to the real causes.

- Radical practice in relation to asylum-seekers and refugees requires particular skill in finding and exploiting areas of discretion, as well as discreet reference to campaigning activity.

- Social pedagogy offers a framework to extend and properly use the relationship-based nature of social work with children into a practice that is not solely deficit-based but, rather, works holistically with children across their lives.

The reason for writing this book was the dearth of literature on radical and progressive practice. However, there are books that are particularly helpful in developing this in children and family work that have been cited in this chapter. Key publications are:

- Cameron, C. and Moss, P. (eds) (2011) *Social Pedagogy and Working with Children and Young People: Where Care and Education Meet*, London, Jessica Kingsley. A good introduction to the theory and practice of social pedagogy.

- Rogowski, S. (2013) *Critical Social Work with Children and Families: Theory, Context and Practice*, Bristol, Policy Press. This welcome text takes the theory of the Radical Literature into ideas surrounding practice with children and families in a mainly UK context. The chapter on asylum-seeking and refugee children is especially strong.
- Scourfield, J. (2003) *Gender and Child Protection*, Basingstoke, Palgrave Macmillan. Essential for avoiding the invisibility of men in child and family work.
- Smidt, S. (2006) *The Developing Child in the 21st Century: A Global Perspective on Child Development*, Abingdon, Routledge. This is a superb reference book for those who want to ensure that their basic knowledge of child development takes account of culture and place in society.
- Welbourne, P. (2012) *Social Work with Children and Families: Developing Advanced Practice*, Abingdon, Routledge. This book explains the importance of linking practice to an understanding of the dynamics of poverty.

5 Working with Adults

Overview

This chapter will take a similar method to Chapter 4: with a focus on possibilities for radical approaches, it will not seek to explore mainstream practice unless this informs suggestions for alternatives. The chapter will examine such possibilities across several of the adult groups who seek the services of social workers: older people, those with learning difficulties, those with mental health problems and, finally, carers. Personalization (a term that is used alongside the concept of self-directed support – they will be used interchangeably) is the main driver for these areas of work in the UK and, in particular, for those with disabilities, so this will be looked at first. The comments about practice within this section apply across groups not specifically covered, such as physical disability. Addiction was considered in Chapter 4.

From community care and care management to personalization

Those of us in practice in the 1990s will recall how the 'community care' reforms in the UK, which were brought together in the NHS and Community Care Act 1990, were surrounded by the atmosphere of positive change. It was as if, prior to that point, no one in social work had provided services that enabled people to stay at home as an alternative to hospital or institutional care. A similar feeling pervades the advent of personalization in present times: that, until the advent of person-centred budgets, people were forced to accept straightjacketed services that were more in tune with the needs of providers than those they purported to serve. This background serves to characterize those who are enthusiastic about such changes as being progressive, and those who are sceptical, trapped in the past and, in effect, obstacles to empowerment and freedom to choose for service users (for example, Scottish Government 2009: 44). Whilst such thinking is associated with the advocates of 'modernization' and 'change' discussed in Chapter 1, the truth, as always, is more complicated. Just as 'community care' was the product of the neoliberal reforms of the Thatcher years and was more about reducing public spending than providing better community-based services (Barnes 1997), so personalization is arguably about transferring responsibility from the state to the individual, as well as further reducing public provision (Ferguson 2007; Galpin and Bates 2009; Rogowski 2013). It would also be an insult to previous generations of social workers to see them as somehow failing to adhere to such a basic social work value as support for independence and choice in the community. Then, as now, we can only provide (or broker for) what is available and feasible. There is no doubt that an emphasis on choice and self-direction of support, as opposed to insistence on prescribed services, provides opportunity for a progressive practice. Similarly, the closure of large institutions (psychiatric hospitals, for example) – whose philosophies sometimes belonged to a previous century – had to be seen as a good thing in the UK of the 1990s.

The community care reforms threatened to change social work practice from a relationship-based profession to one focused on quick assessment, arrangement of services (often purchased from the open market) and then a remote care management model that reviewed matters periodically and, if required, ended or changed a service. Such practice has permeated social work for adults in all service user groups and, arguably, resulted in a managerial invasion not experienced to the same extent in services for children and families. To use the example of mental health, 'bricks and mortar' institutionalization was replaced with the 'constraining institution of care planning documentation and systems' (Bailey 2002: 170). The exercise of professional skill became limited to assessment and, perhaps, advocating for a good level of purchased service provision; and there has been little expectation that social work itself should be seen as a valued commodity. The emphasis has been on routinized work practices with a deskilling of the workforce and a move from care and counselling to administration (Ferguson and Woodward 2009: 40). Management concerns have focused on the freeing up of hospital beds, numbers of assessments turned around and doing more-for-less as a response to increasing demand. It is difficult to locate a progressive practice within such constraints but it would also be wrong to condemn all social workers who were (and still are) encumbered by care management as conforming and uninventive; the street-level bureaucrats discussed in Chapter 3 have been active in community care, trying to enhance service user participation in services and ensuring that real choice has been exercised (White and Harris 2001). Sometimes, this brings practitioners into conflict with powerful groups, such as hospital consultants, over attempts to speed up processes (Community Care 2007).

> ### Research Box 5.1
>
> *Processing older people*
>
> Sullivan (2009) found that social work staff undertaking assessment and care management tasks for old people did so routinely according to implicit understandings about agency expectations and resource availability. They paid little attention to underlying social work values concerning social justice and, effectively, differentiated between the deserving and undeserving. Such practice was validated within their teams and by their agencies. She concluded that this occurred because social work skills and values were unrecognized and unvalued in the real world of day-to-day work.

Personalization is said by its advocates to be the big idea of the early twenty-first century. With origins in the direct payments movement that rose out of numbers of radicalized US veterans disabled in the Vietnam War that sought to increase power and choice for those able to exercise it, personalization takes things considerably further. In the words of its main UK architects:

> [It is] not a set of policies but a general approach to public services and social care that puts the person at the centre as a participant in shaping the services they get, managing risk and providing resources, whether financial or in terms of their own effort.
>
> (Leadbeater and Lownsbrough 2005: 25)

This quotation clearly shows the intent in terms of a relocation of responsibility. Personalization provides a bridge between right-wing neoliberal notions that reject the 'nanny state' and centre-left notions of the 'Third Way' through which state provision should be provided through the market (Jordan and Jordan 2000). Ferguson (2007: 389) comments that, despite language that is rejecting of paternalism, personalization is entirely consistent with the welfare reform of successive governments in their pursuance of a neoliberal agenda, in that it involves 'individualization, responsibilization and the privatization of risk'. In effect, service users are being encouraged to embrace an entrepreneurial approach to service provision that flows from a political and economic system responsible for many of their problems (Galpin and Bates 2009: 10). Those with neither the capacity nor willingness to engage in organizing their own services are in danger of marginalization as state-provided services disappear, and numbers of adults at risk of abuse from unmonitored and unregulated services, provided privately or by family members, increase (*ibid.*). In the meantime, secure and reasonably paid jobs in the public sector associated with provided services disappear as local authorities take the cheaper road of self-directed support, with a consequent effect on the morale and motivation of staff providing services (Cunningham and Nickson 2010). This also takes its toll on carers: as one overburdened parent told the trade union UNISON:

> I seem to spend nearly all my time organizing care for my severely disabled deafblind son. If a carer is ill, there is no cover ... It takes me hours to organise patchy cover. Therefore it is impossible for me to have any job or life as I have to be around constantly. Bring back properly qualified, trained and vetted homecare – they were wonderful.
>
> (UNISON 2009b: 3)

The fragmentation of services will also have a particularly adverse effect in rural areas: critical mass will work against the provision of services for those who would prefer an organized collective resource that addresses geographical isolation, rather than an individual one (Turbett 2010).

stop and think

Despite the criticisms levelled in this book and elsewhere in the literature, a recent survey of factors associated with poor morale amongst social workers did not refer to care management (BASW 2012b).
Why do you think this might be the case?

Possibilities within personalization

Personalization contains undoubted threats in its marketization of whole areas of service provided in the past, even if not always entirely successfully, by state-provided services staffed largely by state employees. However, it potentially creates opportunities for good and innovative practice. These are unlikely to present themselves easily in a climate of cuts and austerity.

One of the first pointers to a radical practice is that personalization recognizes the oppression of certain marginalized groups in society and seeks to enable those within them to exercise power over their lives in a way previously denied. Unlike the care management model that saw social workers as little more than gatekeepers of services and enforcers of eligibility criteria, the new policy has the potential for a practice based on empowerment, enabling the exercise of real choice. For the disabled users movement, the policy represents a move towards their goal of achieving a change in society in terms of recognition that disability is a social construct. The social model differentiates between impairment (however caused) that can result in limitation, and disability which is the disadvantage or restriction of activity that society imposes because of economic, cultural and political norms (Oliver *et al.* 2012). Disabled activists who seek liberation from such restrictions see social workers as a component of a society that continues to oppress them (*ibid.*). This view sees personalized approaches as a potential opportunity for a measure of freedom. All this, of course, depends on the availability of resources to meet needs agreed between service user and worker. The Resource Allocation System (RAS) is a locally applied but universal system within the personalization process that involves service user self-assessment. Once this is agreed with the social worker around recognized needs, it gives a calculation of financial resources that will be made available to fund self-directed care. However, there are no positive signs that this will necessarily work to anyone's advantage: in Glasgow, the value of support packages was cut by between 50% and 80% with the introduction of RAS (UNISON 2012b).

Social workers have a collective responsibility to express their views alongside those of carers and user groups, and to argue for adequate resourcing. However, the focus of this chapter is on possibilities within practice and a good starting point when faced with such reality lies within the blueprint document for the personalization project in the UK. Leadbeater and Lownsborough (2004: 59) emphasize participation by service users in processes and the role of the social worker as an engaged advocate in a continuing relationship with them. This provides opportunity for the type of progressive practice denied within the care management process: one that emphasizes the importance of a sustained social work relationship with the service user and, within that, an advocacy role for services that meet the needs identified by the user on the basis of their empowerment and self-realization. This is consistent with the social model of disability. However, there seems to be incongruence in the fact that a neoliberal society (as described in Chapter 1), based on competition and leading to rising inequality, should give birth to a personalization policy championing an equality agenda resting on privately purchased, rather than state, provision. At this stage, it is too early for research to identify whether the policy will actually increase opportunities for those who use it.

Employment is a key objective of disabled groups (Oliver *et al.* 2012) and self-directed support has the potential to enable access to work for those who might otherwise find disadvantage overwhelming. However, in the UK the government have closed down productive manufacturing employment for disabled people provided by REMPLOY, with 34 factories closing in the last half of 2012 and a threat to a further 18 (*BBC News* 2012b). Reflecting personalization and its effect on services, the reason given by government ministers is that this is based on a belief that funding for disabled services can be spent more effectively (*ibid.*). Disabled activists and their supporters will have to use legal opportunities contained under the provisions of the Equality Act 2010 to ensure that disabled people are not discriminated against, given the dearth of employment generally due to the economic recession.

Perhaps the key for a progressive social work practice is the role that state local authority workers are expected to fill within personalization: that of broker and advocate. This, however, is contested, with the voluntary (or third) sector of not-for-profit organizations arguing that this should be their role because of their independence (Harlock 2009). The concern that trained social workers could be squeezed out of personalization altogether is real (Gardner 2011).

In Chapter 2, a radical practice founded on human rights was considered. The social worker involved in self-directed care in the UK has to be aware that the Human Rights Act 1998 does not apply to independent care providers or privately employed personal care assistants who look after people in their own homes (Galpin and Bates 2009). A radical practice, however, would always be guided by human rights principles and perceived transgressions should be addressed by whatever means are available. This would include reference to adult protection legislation and processes, as there are legitimate concerns about the possibility of abuse and exploitation within self-directed care provided by family members or neighbours (Gardner 2011). As already mentioned in this chapter, the issue of risk associated with unregulated support services is an important one for social workers promoting self-directed support and these should be pointed out on the basis of professional experience. However, within the framework, choice lies with the user who can exercise this just as other citizens can.

One of the main problems within personalization, as pointed out earlier, is for those very vulnerable individuals who just want a basic service, such as homecare. In Scotland, the Scottish government's Self-Directed Support legislation aims to enshrine the right not be the subject of self-directed support (thanks to lobbying by the trade union UNISON, amongst others) and workers there can ensure that this, too, is an exercised choice. However, in England and Wales all services will have to be provided through personal budgets. This problem may particularly be the case for older people; if the choice between unregulated privately-employed individuals or providers is exercised by a relative or someone else on the older person's behalf, is that better than a state-provided service that is regulated properly and provided by staff on decent pay and conditions? Many older people might not think so, especially if they are conscious of the role their generation played in building the welfare state.

■ Personalization (Self-Directed Support) is about empowerment and choice. Why then might it draw criticism from a radical perspective?

Older people

In Chapter 2, anti-oppressive practice was described as a means of understanding how marginalized groups suffer discrimination and it was noted that a reframing was required to consider disadvantage as socially constructed and related to power and class. This way of seeing issues very much applies to older people in western society. Ageing is seen as an inevitability that should be delayed through products such as anti-ageing lotions, hair dyes or even cosmetic surgery. Social policy is often aimed at extending middle-life activities (such as sport), or work-like activities (such as volunteering) – and, increasingly, work itself. This type of approach may seem empowering but, in reality, it ignores the physical realities of later life in a 'blurring of the life-course' (Galpin and Bates 2009: 21). The 'special qualities and attributes' of growing old, which can be seen in the veneration of older people in other societies, are denied (*ibid.*). Because ageing inevitably results in physical deterioration, this also results in a fragmentation of older people into 'third-age' individuals who are active and independent and 'fourth-age' people who are frail and dependent, and therefore excluded and disadvantaged (*ibid.*: 21). Older people who reach this fourth stage where they need support to achieve a quality of life are a 'problem' because of the resources they require, especially if these resources, such as health and social care, might have to be provided from precious public funds.

Phillipson has been writing about ageing and society from a critical Marxist perspective for many years. In the midst of the recession of the early 1980s, he wrote about the emergence of 'retirement' as a phenomenon associated with the development of capitalism and the intensive labour processes it created. The latter left little scope for the productive exploitation of workers whose physical capabilities would be limited (Phillipson 1982). He went on to explain how the tensions between investment in a productive labour force and the requirement to look after those who were no longer required would create tensions in welfare spending, especially in times of resource scarcity. These issues are very much alive in neoliberal economies in the twenty-first century. Phillipson and others have developed perspectives around critical gerontology that show how social policy has adapted to the needs of globalized capitalism: despite superficially anti-discriminatory policies (for example, the outlawing in the UK of explicit ageism in employment practice), 'age is used politically and bureaucratically as a principle of social organization and control' (Baars *et al.* 2006). In the same text, Crystal shows how opportunities in later life are established by the stage of mid-life by socio-economic status and poor health through exposure to stresses and risks (Crystal 2006). The effects are shown in the inequalities, including early death, reported by Wilkinson and Pickett (2010) discussed in Chapter 1. In other words, the opportunity to enjoy 'retirement' is socially constructed by one's place in the class system, with many condemned to poor health (if not an early demise) and reliance on welfare state services.

The 'problem' of old age is increasing in scope as the population ages: frail older people are sometimes described in social work and health settings as 'bed blockers' when they are admitted to hospital and then need support in order to return to their homes (Brown 2010). In the UK, care management arising from the community care reforms of the 1980s and 1990s sought to address such problems and personalization is the latest response, albeit one that challenges some aspects of oppression through practical measures to ensure empowerment and choice. However, as described earlier, it is Galpin and Bates' fourth group who are most disadvantaged by the latest policy.

When looking for possibilities for a radical practice, it is important to seek out the space afforded through government policy and guidance. Although the emphasis in a time of recession is bound to be about affordability around rising demand due to an ageing population, guidelines also make clear reference to human rights considerations arising from UN principles. The Older People's Wellbeing Monitor for Wales lists five aims for services for older people:

- Dignity and social inclusion
- Material wellbeing
- Participation
- Health and social care
- Self-fulfilment and active ageing.

(Roberts 2011: 173)

Research Box 5.2

Assessing older people

Manthorpe *et al.* (2008) talked to older people about their experiences of social workers in the UK. They found that, with exceptions, many workers were perceived as less interested in advocating for and reflecting the views of service users and then taking an interest in what happened afterwards, than in undertaking quick assessments. Many users felt discriminated against and that resources were being diverted away from them to younger people.

In Scotland, the inspection body for social care services lists six guiding principles for services: dignity, privacy, choice, safety, realizing potential, equality and diversity (*ibid.*). As we saw above, these only apply to regulated care services and not to those arranged through self-directed support or private home care providers. In England, the government's Green Paper on adult social care commits social policy to the provision of services that are fair, universal and underpinned by national rights and entitlements (*ibid.*). All these provide a foundation for challenges to service provision considered to fall short. This might not be an easy challenge but, if the role of the social worker is increasingly as a broker and advocate, possibilities should present themselves.

The concept of 'interdependence' or 'reciprocity' provides opportunity to consider how we can move away from stereotyped practice that sees dependent older people as a burden to society (Brown 2010). This shifts the focus from the opposing concepts of independence and dependence, 'implying an equal exchange of balance and power and recognizes the reciprocal nature of caring arrangements' (Galpin and Bates 2009: 20). This is most graphically realized with personalization, where the provider is actually employed directly by the user so that they are dependent on them for income. However, it can be applied to other social care situations: from giving power to user groups within residential or group housing situations, to the social work role itself. Through professional status, the social worker will typically have power over knowledge, resources and access to statutory measures, but should ensure that this is shared as much as possible with the service user so that they can truly exercise power and choice themselves over what happens in their life. Qubain (2010) discusses how reciprocity features in multi-disciplinary team efforts to give older people power to determine their future through intensive short-term intermediate care. This is geared towards re-ablement and avoidance of life changing decisions at times of crisis. It is very much based on a social model of ageing and associated disability, rather than a medical model. It is interesting that Qubain notes that, because of the model used, power does not lie with the medical consultant but with team members (for example, nurses, occupational therapists, social care assistants and social workers) who have 'freedom to practice' (*ibid.*: 55) in close collaboration with the older people themselves.

The final approach that will be noted in this section on older people is that of taking a 'life course' perspective (Galpin and Bates 2009: 31). This is about assessments that embrace the cultural and structural forces that shape lives that were discussed in Chapter 1. It sees ageing not as something separate (a problem that follows on from earlier productive life phases) but, rather, as a part of a continuum that only makes sense when viewed holistically. It also sees social work interventions as opportunities to reflect on past experiences and perhaps reframe them, look at the present situation and then at aspirations for the future. This is in line with 'narrative' approaches that are discussed more fully in Chapter 7. Galpin and Bates quote sources that state clearly that, whilst time-consuming, such approaches lead to good outcomes for older people in terms of appreciation of issues surrounding diversity and oppression, the growth of trust between the user and the worker, and reduced power imbalances – all leading to better decisions about future service provision.

5.1 Katia looks back

Katia has lived in her terraced home since the mid-1950s. Originally from Poland, she found herself in the UK after World War II as a teenage girl together with her mother and older brother, all long since dead. She married in the early 1950s, her husband also being a Polish refugee, but he died several years ago. The couple never had any children and, as the years have gone by, her friends from the Polish ex-patriot community have all gradually died and she is now quite alone, increasingly frail, confused and talking often in her native language, apparently distressed. To date, she has received no services but is known to her GP. She was recently hospitalized after a fall but is now ready for discharge. Social Services have been asked to consider her situation and determine quickly what supports she might need in the future.

Thinking about assessments for older people

You are the social worker tasked to assess Katia's situation. What might feature in a radical approach to assessment and decisions about her future? How might she be involved in making decisions herself?

Learning difficulties

Much of what has already been said in this chapter applies to adults who, for whatever reason, have a learning difficulty. Oppression can often flow from the labels placed on groups, especially vulnerable ones, and this chapter will use the term 'learning difficulty' generically as a preferred term (Willets 2010) over others such as 'learning disability', which have taken over in recent years from dated and pejorative terms such as 'mental retardation' and 'mental handicap'. This group have traditionally enjoyed few rights and little say in what happens in their lives, including fundamental issues such as where they might live. This, too, is because of a social construct that creates a hierarchy within society that leaves, as we saw in Figure 2.1, those with a learning difficulty as one of the most oppressed groups in terms of their distance from power and wealth. Significantly, this makes them especially vulnerable to life-threatening levels of harm from others. These arise from factors such as over-compliance and dependency on others, fear of retaliation from complaint, absence of support networks, social isolation, inability to communicate and (sadly) the low status afforded to those who often provide the care (*ibid.*).

A creative and radical practice therefore has to be about opening up life opportunities involving choice, and also looking at issues surrounding safety and protection from harm. This will involve proper consideration of risk to the individual and not just to the organization. Personalization certainly offers opportunities in line with such aspirations, but it also contains threats to those with learning difficulties: day care centres throughout the UK are being closed as a direct result of the policy (Needham 2012). This may seem progressive to some as the funding is being used to promote choice; however, for many it can now mean days spent tramping up and down shopping malls in the company of personal assistants, this being especially the case when other community resources such as libraries, community centres and swimming pools are having hours cut back or are even closing (UNISON 2012b). Day centres were places that offered activity, training and support as well as warmth, company and safety. Their closure on economic grounds does not fit well with the broadening of choice and opportunity promised by personalization.

When asked, those with learning difficulties (bearing in mind that this covers a continuum from mild to profound) say that what they want is to have their own home, have friends and be able to go out more (Rowley and Hunter 2011). Although policy strands in the UK have different origins, it is now generally recognized that, underpinned by personalization, person-centred planning (PCP) is the mechanism for ensuring that the process of meeting such aspirations is participatory and self-directing (Cambridge 2008). Progressive social work practice should ensure that this really is a democratic process and that resources are not simply directed towards those carers who are able to articulate most effectively, which of course will be those from middle-class origins. The latter may well over-estimate need and, conversely, working-class carers and service users who have lower expectations will under-estimate need. Whilst class origin might mean little to users themselves, it will affect the services they are likely to receive.

Many adults with learning difficulties, like disabled people in general, as discussed earlier in this chapter, would like to work and contribute. In the past, when there was more employment available generally, work placements, whether organized formally or informally, were a possibility. With unemployment high in many western democracies, such opportunities will be very limited: indeed, it is probably not an exaggeration to state that many university graduates are filling posts that might in past times have been undertaken by employees who might require support, albeit low-level. With dozens of people typically applying for every vacancy, why would an employer want to take on an employee who might require assistance to travel to work, close supervision and support, and whose productive output might be limited? Legislation beyond the Equality Act would be required to open up such opportunities and this runs counter to basic neoliberal principles concerning free markets. In the meantime, social enterprises should be persuaded to offer such opportunities.

5.2 Eddie and Mary

Eddie is now nearing 55 years of age and has a severe learning difficulty. The extent of this has never really been assessed as he has been cared for his entire life by his mother Mary, who is now 75. When he was very young, she rejected a suggestion from a GP that perhaps Eddie should be admitted to an institution and looked after there. He never went to school and has never spent a night apart from her. Eddie is therefore quite dependent on his mum and the two have shared a home since his younger brother grew up and moved away many years ago. Over the years, more enlightened health and social work professionals have tried to get Eddie to attend day services but Mary has always insisted on going too, and then withdrawing him on the basis that he did not enjoy them. Eddie however has always been regarded as happy and well cared for, and he and his mum were a familiar sight around the rural community where they lived.

All this began to change two years ago when neighbours and the social worker who kept an eye on the family began to notice changes. Mary became confused and forgetful, and her routines began to fall away. She became suspicious and hostile of family and former friends and neighbours, and decided to sell her house and move. Social Services were alerted by the estate agent and Mary's lawyer was contacted. By this time, her house sale was almost completed despite some doubt about her capacity to undertake such a transaction. In the event, hosted by the social worker, agencies met together with her lawyer to determine what was in the best interests of Mary and Eddie from this point on. By this time, there was also concern that Eddie, whilst he remained inseparable from his mother, might be suffering some degree of physical neglect. The plan was agreed.

A day or so prior to the date of her house transfer to the new owner, Mary was reminded that she and Eddie had nowhere to go and that a place had been found for them in a local care home. She agreed to go with Eddie until such time as she found somewhere for them both. Once in the care home, a very carefully worked out care plan commenced to help them settle in a dignified fashion into their new environment. Prior to the move, considerable negotiation had taken place with the external inspection body, health professionals and the local authority to permit this unheard of arrangement. Social Services managers had to be convinced that Mary and Eddie should not simply be prised apart. That would probably have resulted in Eddie being placed in a specialized care home setting some distance away and a likelihood that resistance and deterioration would be such that Mary would have to be detained in a psycho-geriatric hospital setting. Old age and learning disability psychiatrists who examined them both were of the opinion that separation would probably prove very problematic and possibly fatal for them both. The social worker used their support to successfully argue for the finances involved to place them together, which involved a supplement to the care home for the additional staffing this would involve.

Two years later, Mary and Eddie are settled into the care home. This has not been without its problems and legal issues that have been resolved through the combined efforts of social worker, lawyer, family members and other professionals. Doubts about the arrangement from those managers who hold the purse strings continue but the social worker has stuck to her guns. The government body who oversee the legal guardianship that was required to secure Eddie's situation have commented favourably on the imaginative solution found to the problems facing all concerned at the time of crisis.

Exercise 5.2

Care planning: thinking out of the box

What was radical about the care plans for Mary and Eddie, and how might they have cut across proceduralized and man-agerially-driven practice? What can we learn from the tactics used by the social worker concerned? Given the way services are organized, what would be the greatest obstacle to such an approach and how might it be tackled?

stop and think

It is argued that learning difficulty, in common with other types of 'disability', is a social construction, rather than an absolute fact.

If this is so, why, and how, might such an explanation guide social work practice?

Mental health

Over the years that psychiatry has grown as a branch of medicine, there have been many professionals who have contested basic concepts of mental illness from a critical and radical perspective. Contemporary with 1970s radical social work are the popular writings of the psychiatrist R.D. Laing (for example, *The Divided Self* 1969) and the sociologist Erving Goffman (for example, *Asylums* 1968). Psychiatry itself, the basis of treatment methods for those who suffer the most severe disorders, might also seem the antithesis to radical approaches with its over-focus on organic, rather than social, causes of mental ill health. Similarly, psychoanalysis, a major contributor to psychiatry, with its emphasis on tensions within the inner world of the individual, might also seem at odds with radical social work (it is also a major contributor to very traditional forms of individualist social work discussed in Chapter 1). However, both have adherents who have adapted their methods in the critical radical tradition (Wolfenstein 1993; Roy 2007). These trends have been influenced by some of the same sources as the radical social work developments discussed in Chapter 2 through such writers as Franz Fanon (1967).

It follows that treatment and therapy are also contested, with radical ideas being presented that counter mainstream treatments. These draw inspiration from Freire, whose work is discussed elsewhere in Chapter 2, and narrative therapy, which is discussed in Chapter 7 (Martinez 2005). The radical alternatives stress the place of social class and place in unequal societies. In neoliberal-driven states, it is no accident that research programmes tend to reflect the priorities of the global pharmaceutical corporations with their emphasis on the chemical suppression of symptoms, rather than the cure of the issues that underlie them (Barnes and Bowl 2001; Martinez 2005). The Mental Health Survivors Movement, which started in the USA in the 1970s and which is now influential elsewhere (Ferguson 2008), rests on non-acceptance of the medical model of illness and a belief in a different kind of society. The Mental Health Survivors Movement, and its insistence that user-controlled services are more effective than traditional treatments, is a cornerstone of radical alternatives. Martinez (2005) lays out a vision for post-capitalist mental health services which echo the calls in the Radical Literature for a challenge to the hierarchical privileges associated with 'professionalism'.

Mental disorder is a concept defined in law which has widespread general acceptance, including by those diagnosed as sufferers. So, whilst it is important to recognize the social construction of mental illness and mental disorder, its varied presence and effect should not be denied. As with other aspects of state social work, which is the subject matter of this book, social workers can find themselves involved in statutory functions with the mentally ill which can be experienced as oppressive and disempowering. Social workers in mental health settings will necessarily be involved in bringing the service user's social context into a framework where medically trained doctors hold authority, especially in situations where detainment in hospital is a consideration. This can involve conflict and challenge amongst the actors involved (psychiatrist, social worker and patient) who all hold very different levels of power. The focus on biological 'illness' can shift focus away from issues of gender, culture, class and poverty, all of which impact on mental health, with the risk that oppression and discrimination are confirmed (Thompson 2001). Radical practice in mental health therefore involves skills in bringing the reality of social situations to the attention of medical professionals despite differences in status and authority. The legal framework in Scotland for interventions in compulsory treatment situations aid this process through the requirement to consider social circumstances reported by mental health officers before compulsory orders can be made. However, the Mental Health Act 2007 has reduced the role of social work involvement in compulsory treatment and detention in England and Wales, and does not have a place for social circumstances reports (Johns 2011). A progressive approach would promote this practice despite this legal deficit.

Lymbery and Butler (2004: 107) postulate that there is a tradition of distrust between those who use mental health services and those who provide them. The radical movement of the 1970s did not help this by being based on practitioners and largely ignoring the contribution and experience of users of services (Barnes and Bowl 2001). This reflects medical hierarchies and also the fact that, as these writers discuss, the emphasis for mental health professionals has always been on addressing the immediate presentation of acute symptoms. Since the 1990s, the focus has become centred on public safety as a result of some high-profile murder cases involving a very small number of individuals with acute mental health problems. Community inclusiveness has had less prominence. In the writer's experience, the support given to those with mental health issues who are considered 'stable' is poor, even in comparison with people with learning difficulties. It is therefore not uncommon to come across individuals living in impoverished and neglected situations in the community, sometimes characterized by a downward spiral into homelessness in the big cities. This has only been partly challenged through the emerging *collectivism* of the mental health user/survivor movement (Barnes and Bowl 2001; Bailey 2002). With an emphasis within health services (Community Mental Health Teams) on short-term therapeutic interventions and public safety, it cannot be assumed that anyone will accept responsibility for socially isolated and poorly-functioning adults with mental health issues. Sometimes, interested and caring social workers are the only ones willing to carve out time to offer support and this itself is radical practice. Lymbery and Butler (2004: 124) emphasize the role of 'bridge builder' between the service user and the community in all its aspects: a straightforward task and one not necessarily associated with the role of social worker, but the question remains as to who else might fulfil such a function.

Research Box 5.3

Carers' assessments

Seddon *et al.* (2007) conducted research into carers' assessments in the UK and found a wide gap between policy and practice reality.

- Neither practitioners nor carers saw them as being of value.
- Assessments focused on the practical components of care and tended to minimize the emotional needs of the carer and the effects of stress.
- Local authorities seemed more concerned with numbers of completed assessments, rather than their quality.

The authors conclude with suggestions for a practice that is carer-generated and outcome-centred, with assessments that are reviewed regularly.

stop and think

- With work with mental health users, it is also worth considering the difference between 'interventions', with their association of intrusion, and 'interactions', which have connotations of partnership and help (Dalrymple and Burke 2006). These issues are explored in the practice example in Chapter 8 concerning Maureen and the two approaches to her difficulties. This example also explored other practice themes relating to mental health social work.

Carers

The welfare state has always rested on the idea that families should be supported by state-provided services to care for their own vulnerable members from birth to old age. In recent years, the fragmentation of communities through industrial decline, as well as ease of travel and relocation, has resulted in greater expectation and requirement that the state should provide more – different generations might no longer be living within easy reach of one another. Another factor is the social change that has brought equality onto the agenda for women who work outside the home. In times of economic hardship, women's financial

Table 5.1 Carers in the UK

	2001	2011
Total number of unpaid carers (% of all residents) in England and Wales	5.2m (10%)	5.8m (10%)
Providing 1–19 hours care per week	3.556m (7%)	3.665m (7%)
Providing 20–49 hours care per week	574,000 (1%)	775,000 (1%)
Providing 50 hours or more care per week	1.088m (2%)	1.360m (2%)

Source: Office for National Statistics (2012).

contribution to family income has become an essential for many and work has been added to their traditional role as homemaker and mother. Despite social changes, the burden of caring responsibility continues to fall on women (Carers UK 2012), with an expectation that this should be, if not cost free, then of less cost to the state than provided care. In the UK, the notion of the 'Big Society' celebrates the idea that voluntary unpaid activity might replace unaffordable state services such as public libraries; it also reinforces the idea that unpaid care of the old and the sick through family members or informal networks is a desirable alternative to state provision, rather than just a cheaper option. The organization Carers UK states that caring responsibility takes a particular toll on carers when it is over 20 hours per week, at which point it impacts on health and the ability to work outside the home (*ibid.*). They estimate that savings to the state from this burden amount to £119 billion per year, a main reason being that the principal benefit for carers is £58.45 per week, or £1.67 per hour – well short of the national minimum wage of £6.04 per hour (*ibid.*). The number of carers in the UK is rising (see Table 5.1).

Neither is this just about the old, the disabled, or the sick: few would question that children, whose own parents are unable to care for them, are usually better placed with extended family members (kinship carers) who can continue to give them their own family identity. However, they and foster carers are usually treated very differently: foster carers can now expect to receive an equivalent amount to the income from work they have to give up because of their fostering duties. The equivalent kinship carer is supposed to receive the maintenance proportion for children who are looked after by local authorities, but will typically receive a fraction and will have to work as well as care for children probably damaged through their experiences.

Carers are, therefore, a large and diffuse group of mainly women who sit on the margins of society, many of whom many are in poverty (Oliver *et al.* 2012). They occupy a politically important role because of their potential impact on public spending. Carers are typically praised by politicians on all sides but, as we see with the Big Society vision, are at the same time exploited for the savings they continue to make for the public purse in a time of austerity. In the UK, the Carer's (Recognition and Services) Act 1995 gave carers the right to have their needs assessed alongside the person they care for (in relation to disabled and sick adults and children) and such assessments should highlight conflicts of interest (for example, the health of the carer versus the health of the person they care for) that indicate the need for respite and other forms of support. Such assessments should be done robustly and viewed not as an optional adjunct to the assessment of the cared for person, but as an important piece of work in their own right. A radical practice flows from recognition of the exploitation of carers by society in general, is influenced by a feminist view and is focused on rights and the supports that should flow from them.

As with any marginalized group in society, carers are stronger when they organize together and advocate for their rights collectively, as well as provide support to individual members: workers should signpost towards such groups and promote their establishment when they do not exist.

main points

■ Assessment and care management models that have dominated adult services since the 1990s have their roots in neoliberal attempts to reduce public spending on a burgeoning elderly population and increase the marketization of social care. However, they contain progressive possibilities in terms of their emphasis on caring for people in their own homes and with user choice.

■ Assessment and care management models do not, in themselves, promote practice based on social work values of social justice, or knowledge; there is evidence they do the opposite.

■ Personalization is replacing the care management model with one based on the creation by the user of their own services to meet their self-identified needs. This holds out threats to welfare state provision, but also opens up opportunities for empowering practice.

■ All adult care groups suffer different aspects of oppression. Radical practice starts from a recognition and evaluation of the impact of oppressions, and seeks out opportunity to address them. This also applies to informal carers.

- Carers UK Website: www.carersuk.org. This contains a wealth of factual and campaigning information useful to carers and those advocating for them.
- Ferguson, I. (2007) Increasing User Choice or Privatizing Risk? The Antinomies of Personalization, *British Journal of Social Work* **37**(3), 387–403. A scholarly critique of personalization and its implications.
- Galpin, D. and Bates, N. (2009) *Social Work Practice with Adults*, Exeter, Learning Matters. This is one of the best of the straightforward contemporary accounts of the field in the UK, containing excellent critical material.
- Leadbeater, C. and Lownsbrough, H. (2004) *Personalisation Through Participation: A New Script for Public Services*, London, DEMOS. Like it or loathe it, this is the blueprint for the pervasive policy of personalization.
- Oliver, M., Sapey, B. and Thomas, P. (2012) *Social Work with Disabled People* (4th edn), Basingstoke, Palgrave Macmillan. An essential text for achieving understanding of the social model of disability.
- Phillipson, C. (1982) *Capitalism and the Construction of Old Age*, London, Macmillan. This, and other more recent works by Phillipson, lifts the lid on how neoliberal societies construct old age and deal with the consequences.

6 Community Social Work in the 'Big Society'

Overview

Throughout most of the twentieth century, coal mining communities in the UK were known for features such as enduring solidarity in the face of adversity, working-class culture and self-help through trade union, cooperative and other organizations. Some were so resistant to the norms of capitalism that they were known as 'Little Moscows' because of their collective socialist aspirations and communist political representation (Macintyre 1980). Such traditions were inevitably eroded through the course of the century but were revived in the mid-1980s (Freese 2006) when miners fought back against the destruction of their communities through a bitter year-long strike. The organization shown by the women as well as the men strikers helped unite the communities against an orchestrated onslaught from the media, most mainstream politicians, the police and the courts. The strike was, however, lost, the pits were shut and these same communities have gone into rapid decline. This was due, at least in part, to the splits (for example, the criminalization of strikers and open encouragement given to strike-breakers) deliberately engendered by government in order to defeat the miners. A generation later, former pit communities are characterized as 'trainspotting without the glamour' (Jones 2011: 216) because of their drug problems that flow from unemployment and despair; elsewhere, they are described as having a 'unique combination of concentrated joblessness, physical isolation, poor infrastructure and severe health problems' (Coalfield's Task Force, quoted in Freese 2006: 247). The social cohesion that grew from a shared adverse working environment has largely disappeared. Clearly, traditional mining communities are very different places to practise social work than they were in the 1980s and earlier. This is one example of how social trends can shape communities and lends proof to the contention that context needs to be understood if effective practice is to be pursued.

This chapter will examine communities and their meaning for practice, look at how neoliberal politicians are trying to use such notions to reduce public services and, finally, at radical possibilities.

Defining community

The mining communities of the UK have come to idealize a type of close community generally believed to have been lost with the advent of globalization described in Chapter 1 (Freese 2006). Outside of similar isolated industrial communities (most probably located in otherwise undeveloped parts of the world), it might be difficult to find such communities in western societies. Communities are loosely defined and tend to describe some aspect of commonality, whether that is achieved through a shared history and culture (as would be the case with the Gypsy Traveller community), or some other feature, whether chosen or not. In contrast to past descriptions with their emphasis, as with mining villages, on locality and other aspects of shared identity, modern interpretations place emphasis on other shared traits that potentially unite or divide: culture, values, religious belief and ethnicity all being examples. There might therefore be many communities within a geographical locality (Pierson 2008). Unless individual members accept their community identity, the concept might be an idealized one constructed by others, so individual membership could be contested from within or without and there may be eligibility criteria (as, for example, with a religious community).

A shared feature of all communities is that members have things in common with one another. To the Marxist-inclined radical, the social divisions described in Chapter 1 that become more prevalent the more unequal society is would reinforce the old adage that common class interest will tend to underpin notions of community identity. The concept of community becomes confusing: is the mass expression of patriotism said to be behind the UK's support for its Olympic team in the summer of 2012 a sign of community spirit or a transient manufactured feeling? Could it be compared with that felt by the people of the European warring nations at the start of World War I (but entirely fragmented at its end four years later)? This difference is important: ardent patriots, or even those who support the UK Prime Minister David Cameron's 2010 notion of the 'Big Society' (see p. 123), might wish to make us all believe we live in a large community of interest. However, that description essentially diverts us from the real meaning of community and the strengths and positive accomplishment, but also divisions, it can bring to people's lives.

Research Box 6.1

The importance of community

Pierson (2008) draws together evidence from research into neighbourhood effects that show that material conditions in local areas influence:

- Local labour markets
- Peer groups
- Social conduct of neighbours
- Aspects of physical environment
- Quality of services
- Prevailing social norms
- Levels of health and wellbeing (including infant mortality and life expectancy)
- Quality of social interactions and networks
- Presence of local organizations and institutions.

(Pierson 2008: 12–13)

Martinez-Brawley (2000) writes about rural communities and their particular strengths. She uses the nineteenth-century German sociologist Tonnies' descriptors, which divide communities into two types: *Gemeinschaft* describes one based on close relationships within a defined locality, shared knowledge, culture, values and history with a clear sense of belonging and identity. The antithesis of *Gemeinschaft* is *Gesellschaft*; this describes the impersonal relationships and contractual ties that typically exist in cities where people gather in order to access work opportunity. Within cities there will be *Gemeinschaft* communities and it is these that afford individuals a warmth and sense of belonging. This model sees *Gemeinschaft* (associated in rural communities with church and family) as constantly under threat as the ties that bind people together in localities are undermined by the advance of capitalism and, in modern times, globalization and neoliberalism. This is a useful model because it emphasizes the psychological aspects of community and their importance for wellbeing. It also makes it clear that the protagonists of a society united around a community of interest are basing their argument on impossible notions: indeed, attempts to do so rest, like the fascist states of the twentieth century, on a common hatred of a particular group as the binding factor.

Neoliberal commentators have argued that community has no value in terms of economic practicality and therefore serves no purpose (quoted in Hardcastle *et al.* 2011: 95). Countering this, Ledwith (2012), from a radical community development perspective, argues that communities can be 'contexts for liberation as well as domination' (*ibid.*: 32) and that the task is to find opportunity for empowerment and change. This also involves seeking out the opportunities and spaces for discretion that neoliberal societies create through their inherent contradictions, as discussed in Chapter 3.

For the radical social worker, these concepts of community are important. Although we may struggle to find neighbourhoods or localities that can be described homogeneously as communities, it is suggested that their existence is based on other identities. These may or may not be supportive to vulnerable individuals but, the more identity communities believe they share, the stronger the locality or neighbourhood will be as a broader community. Some examples of the possibilities for community social work arising from this will follow later in the chapter. The opposite is the reality experienced in Bosnia during the conflict of the 1990s, where neighbours who had lived together in harmony for generations were encouraged to divide and murderously fight one another on religious grounds. There are far too many examples of this in recent human history and far too many politicians at home and abroad who thrive on such division.

Community social work

The idea of fusing community work with social work should take account of the development of community work and the experience of putting radical ideas within practice. In the UK, this could be said to have reached a peak in the 1980s, with local authorities employing community workers in large numbers as a result of the welfare state developments of the 1970s discussed in Chapter 1: they organized in some cases against their own employers and certainly against other public sector bodies. A group of radical community workers in Scotland published a collection of papers in the mid-1990s which reviewed activity against the reality of developing neoliberalism (Cooke and Shaw 1996). They remained generally optimistic that their aim of helping raise collective voices against increasing poverty and inequality was still possible, especially in the area of public housing. Over 15 years later, the reality is that there are now few community workers undertaking such work and that most who are in employment (cuts in spending have greatly reduced their numbers) are involved in specific outcome-focused youth work or adult education, rather than general support to community or tenants' groups. Community work has, in the process, become depoliticized and 'misappropriated in the interests of top-down agendas' (Ledwith 2012: 198). Critical community development work within the context of the 'Big Society' will be considered later in this chapter.

Community social work was much talked about in the late 1970s and early 1980s in the UK, and featured prominently in the official government Barclay Report into social work published in 1982 (Barclay 1982). The UK notion of community-orientation in social work was recognized internationally and influenced developments elsewhere (Martinez-Brawley and Delevan 1993). Although Barclay was quite vague in his notion of community social work, the favoured method (as proposed in a minority report) was through locality-based generic 'patch teams' who would work closely with local agencies and groups within neighbourhoods, and which might or might not include specialist social workers for particular client groups (Hadley *et al.* 1987). At its most pure, such teams worked in small areas and might include staff who moved into the neighbourhood and who were prepared to blur the differences between work, social and personal life (Hardcastle *et al.* 2011). The trend for community-orientation failed to take a real grip of social work practice and, almost without a murmur of dissent, such teams had largely disappeared in the UK by the early 1990s. Whilst this was driven by the neoliberal priorities of government (see Chapter 1), it also reflected a feeling on the ground that genericism (practice across specialist boundaries) had resulted in a loss of expertise: social workers preferred to feel that they were not jacks-of-all-trades and masters of none. Even in remote rural areas where economies of scale and efficient use of resources had resulted in a celebration of community-orientated generalist social work approaches (Turbett 2004), managerialist agendas have forced change towards silo-like structures (Martinez-Brawley and McKinlay 2012).

Although the idea of the patch-based locality social work teams in the UK has passed into history, ideas surrounding community social work are still influential because of the social policy gearing towards locality-based services that began with the election of the Labour Government in 1997 (Pierson 2008). The notion that context should be taken into account when planning service provision is obvious and resource allocation is usually based on the demands likely to be made in any particular area. There is a wealth of research that examines the effects that the environment in neighbourhoods has on family life and the wellbeing of individuals over their life course, and these are demonstrated in Research Box 6.1. In Scotland, the major report into social work delivery talked of the need for an approach that 'positions social work at the heart of communities delivering a combination of individual and community based work alongside education, housing, health and police services' (Scottish Executive 2006: 38). Whereas Barclay talked of community social work as a specialism, the concept has moved on to encompass all social work fieldwork services and describes an approach, rather than a stand-alone concept.

Community social work rests on the idea that most people manage their situations without the help of social work agencies, even under adverse circumstances, through natural helping mechanisms provided through family or informal networks within communities (Hardcastle *et al.* 2011; Pierson 2008). Hardcastle *et al.* suggest the following themes for a community social work approach:

- Individual lives are entwined with and inseparable from their social environment.
- Social networks and organizational infrastructure affect professional practice.
- Strengthening community helps to solve individual and community problems.
- Community is currently important to government at every level.
- Knowledge of the larger world is empowering.
- Collective as well as individual activity is valuable.
- At every system level, there are many ways to exert influence.
- Collective and individual social involvement and action builds social capital and avoids social marginalization.
- Collective and individual social involvement and action is empowering.

(Hardcastle *et al.* 2011: 404–5)

The approach therefore looks to locate, facilitate and build such supports around vulnerable individuals. Social workers are especially well-placed because of their training in the interplay between individual and environment to play such a role (Pierson 2008). This may involve community capacity building: carefully encouraging local leadership and activity, even if that challenges the *status quo*. The classic advocate of a more confrontational approach was the American Saul Alinsky whose book *Rules for Radicals* (Alinsky 1971) inspired generations of community workers and activists. Alinsky was no revolutionary and was criticized from the left for his philosophy based on manipulating capitalism for the benefit of the dispossessed, rather than seeking its overthrow. However, his campaigning ability to seek advancement for very oppressed groups in US society through tactical manoeuvre is of huge interest to radicals seeking social justice today, even if some of these might be used cautiously within employing organizations.

Alinsky's 13 tactical rules for community campaigners:

- Power is not what you have it is what your enemy thinks you have
- Never go outside the experience of your people
- Wherever possible go outside the experience of your enemy
- Make the enemy live to their own book of rules
- Ridicule is a potent weapon
- A good tactic is one that your people enjoy
- A tactic that drags on too long becomes a drag
- Keep the pressure on
- The threat is usually more terrifying than the thing itself

- If you push a negative deep enough and hard enough it will break through into its counterside
- The price of a successful attack is a constructive alternative
- Pick the target, freeze it, personalize it and polarize it.

(Alinsky 1971: 126–30)

Exercise 6.1

Community profiling (or mapping)

Either individually or in a small group choose a locality known to you through work, placement or personal experience. Using the Internet, spend half an hour finding out what you can about the chosen area's economy and population, paying attention to features such as ethnic diversity and density, unemployment, age profile, poverty indicators and anything else you think might be relevant.

On the basis of the section of this chapter which discussed how communities might be defined, list those features you consider exist in your chosen locality.

Once you have this information, list the factors that might create adversity for the people who make up communities in the chosen area and then construct a list of features of resilience. These can be based on anything known to you, or arising from the information you have found.

You can then begin to analyse this information to identify the most vulnerable members of the population.

Finally, you might consider whether the resources available to social workers match the issues you have identified.

NB This exercise could be a major research task, but the object here is to gather information quickly and then analyse it so that the issues facing social workers can be examined. Further information on community profiling or mapping can be found in Hawtin and Percy-Smith (2007) and, with particular reference to social work, Smale et al. (2000).

stop and think

There are many people in social work who believe that it should be about casework with individuals to address psychodynamic issues and that such help will enable individuals to participate more fully in wider society without social work itself being concerned with that dynamic.

How would you challenge such a position?

Neoliberalism and community: the 'Big Society'

The notion of the 'Big Society' is of concern to social workers because of its premise that important public services should cease to be the responsibility of the state and be that of the community and individual: where provision is required, it should be provided by voluntary organizations, or through private businesses. Within a year of the Coalition government's election, the UK saw collective action, but not as envisaged by the doctrine of 'Big Society'. The action took the form of riots in English cities and mass student protests against the austerity policies that were the other side of attempts to cut the national financial deficit (Jordan and Drakeford 2012).

In a *Guardian* website article (2011b), the UK social policy academic Peter Beresford compared past Conservative Prime Minister Margaret Thatcher's 1987 pronouncement that 'there is no such thing as society' with the 2010 Conservative Prime Minister's advocacy for the 'Big Society'. In her 1987 interview with the magazine *Woman's Own*, Thatcher had attacked those who were dependent on state benefits, arguing that they should take responsibility for themselves rather than relying on 'society' (Thatcher 1987). Twenty-four years on, David Cameron seems to be talking up society, rather than belittling it. In his speech in Liverpool in 2010 (Prime Minister's Office 2010), Cameron suggested that the role of government is to facilitate services that business will provide in local communities alongside citizens who will exercise directional control and responsibility, as well as direct voluntary participation. He outlined three strands: *social action, public service reform* and *community empowerment*. Beneath the spin, as Beresford points out, lies the same agenda of cuts in services and welfare benefits for which Thatcher stood. Already, it has provided a cover for the widespread closure of such public assets as libraries (in some places, replaced by volunteer-run book-lending services). Irony also looms large: as we have already seen in this chapter, Thatcher's industrial policies destroyed communities and actually led to increases in welfare benefit spending to cope with the mass unemployment that followed. In Cameron's case, his choice of Liverpool for his speech was also cruel. This working-class city had suffered throughout the Thatcher era: in the view of some, being punished for electing a left-wing council in the 1980s. This led to official and permitted attitudes to the Hillsborough football disaster in 1989 (involving the death of 96 Liverpool fans through criminally poor crowd-policing), which resulted in the fans themselves being wrongly blamed and ridiculed in the national press (Jones 2011). As recently as 2008, a Conservative think-tank had suggested that Liverpool, together with certain other Northern English cities, was beyond economic redemption and should be depopulated, with its residents moving south to areas of prosperity (*ibid.*).

Whilst it might seem easy, from a left-critical stance, to ridicule the 'Big Society' and its millionaire architects, it also seems to be failing by its own criteria to deliver on its promises. As a policy initiative, its content (as in the three strands quoted above) was similar to policies of previous Labour governments. An official audit published in 2012 was concerned at what it described at the 'Big Society Gap' (Civil Exchange 2012). This showed that positive results from the policy were lacking in the most deprived areas of the country most badly affected by government spending cuts. This applied to:

- aspects of *community empowerment*, such as trust, civic engagement and sense of belonging
- to *public service reform*, in that the voluntary services that were to take over from publically-provided services lacked funding and resources to deal with disadvantage
- and to *social action*, in that volunteering was predominantly undertaken by people aged over 65 who were well-educated and from professional and management backgrounds; volunteering was in decline with all other age groups.

(Civil Exchange 2012: 16–17)

In other words, those who were least dependent on public services were in the best position to take up the challenge of community empowerment and benefit from the other aspects of 'Big Society'. If, however, you were already in poverty and lived in an area where others shared this burden, then social divisions would be perpetuated.

The London Olympics referred to earlier in this chapter were seen to unite the nation and even resulted in a short-term dip in unemployment. The efforts of the volunteer 'games-makers' who provided much of the marshalling at the events has since been praised by politicians and is clearly seen as representing the spirit of the 'Big Society'. One of the main sponsors of the 2012 Paralympics was the company ATOS, who held a reported £3 billion-worth of UK government contracts at the time. Their main role was to reduce benefits claims by disabled and sick people through assessing them for transfer to the new claim system and, to do so, ATOS employees were given targets (*Guardian* 2012a). Of the 40% of claimants deemed by the ATOS assessors to be fit for work who had appealed the decision, 38% had been successful (*ibid.*). Irony, referred to above, features here, too: a games that celebrates recognition of disabled achievement being actually sponsored by a company who are fulfilling the government's objective of denying disability because it means benefit entitlement. However, as the *Guardian* article quoted argues, outsourced companies such as ATOS and G4S who run large parts of the

Criminal Justice System are a convenient cover for government (who decide policy) when things go wrong.

The 'Big Society' idea is persuasive: its major selling point is the idea that citizens should contribute their time and energy to make our communities better places. This has always happened, and participation and contribution towards voluntary organizations and self-improvement has a long and honourable history: from the crewing of lifeboats to the creation of cooperative societies. Those who understand this should make it their business to ensure that a notion fundamental to a decent democratic and sharing society should not be hijacked by those bent on increasing market opportunity and destroying public services.

Research Box 6.2

Reality of the 'Big Society'

Whelan and colleagues from the Australian-based Centre for Policy Development conducted a study into the impact of the 'Big Society' in the UK and the lessons for Australia, where similar policies were under consideration (Whelan *et al.* 2012). They found that:

- Public services were being outsourced without public interests being safeguarded.
- There was a disconnect between pro-community rhetoric and small government reality.
- Promises to build the not-for-profit voluntary sector had not materialized and large corporations such as Deloitte, Serco and A4e were dominating outsourced service contract awards.
- Volunteering was being used to fill the gap created by spending cuts.

---

stop and think

The Civil Exchange Audit of the 'Big Society' (see p. 124) advises that, in the UK, half a million people were members of one of the three main political parties in 2012, compared with 2 million in the 1970s. It also states that 40% of the population do not believe that any government would place the nation's needs above that of their own party, compared with 10% in 1987.

Think about these statistics and give ideas about why you think there is so little trust and interest in mainstream politics. How might this affect community participation in its broadest sense?

Radical opportunities within a community orientation

Chapters 4 and 5 of this book focused on practice opportunity afforded with client groups within contexts defined by statute and service expectation. This section looks forward to Chapter 8, in that it suggests that, as well as the obvious linking of individual problems with community solutions suggested earlier in this chapter, social work seeking social justice should also be about campaigning and how we link individual need to such activity. Chapter 8 will look at ways that legitimize campaigning and insure against attack but this chapter suggests opportunities that present themselves within contemporary practice contexts.

Radical community social work is informed by critical community development strategies as suggested by Ledwith (2012). These are influenced by the work of Freire, the South American philosopher, educationalist and political activist. Ledwith's ideas about collective action built on Freireian concepts of critical reflection, developing consciousness (or conscientization), and problematizing (identification of problems) involve the professional community worker as a facilitator, rather than expert. This theme will be returned to in the focus on groupwork in Chapter 7.

One of the biggest issues facing social workers in western societies driven by neoliberal reform agendas is the impact of welfare benefit spending reductions. In the UK, Housing Benefit ensures that those on low incomes and dependant on benefits receive help with rent payment. Under government reforms, it will be capped at a certain level and paid direct to tenants to increase their financial independence. The reforms will cap benefit and will mean that tenants in areas where rents are high will find their homes unaffordable. According to research published by the National Housing Federation (an umbrella group for social housing provider Housing Associations), the reforms will increase financial and housing insecurity for a group who actually budget well, will increase debt (including rent arrears) and will have a knock-on effect in terms of reducing people's capacity to get back into work (Policis 2012). Private landlords are certain to respond by evicting tenants and this is likely to become a major issue. Over the past one hundred years, there have been numerous examples of how such policies have been resisted successfully. Here are only a few:

- During World War I, attempts by landlords to raise rents in Glasgow were met by mass opposition that included organized resistance to evictions (Melling 1983).
- During the depression of the 1930s, slum conditions, house sales racketeering and rent increases were successfully resisted across the

country by organized groups of tenants culminating in the formation of the National Tenants Federation (Piratin 1978).
- In the 1990s, the Poll Tax was introduced, first to Scotland and then to the whole of the UK. Resistance based on widespread perception of its unfairness resulted in its downfall and, ultimately, that of the Conservative government who had championed the policy (Jordan and Jordan 2000: 149).

Such campaigning activities were never easy but tend to be viewed, in hindsight, as essential components of a vibrant democracy. Their success depends on efficient organization along the lines of the tactics proposed by Alinsky (pp. 121–2). Radical social workers may find themselves signposting families they work with towards organizations prepared to take direct action to resist eviction. They might also become involved themselves as individuals, trade union or professional association members. This requires exposure and risk, especially when disciplinary action by an individual employer can threaten professional registration (these issues are discussed in Chapter 8).

practice example

6.1 Resisting the 'Bedroom tax'

A national campaign developed in the UK in the spring of 2013 around implementation of the aspect of government welfare reforms that involved reducing housing benefits (assistance with rent payment) for those people considered to be in social housing of a size that exceeds their needs. The new tax was widely seen as unjust, and an attack on the poorest and most vulnerable. Because of the general shortage of social housing and, in particular, the non-availability of smaller homes, the policy was considered to serve only to further impoverish individuals on the lowest incomes and force them into debt and homelessness. Public meetings were held throughout the country, organized by opposition and left-wing political parties, as well as spontaneous local groups. All sparked interest and support from some of the most marginalized members of society, supported by trade unionists and community activists who were not directly affected. All were brought together in large public demonstrations in the major cities. Campaigners pointed out that savings from the new tax were likely to be greatly exceeded by additional expenditure on homelessness and other unintended consequences of the new policy. They also pointed out that injustice was confirmed by the savings for the wealthy that would be achieved through tax changes that were taking place from the same date. Local groups vowed to offer collective resistance to attempts to evict people who were in rent arrears because of the tax. Social housing providers were forced into declaring non-eviction policies and moves such as redefining spare bedrooms in homes as storage spaces, in order to avoid imposing the tax. The coalition government, whose members typically lived in huge properties containing large numbers of spare bedrooms, were being shamed into looking again at the policy. The Minister responsible for welfare reform, Iain Duncan-Smith, when challenged on radio about how he could live on what a single person hit by this tax might be left with (£53 per week, rather than the £1500 he receives as his ministerial salary), stated he could do so if he had to. This was countered with an online petition that attracted 300,000 signatures within a few days calling on him to try (*Scotsman* 2013).

Exercise 6.2

Tactical campaigning

Look at the list of 13 tactical rules for community campaigners suggested by Alinsky and quoted earlier in this chapter (pp. 121–2). Which of them could be identified as applying to the campaign against the UK 'Bedroom Tax'? How might social workers involve themselves in such campaigns?

There are other less confrontational examples of radical community-orientation. For example, as seen in Chapter 4, work with ethnic minorities and asylum-seeker groups is likely to bring workers up against discrimination and injustice. This might be found within official reactions to asylum-seeking and illegal migration by some of the world's most oppressed people to wealthy nations such as the UK. Illegal migrants are regularly detained in UK Border Agency raids and then sometimes released back to the illegal, unregulated and very poorly-paid employment that suits the market economy. There are groups that can support individuals and some social work representative organizations have taken up the human rights cause of children affected by refugee status or non-status (UNISON Scotland 2006). Other forms of social work may involve linking individuals with organizations and groups that provide support for ethnic minorities facing discrimination and isolation.

main points

■ Community-orientated social work has a long tradition and, although no longer discussed as a particular mainstream approach, is still considered central to effective practice.

■ The notion of effective community capacity-building and empowerment should not be confused by neoliberal ideology such as that expressed in the 'Big Society' idea of the UK Conservative Prime Minister David Cameron.

■ Radical ideas around community-orientation will always include possibilities in day-to-day practice for linking individuals with community supports and networks. This might also extend into campaigning around issues concerning the victims of social injustice but skill and discretion will be needed to link these two approaches.

■ Empowered communities (such as the mining villages of the past) are best able to unite within and between themselves to resist external threats to their wellbeing and existence. Whilst there are many middle-class examples of this in the UK (for example, where rural school closures are averted), there are also working-class examples, such as the campaign against the 'Bedroom Tax'.

taking it further

■ Alinsky, S. (1971) *Rules for Radicals: A Pragmatic Primer for Realistic Radicals*, New York, Random House. Although decades old, and therefore lacking in advice about the effective use of social media and modern technology, this is still a basic book for campaigning activists.

■ Hardcastle, D., Powers, P. and Wenocur, S. (2011) *Community Practice: Theories and Skills for Social Workers* (3rd edn), New York, Oxford University Press. A superb and very full US book updated regularly since its first publication in 1997. Absolutely jam-packed with advice and ideas for social justice-seeking social workers.

■ Ledwith, M. (2012) *Community Development: A Critical Approach*, Bristol, Policy Press. Margaret Ledwith's updated book could be described as providing for community development workers what *Doing Radical Social Work* should for social workers, but with an emphasis on theory.

■ Pierson, J. (2008) *Going Local: Working in Communities and Neighbourhoods*, Abingdon, Routledge. Although it has no radical pretensions, this book has all the basic tools for effective community-orientation and argues well for the social justice agendas that are implicit in such approaches.

■ Whelan, J., Stone, C., Lyons, M., Niamh-Wright, N., Long, A., Ryall, J., Whyte, G. and Harding-Smith, R. (2012) Big Society and Australia: How the UK Government is Dismantling the State and What it Means for Australia, http://cpd.org.au/2012/06/australian-policy-online-big-society-and-australia/ This Australian study of the UK 'Big Society' exposes the concept for the cover for neoliberal policies it actually is.

7 Radical Social Work with Individuals and Groups

Overview

So far, this book has placed considerable emphasis on the need to consider social context and to regard individuals with problems as reacting to situations beyond their control, rather than necessarily choosing their lot in life. That said, social work, as referred to in earlier chapters, is primarily about working with individuals: just as some people have resilience to deal with life's problems, others require support to do so and, under certain circumstances, that becomes the role of social workers. This chapter will look at approaches to working with people individually and in groups that are consistent with radical theory and social justice aims.

Relationships

Chapters 4 and 5 referred to the fundamental social work skill of working with people through relationships that are:

- Honest
- Empathetic
- Helpful
- Involve reliability.

Before commenting on what these relationships might be used for, it is worth looking further at their importance. A book written about radical approaches 20 years ago would have found it unnecessary to do this, as there was a universal and uncontested assumption about the importance of relationships. However, the onward march of managerialism and pre-scribed social work practice based on neoliberal agendas, rather than social justice and ethical practice considerations, has rendered this task necessary. As Ferguson and Woodward (2009) remark, relationship-based good practice is itself radical in its defiance of these trends.

In a largely forgotten text from the 1980s, Hugh England (1986) argues that social work relationships cannot be framed by scientific understanding in order to determine a correct formula that will work on every occasion. Instead, he contends that, as in art and literature, skills in social work help relationships flow from intuition, experience and imagination. He bases his understanding of the processes involved on the practice of literary criticism as developed by the post-war English Marxist academic Raymond Williams. England's contentions explain why some people are suited to social work and some are not, although skill will always be improved by learning and experience. He writes:

> social work cannot be confined as a 'clinical activity'. The old (always unreal) stereotype of casework with its focus solely upon the individual is evidently untenable ... Thus the plausible strength of good social work and literature is that they examine the interaction of the general way of life and the closest personal experience.
>
> (England 1986: 115–16)

England's explanations of how successful relationships in social work involve this fusion of personal approaches with wider understanding of social processes and contexts seems to fit with the radical argument of this book and his work deserves a wider audience, given developments that are trying to reduce the importance of relationship-based social work.

Working with individuals at the therapeutic level and the use of narrative approaches

If asked, most experienced social workers would find it easier to describe what they are not, rather than what they are. It is likely that few would say they are counsellors and even fewer would say that they employ psychotherapy, even though in the past casework theory was largely based on these two disciplines. The tasks prescribed by society through role descriptions and legislative remits do not make self-description any easier and, as commented in particular in Chapter 5, many social workers find that their professional training ill-prepares them for the mainly administrative tasks expected of them in practice. Social workers who recognize structural oppression would probably agree with Mullaly (2010: 223) that their activity:

- Links personal problems with their structural causes
- Links therapeutic insights with actions so that service users cease to see themselves as inferior beings

■ Links denial of rights with the collective action required to attain such rights.

However, as seen in Chapter 1, this vision of social work does not chime with the neoliberal drive to blame the poor for their situation, and has to be fought for and carved out through the opportunities discussed in previous chapters. In this sense, radical social work has much in common with critical psychology in its ideological battle with traditional psychology and psychiatry, which seek to medicalize psychological suffering. The classic example is post-traumatic stress disorder (PTSD): this came to the fore when the Vietnam War exposed US soldiers to horrific experiences that affected the psychological wellbeing of many who took part. As time went on, PTSD became pathologized as an illness with origins in the brain chemistry, vulnerabilities and predisposition of sufferers, rather than a reactive disorder. This effectively de-politicized PTSD and removed it from difficult moral issues concerning the war itself (Marecek and Hare-Hustin 2009).

If we accept that individuals can be emotionally damaged by their situations (see Research Box 7.1), then it follows that a social work practice aimed at helping them deal better with their situations will work at what Mullaly describes (2010: 223) as the 'intrapsychic' level.

Research Box 7.1

The effects of oppression

Moane (1999, cited in Mullaly 2010: 81) reviews research to find that oppression negatively affects personal functioning at the levels of:

■ Loss of personal identity
■ Sense of inferiority and low self-esteem
■ Fear
■ Powerlessness
■ Suppression of anger
■ Alienation and isolation
■ Guilt and ambivalence.

A practical tool for social workers that recognizes oppression and its negative role is that of *narrative therapy*. This was developed by the Australian Michael White in collaboration with the New Zealander David Epston (White and Epston 1990). Although it is associated with post-modernist approaches (see Chapter 2) because of its concern with language and personal experience, it is an example of how a model that can be assimilated into a radical approach moves away from the individualism of post-modernism. Anti-oppressive authors concerned with practice have adopted it as a valid method that requires an understanding that is within the remit of social workers (for example, Goldberg-Wood and Tully 2006; Mullaly 2010; Payne 2011). The idea behind narrative therapy is that the problems of individuals are manufactured within social, cultural and political contexts. People create meanings and understandings within their own lives based on how they frame their own experiences. Such accounts build up over time so that when we look back, certain events select themselves as dominant over others. This can lead to individuals becoming overwhelmed with oppressive aspects that lead them to believe, for example, that they have always lacked hope and aspiration, that they are hopeless compared with others, that they have always been depressed, that they will always be victims of domination by others. Recounting such narratives with a therapist (the social worker) can help them reframe experience and discover positives that have been pushed into the background, so that they can begin to re-establish hope for the future.

The therapist is not an expert but a listener who prompts and encourages the narrator to uncover their own past and discover previously hidden possibilities than might open up a new future. Payne (2011: 78–9) suggests types of questions that can aid this process. The first concerns the *landscape of action*: this looks at how understanding the detail of what actual events took place might help see how things need not have happened, that events are not the fault of the client and are different now, or could be in the future. The second concerns the *landscape of consciousness*: this involves a reflective focus on what was being thought at the time of the event, by self and others, so that different perceptions are considered for alternative futures. The next concerns *experience of experience*: this looks at how different people will view the experience differently and that perceptions can change, as can future possibilities. Finally, there are questions that look at *deconstructing patterns of power*: this looks at the power held by others and on what it might be based, and how this might be changed.

Narrative approaches can be used across the life course and in widely different settings. Buckley and Decter (2006) report on their work in the US with families in crisis in the wake of school shootings in the late 1990s. Children displaying behavioural problems, often in response to very adverse circumstances, were being assessed and labelled in clinical settings by psychiatric professionals. Their work sought to use narratives with family members to explore the causation of crisis and seek to mend, rather than simply treat medical symptoms. Barnes (2006, cited in Payne 2011) showed how the life histories of informal carers affected their view of themselves and their present circumstances. A BASW conference on social work in Palestine held in Durham in November 2012 heard of the use of such approaches with individuals suffering from trauma as a result of the ongoing military occupation by Israel of the West Bank. Elsewhere, similar approaches have been used to help Holocaust survivors entering old age and reflecting on their experiences (Hunt *et al.* 1997).

7.1 Using narrative therapy in a child protection context

Mandy was 35 years old and lived alone with her seven-year-old daughter Debbie in council tenancy accommodation. Debbie had been brought to the attention of Social Services by her primary school because of late and erratic attendance, poor presentation and personal hygiene. On visiting the home, it was clear that Mandy was finding it difficult to maintain routines, was turning night into day and drinking heavily in order, she said, to sleep. She was becoming reclusive and complained that she was agoraphobic, although she had never discussed this with her GP. Debbie was often left to feed and put herself out to school as her mother slept. Although Mandy's self-esteem was at rock bottom, it was clear that she and Debbie had a close bond and that she cared deeply for her. Rather than focus entirely on the presenting issues of child neglect, the social worker encouraged Mandy to talk about her life and the issues she felt had led to the situation in which she and her child now were. Mandy recalled sexual abuse at the hands of her father before his death when she was eleven years old, alienation from her mother and family as she grew older, drug experimentation when she was a teenager, and an abusive relationship with Debbie's father which had ended some years ago, although he still featured in her life as an occasional visiting critic, rather than a support. She had worked prior to Debbie's birth and had been an office supervisor in a large public enterprise but had left this after going off sick for a long period.

Over a period of child protection planning, through which Debbie was also supported, Mandy was helped to reframe her life experiences and overcome the hopelessness and despair she felt at her situation. She received support from an alcohol counsellor who worked closely with the social worker. Eventually, she was able to look anew at work possibilities and began to network socially. The latent qualities Mandy had as a parent were brought to the fore and Debbie ceased to be a source of concern. Mandy was also able to bring some control into the involvement of Debbie's father in the life of the family.

Unintended consquences in busy settings

Mandy's story illustrates how an alternative approach that looked at issues other than the presenting ones succeeded in positive change. Think about where a focus on change surrounding the presenting issues alone might have taken Mandy (and you as a worker), and what the consequences for Debbie might have been. Is this what happens in busy settings?

Interpersonal approaches

Interventions with individuals that are not designed, in themselves, to be therapeutic are described by Mullaly (2010: 228) as 'interpersonal'. The broad underlying theme is that the social work task is to connect the individual with other people or agencies that can help with a problem or issue. There are various levels in which this might be focused in a radical practice and the list below (with the exception of conscientization) is informed by Goldberg-Wood and Tully (2006).

Research Box 7.2

Perceptions of social workers

Beresford *et al.* (2008) undertook qualitative research into service users' perceptions of social workers involved in palliative care. They found that workers used a variety of methods (individual, group and family work, crisis intervention, advocacy, counselling, support and empowerment approaches). The method used was matched to the needs of the particular service user. What marked out practice that was most appreciated by users was that it was 'truly psycho-social' (*ibid.*: 1405), combining attention to individual psychological need with broader social circumstances. A combination of practical help and support with a relationship and 'friendship' were seen as 'valuable and unique' (*ibid.*). Managerial approaches based on formal assessment as a rationing device which pre-empts supportive social work were criticized.

The first level is that of *advocacy*. Advocacy, in the sense of a discreet and impartial activity where all goals are set by clients, is not a role in which social workers usually engage. It is seen as a specialist activity usually undertaken by agencies established for the task and funded so that clients' voices can be heard in particular processes (for example, statutory mental health treatment processes such as that in Scotland, prescribed in legislation). However, all social workers find themselves advocating for service users at one time or another. Often, this involves housing or benefit agencies but can also involve the worker's own agency (especially in a climate of diminishing resources) and the role is to ensure that rights are met and effective resources deployed to meet identified need (Baldwin 2011). As Goldberg-Wood and Tully (2006) point out (from a US but, nonetheless, universal perspective), advocacy is fundamental to human rights and social justice social work, and especially so in a regime that can be oppressive and has neoliberalism as its driving force, as described in Chapter 1. Advocacy is not necessarily welcomed by social work employers, as it can lead to friction within the agency or with other agencies.

The next level is that of the role of *broker*. In Chapter 5, a description was given of this facet of a social work role in personalization. Whereas advocacy concerns an active and persistent role on behalf of an individual who lacks the personal ability to argue for themselves, brokerage is about holding an expert knowledge of community resources that can be linked with the client. In the words of Goldberg-Wood and Tully (*ibid*.: 115), this is intervention at the point of 'least contest', as it involves matching client with provider. This, of course, fits with the market model of public service provision, especially if it is also linked with value-for-money criteria and even competitive tendering at a basic level, which are part of the ethos of self-directed support. It is, however, a traditional and long-standing task of social work and involves the building up of knowledge, as well as networking skills and the ability to cultivate and create supporting resources. This is in tune with a radical community-orientation role discussed in Chapter 6.

Social workers are also required to work with service users in the role of *mediator*. This involves the bringing together of individuals within a family or group who are in conflict and have somehow lost sight of the common ground or aims that they share. Just as mediation between warring nations assumes that both want peace, so the types of mediation in which social workers might be involved assume that it is in the interest of both parties to seek resolution, so that lives can continue unimpeded by conflict. Commonly, mediation involving a social worker will take place within a family, and the worker concerned has to be careful to be impartial and recognize the validity of positions adopted by all sides. The anti-oppressive radical element of this concerns the fundamental value of mutual aid as a necessary requisite of social justice and progress.

Some elements of mediation will arise from situations where advocacy might have appeared to be indicated. An example of this would be when a relationship has broken down between a client and an agency whose service they require: whereas advocacy involves challenging on behalf of the client and will not necessarily resolve confrontation, mediation accepts that resolution will require a bringing together of both parties. Skill and judgement are needed to determine which method should be adopted in order to get the outcome desired. Unfortunately, the citizens' charter culture (discussed in Chapter 1) assumes that customers should have power as consumers in a market situation and has resulted in a belief that resolution of difference in viewpoint between a service user and an agency requires a formal complaint that is either upheld or turned down. A mediation approach does not assume winners or losers and tries to leave each side with dignity intact.

Finally, *conscientization* is a part of the radical social worker's armoury when working with individuals. This is both an interpsychic and interpersonal approach. Conscientization (mentioned in Chapter 6) is informed by the work of the South American philosopher, community activist and educationalist Paulo Freire (1996), whose work was first published in the early 1970s. He believed that oppressed people needed to come together to discover their common identity and that this occurs through the encouragement of critical thinking about their lives and the forces that shape them. He applied these ideas especially to education, contending that traditional one-way education reinforces dominant ideas and that it is only through dialogue and self-discovery that it becomes truly liberating. This is fundamental to the feminist ideas discussed in Chapter 2, but is carried over into other individual interventions aimed at changing people's lives through 'empowerment'. This is a contested term within the literature of social work and can mean little if it means simply that people should be helped to help themselves. Mullaly (2010) contends that empowerment is crucial to anti-oppressive practice and should involve effort to help people discover their histories and the origins of their oppression. This might be difficult to justify to an employing organization within a social work relationship but, if a worker is being true to the ethical code that seeks social justice as underlying social work (as discussed throughout this book), this should not be avoided. 'Conscientization' is 'empowerment' with a radical tinge.

7.2 Jean looks to the future

practice example

Jean is now in her mid-forties and all but two of her six children have now left home. As a child, she was physically abused by her father and she went on to be similarly abused by the three successive fathers of her children. She has been brought to the attention of Social Services because of police involvement in domestic violence from the father of her two youngest children who has been intermittently involved in her life for over 12 years. After this incident, bail conditions had promoted his removal from the family home and relocation elsewhere. On this occasion, the oldest child at home, Darren (12 years) had run out to alert neighbours who called the police after his mother was subjected to a savage beating after an argument over the TV remote control. Further assessment highlighted concerns about his and his younger sister's safety and his erratic school attendance, which seemed to revolve around anxiety over his mother. It also emerged that the children were also witnessing violence and threats towards their mother from two of their older brothers when they visited the family home looking for money or overnight stays. The risks to the children were managed through a multi-agency child protection plan which included referral to Women's Aid for both children and mother. Jean responded well to this and, over a period of time, which included groupwork with other women who were victims of domestic violence, she seemed to be taking on a new confidence to deal differently with relationships and a more robust parenting style. The Women's Aid workers considered that this involved empowerment through a conscientization process. Darren and his sister were also helped to understand that the relationships between adults they had witnessed and internally normalized were dysfunctional. After six months, the children were no longer considered at risk but support continued to the family to promote their improved functioning and issues such as school attendance.

Exercise 7.2

Using empowerment strategies with women

How are Freire's ideas illustrated in this case study? What other ideas discussed in Chapter 2 and elsewhere in this book can be seen, and what others might have been applied?

stop and think

SMARRT objectives are now widely used in social work organizations to focus interventions. These point to steps that are: *Specific* – meaning that goals and objectives should be clear and understandable, and not couched in vague generalized language; *Measurable* – meaning that it should be possible to measure and validate achievement of goals and objectives; *Acceptable* – in that goals, objectives and plans must be agreed by all parties including services users and involved agencies; *Realistic* – in the sense that goals and objectives should be achievable given resources, complexities and timeframes; *Results orientated* – meaning that goals and objectives are based on outcomes and not on processes of service delivery or service user engagement; *Time specific* – meaning that time limits are set so that achievement can be reviewed and measured, and that adverse situations do not drift on interminably. (There are many examples in the literature but this is based on description in Hardcastle *et al.* 2011).

Are SMARRT objectives compatible with a radical practice that is based on social work relationships? How can they be used to demonstrate effectiveness using approaches consistent with social justice and anti-oppressive goals?

Working 'upstream'

Preventative work is often quoted in government initiatives aimed at improving outcomes. This is exemplified by the Surestart initiative of the

UK Labour government of the early 2000s, which aimed to invest in early years services aimed at lifting children out of poverty and compensating for their disadvantage. As will be seen in the case example concerning Maureen in Chapter 8, upstream work is attractive to the radical worker because it seeks to address problems before they become acute. It is also attractive as a method that tries to address the source of problems, rather than focusing solely on their consequences – a premise that is not helped by the specialization and gatekeeping encountered in many agencies. Smale *et al.* (2000: 33) illustrate this with their example of people falling into a river and drowning, some of whom have coloured hats and some none. Downstream, lifesavers with different coloured hats are jumping in to save lives, as they are only paid when they enter the water and only for those who have the same colour hat as them. Consequently, those who are drowning try to get the right hat in order to get help, whilst those with no hat at all pass on by and drown. Upstream work to prevent people from falling in is problematic: not only will you not get paid because nobody is counting those who do not fall in, but you might also incur the wrath of the downstream colour-coded specialists whose heroic role you are preventing! This rather neatly illustrates the straightjacket effect of 'silo' specializations in social work, especially if they are also tied to performance indicators whereby certain actions are rewarded with recognition whilst others are ignored or considered of lesser importance or status. However, whilst that is an organizational problem, this book is concerned about what practitioners can do; so, having identified the issue, reference must be made to Chapter 3 and its emphasis on seeking out opportunities for discretion. This matter also involves choice about work setting, a matter that will be considered briefly in Chapter 8.

Groupwork

Groupwork is not an exclusive activity confined to experts and most of the ideas already discussed in this chapter can be applied in groupwork settings. There are clear differences between groupwork and individual work that can be summarized as follows:

- Groupwork requires a high level of commitment (it cannot be easily cancelled or deferred)
- It also requires thought and planning
- It is proactive, in the sense that it does not occur spontaneously
- It is a highly visible activity and results are often evaluated more closely than they might be with individual methods of working
- It can arouse anxiety, and permission within agencies for it to take place at all is the norm

- It involves technical and values issues: recording, contracts, manipulation, self-disclosure, confidentiality, power and issues about group dynamics
- It can be especially exciting and rewarding when the potential within individuals is realized and confidence built.

(From Brown 1994)

These basics hold great potential for radical practice and, when looking at such approaches to groupwork, reference has to be made to the classic text *Self-Directed Groupwork* (Mullender and Ward 1991). The authors start with a summary of how radicals in social work have failed to connect their theory with their practice, and go on to demonstrate with real-life examples how particular approaches to groups and their activities can empower participants. This essentially involves the processes and outcomes Freire suggested that have been discussed above. Examples given include a teenage action group on an English city estate that moved, over a period of years, from being troubled young people whose behaviour was seen by others as offensive to a group who had won community and family respect for taking up collective issues constructively and that grew to recognize and challenge the structural nature of the oppressions they were facing (*ibid.*: 106–19). Five underlying principles are put forward for workers involved in groups:

- All people have skills, understanding and ability.
- People have rights that include whether or not to be involved in groupwork, to define the issues the group will address and the actions that might follow.
- People's problems should never be seen as the result of personal inadequacy, and issues relating to oppression, social policy and the economy should be reflected in practice.
- People acting together will effect more power and influence, and this can be achieved through groups.
- Workers should be non-elitist by facilitating, rather than leading, groups; and all work should challenge oppression.

(Based on Mullender and Ward 1991: 30–1)

Research Box 7.3

Empowering groupwork in a Norwegian child protection setting

Slettebo (2013) studied a group of parents of children who had been removed through child protection processes. This group involved them, alongside social workers and foster carers, looking at services and support. Not only were the parents themselves empowered and able to reflect on their own experiences through this group, but the services gained insight that enabled them to consider changes. The author contrasts this with the negative perception of

---

services normally experienced by such parents. He considers that the study shows how 'Despite obstacles ... an empowerment-based approach may counterbalance interventions that are perceived as a measure of social control of families' (*ibid.*: 593).

Some writers have pointed out that groups can reinforce segregation and that separatism can become an end in itself, rather than a means to an end (Mullaly 2010: 232, reviews this discussion). This was touched on in the section in Chapter 2 on feminist practice in the 1980s. The same theme was considered when looking at the role 'parenting groups' can play in reinforcing personal responsibility and perceived failure amongst oppressed working-class people discussed in Chapter 4. However, groups can meet for diverse reasons and, nonetheless, have an anti-oppressive purpose:

- *Therapy* – the acknowledgement and addressing of negative identities and the alteration of destructive relationship patterns. Some types of family therapy fit this category as do groups that are aimed at addressing criminal or anti-social behavioural patterns.
- *Consciousness-raising* – where members challenge their victim/survivor identity and develop a sense of positive commonality. This could apply to women who have suffered domestic abuse.
- *Social or political campaigning* groups around particular community issues (as seen in Chapter 6). An example would be a group set up to lobby for traffic-calming measures in a locality with low car ownership, where it is particularly dangerous for children because the streets are used for short-cuts by commuters who actually live elsewhere in more affluent suburbs.

(Mullaly 2010)

Social workers might see a group promoting any of these aims as useful, and approaches can be based on the principles espoused by Mullender and Ward. Trevithick (2005) warns against groupwork designed to fit a managerialist agenda for efficiency and one-size-fits-all outcome-focused interventions. Such initiatives are designed to meet targets (she cites examples within criminal justice work) that ignore group dynamics and outcomes for individuals. Dominelli (2002) also reminds us that groups can be used by those with an interest in the *status quo* to reinforce privilege and power. However, she contends that groupwork practice is a fundamental tool for anti-oppressive social work. Whilst focusing on common identity (for example, women), groups should not override individuality and individual thinking. Dominelli emphasizes how empowering groups can be as members discover that their private negative experiences are common and that people can support one another to resist exclusion and oppression. Examples of this were presented in Chapter 6 when discussing collective community approaches and a further example is given in Research Box 7.3. Preston-Shoot (2007), in his social work basic primer, is clear that anti-oppressive practice is fundamental to effective groupwork.

7.3 Billy's story

Billy is a white 15-year-old resident in a small group home for teenagers who are looked after and accommodated. Coming from a fragmented, abusive and neglectful family situation from which he was removed a number of years previously, he is desperate for identity and a sense of belonging somewhere. He is failing at school and has little to look forward to once he leaves. Staff are concerned that Billy is becoming racist and intolerant, and his well-versed arguments suggest that he is in online communication with hardcore extreme right-wing groups. This is causing conflict with staff from ethnic minority backgrounds and with other residents, leading to his increasing isolation and concern that his placement might break down.

Challenge in a group setting

As Billy's social worker, you have been made aware of the issues outlined above. If you think concerns should be addressed, devise a plan to help Billy move on from his right-wing political leanings. What might this involve, and what resources or outside help might you call on? How might you use his residence in a small group setting?

- Good social work, regardless of the method used, is based on relationships and involves skill and artistry.

- The two types of relationship-based approaches to social work, therapeutic and interpersonal, both offer opportunities for radical practice that are consistent with social justice aims and ethical practice.

- Managerialism threatens relationship-based social work because of its emphasis on prescriptive interventions – sometimes designed to ration resources, rather than provide the help that is required. 'Good' social workers are seen within managerialist-driven organizations as those who fulfil such expectations through administrative expertise. Such approaches should be rejected by radical social workers.

taking it further

- England, H. (1986) *Social Work as Art*, London, Allen & Unwin. Hugh England's book was never a part of the radical literature of its day, but deserves to be rescued from obscurity because its messages about relationship-based social work have almost become radical.
- Freire, P. (1996) *Pedagogy of the Oppressed*, London, Penguin. Freire fought oppression by empowering the most disadvantaged people in his native Brazil to take control of education and ensure it met their needs, and not those of ruling elites. This book outlines his basic philosophy.
- Mullender, A. and Ward, D. (1991) *Self-Directed Groupwork: Users Take Action for Empowerment*, London, Whiting & Birch. Although over 20 years old, this book has basic ground rules for groupwork that are fundamental to radical approaches. The book has now been updated and extended: Mullender, A., Fleming, J. and Ward, D. (forthcoming) *Self-Directed Groupwork Revisited*, Basingstoke, Palgrave Macmillan.

8 Prospects for Radical Practice: Survival in the Front Line

Overview

Radical practice carries the danger of attracting adverse attention from senior managers; employing organizations will present difficult environments within which to operate effectively. The final chapter of the book will look at practical challenges faced by frontline workers, and the measures and systems they can use to keep safe so that they can promote a practice that challenges the orthodox agendas prescribed by a framework of managerialism. It will end on a note of optimism with some thoughts for the future.

Stress and burnout

The literature is full of examples of the risks and effects of stress and burnout on social workers, especially in the state sector. Research box 8.1 shows some findings for the UK. Social work is clearly a hazardous profession but we should take heart from Mullaly when he writes:

> I think that mainstream social workers are much more susceptible to burnout than anti-oppressive social workers. Their analysis and explanations of social problems do not explain the persistence of problems, nor does their analysis explain why their interventions and practice seem so ineffectual. Over time, with few limited, short-term successful outcomes and many failures from their interventions, they will naturally begin to question themselves and their competencies. Anti-oppressive social workers at least have an analysis that explains why mainstream interventions and traditional approaches to social problems do not work.
>
> (Mullaly 2010: 276)

This theme was illustrated in Figure I.1 in the Introduction.

Stress and burnout

In a survey in English local authorities, Jones (2001) found that social workers complained that stress arose from their organizations more than from their clients. Managerialism and government policy were located as responsible for this, with social work robbed of its meaning, and routinized and driven by budget-saving and administrative requirements. Similarly Balloch *et al.* (1999) found that whilst one quarter of those surveyed reported stress from clients' problems or issues with colleagues, two thirds were caused stress by not being able to obtain what clients needed, and half that they had accountability or responsibility but no power. A more recent BASW survey (BASW 2012b) found that the vast majority of the 1100 respondents felt adversely affected by such workplace issues as cuts in services and unfilled vacancies; nearly half felt their workplace environment made safe practice impossible and one third were considering leaving the profession.

The rise in concern about stress and burnout within public services parallels the onset of neoliberalism since the 1980s (Maslach and Leiter 1997). Both are associated with the drive discussed in Chapter 1 to get workers to do more with fewer resources. Autonomy and trust have been replaced with micro-management, control and human resource policies (such as those that deal with sickness absence) that put pressure on frontline workers. Whilst managerialism professes to decentralize power the reality is that 'problems are delegated but the power to address them is not' (*ibid.*: 7). It is basic to physical science that if you pile on pressure and, at the same time, reduce the resources needed to absorb it, something has to give: often, this is the workers who provide the services. The effect is compounded by the trend within managerialism to turn the concept upside down by using stress as a form of control.

8.1 Stress and managerialism

practice example

I recall a number of years ago being in a new job where there were several issues on which I required support. My emails outlining the issues and the advice required to enable me to carry out my work were ignored and this affected my ability to get on with things. I suffered headaches and sleeplessness, became irritable at home and my overall efficiency must have reduced along with my general wellbeing. I knew enough about stress to recognize its symptoms and, when I was eventually able to sit down with my manager, I outlined the issues and the stress they were causing me. Immediately, the supervisor's attitude changed: we were no longer talking about the matters I had originally raised but about my 'stress', as if this was an organic illness with which I had become infected. This was something we could look at, whereas my previous questions were ones to which he admitted he had no answers, as they were largely about resources. Of course, I turned it quickly back to the causes of my stress and avoided this becoming about me. How many workers faced with this find themselves in 'stress management' meetings, or referred for occupational counselling, as if they were the problem? Such efforts to individualize the cost of cuts and staff shortages will be more cost-effective than increasing staff or resources. They should be seen for what they are.

Exercise 8.1

Worker stress and client problems

Think of other examples of where problems are personalized: is this how service users are often made to feel?

In Chapters 1–2, Marxism was introduced as a theory that can help us understand tensions, contradictions and possibilities within society. The Radical Literature authors Ferguson and Lavalette (2004) have shown how the Marxist concept of *alienation* points to where social workers find themselves within state organizations in the neoliberal welfare state. This moves us beyond individual responsibility for stress and burnout, as it highlights how the work process is determined by others and how workers feel a loss of control and power over what they do. Work that could be fulfilling and creative ceases to be so: as the welfare state reduces and managerial control tightens around agendas that are not those that social workers were prepared for in training, it is no surprise that, as found in the research cited in Box 8.1, workers do not cope. Marx contrasts this with his view that, in a future 'communist' society, work would be undertaken that would fit the creative and other needs people have to fulfil themselves and one another. Capitalism, on the other hand, whether we enjoy our employment or not, creates a sense that work is a means to an end and that human enjoyment lies outside work in what we do with our leisure time (for an explanation of this general concept, see Collier 2004, who refers to the early works of Marx).

Supervision and support

Whilst the state of society explains much when looking at the features that cause stress and burnout, there are factors that are potentially controllable within any work setting. Research can tell us something about the forms and supports that can help prevent organizational pressures on social workers. These are examined in Research box 8.2. What seems clear is that social workers do better when they feel supported in their workplaces through good supervision and management of workloads. Whilst this might seem obvious, it cannot be taken for granted. The recent review of social work in Scotland, referred to in positive terms in Chapter 6, makes no mention of these matters and talks contrastingly of the need for 'professional autonomy within a framework of accountability' (Scottish Executive 2006: 51). This rather ambiguous statement appears to be saying that social workers should be prepared to take responsibility for their own practice but be answerable if this is in question (rather, perhaps, than their employers who provide such frameworks and the resources to provide services).

Research Box 8.2

Work satisfaction
Collins (2008) in the UK, looked at the positive factors that make social work a rewarding task. He found that group and peer support, good supervision, manageable workloads and essential resources can all build resilience, self-esteem, appropriate feelings of control and autonomy. All these combine to create job satisfaction.

In Canada, Baines (2010) undertook a study of what had drawn people into social work, and what were the positives and negatives of the job. Values played a key role in the answers to what had attracted people, ranging from political to religious beliefs and core values; belief that their role made a positive difference to clients' lives summarizes most of the responses to positive aspects of the work; the managerial environment accounted for most responses in the range of negatives, including lack of helpful supervision.

Whilst there is enough justification in the literature of frontline social work management to justify proper supervision arrangements in any setting (for example, Coulshed *et al.* 2006), the quality will vary. Most writings referring to supervision discuss the main elements as *support* (involving issues surrounding morale, job satisfaction and a manageable caseload), *education* (issues such as reflection, personal development and best practice) and *administrative* elements (issues surrounding agency policy and standards). There are various workload management models but few seem to be implemented outside particular localities where managers and workers are committed to them as a means to systematic task-based focus and avoidance of overload. Both these issues are covered well in a brief guide for social workers produced by the trade union UNISON for social workers in Scotland (UNISON Scotland 2010).

Workload management systems will not, in themselves, create time for social workers, but they can be used by workers to argue for what a particular situation demands. However, systems based on prescribed hours for particular tasks are not helpful and can be overtly oppressive. The argument by individual workers (backed by their trade union organizations) should be that a decent job leading to a good outcome will require a fair time allocation. Workplaces that deny this will be neither popular nor productive.

Technology has changed social work in the twenty-first century. Increasingly, electronic systems have improved communication and recording. However, this has come at a cost. Managerialism and top-down control have introduced expectations about conformity to recording, assessment and report-writing styles that have, according to Lancaster University academic Sue White, chained social workers to their desks for between 60% and 80% of their working time (*Guardian* 2008). The introduction of an electronic universal information system for children's assessments in England and Wales has been criticized for its time-consuming rigidity and failure to improve practice (Munro 2011).

Recording and electronic systems have their upside, from a resistance point of view: they can be used to gather evidence of excessive workloads so that demands for additional resources are well-founded. I have worked in several settings where this has been successful and additional staff members have been employed, countering arguments from well-meaning critics that see such systems as nothing other than *Taylorist* management tools to measure time and motion and improve efficiency. They can also be used to evidence requests alongside management response for additional resources within individual cases.

Social workers value group and peer support. However, there is a trend towards hot-desking (sometimes called, in friendlier terms, 'agile working'), the practice whereby desks, and even offices, are shared so that workers do not have personal space within workplaces. This is based on the ease of such mobile working through personal laptop computers and smart phones with Internet access, and even technology that can locate the whereabouts of staff. Such advances must be treated with caution, whilst recognizing that some systems enable greater safety for workers who are working, at times alone, in communities where hostility might be encountered. Technology might seem neutral but loses that neutrality as soon as it is applied in practice situations where it can be used to degrade, rather than improve, the quality of life. This caution includes use for social work purposes (Weiner and Petrella 2007; Gillingham 2012).

8.2 Mainstream and radical approaches compared: a practice example of applying discretion

This final and longer practice example shows differences between mainstream and radical approaches with themes that include discretion, power, inequality and disadvantage, explored throughout the book. It is included in order to illustrate differences in both processes and outcomes.

Maureen's story

Maureen is 41 years old and lives on her own in a local authority tenancy. She does not work but claims sickness benefits as a consequence of several years of chronic mental health problems. Prior to this, she has been self-employed as a hairdresser. Four years ago, Social Services were involved when her mental health problems first became apparent. At this time, her 14-year-old son, Paul, lived with her but left to live with his father in another town. After this, her situation deteriorated and she was eventually detained in hospital for treatment. During this time, she lost her private tenancy (she had built up considerable rent arrears as her life became more and more chaotic) and, when she was discharged from hospital after six months or so, she went to live with her mother. Her mental health was so improved by this time that she was able to work well with Social Services to get a council tenancy and move in. Soon after this, her social worker moved to another job but support continued through the community psychiatric nurse, who reported to her psychiatrist. Maureen was seen to be doing well and it was considered that, as long as she maintained her medication, this stability would continue. Although no longer living with Maureen, her son John (now 18 years old) continues to visit her at weekends.

Social Worker (1): Helen is a social worker trained to undertake legally prescribed work involved in safeguarding patients who have been identified for possible compulsory hospital detention for treatment of mental illnesses. She also works with other adults requiring social work assessment and support, but enjoys her mental health work having established a close working relationship with the psychiatrist involved in the local area. Helen is an organized worker who likes to plan what she does each day and work out her interventions with her allocated caseload. Her reports have been commended for their attention to procedural detail and for the required assessment purposes, and Helen generally enjoys her care management and assessment role. Her desk is neat and tidy and cleared every night before she goes home at close of business; on it is a copy of the mental health legislation, an explanatory text, a fairly up-to-date copy of the MIMS directory of medication used by medical staff, and a medical dictionary.

Social Worker (2): Debbie prides herself on her good relationships with the service users who come her way. She tries hard to see things from their perspective and work out with them solutions to their issues, whatever they are. Once she sets out to help, she will go the extra mile to ensure that supports are in place and often works late if there are things to be done. Debbie is responsive and sensitive to the needs of her service users and consequently juggles her day to fit everything in. Her paperwork and recording are of a high standard but Debbie often struggles to keep them up to date with her activity and interactions with her service users. She has a heavy caseload. Debbie tries to keep up to date with her knowledge of social work and enjoys the stimulation of training and reading. Her politics are on the left and this is reflected in her view of the issues in the lives of the service users in the town where she works. On her desk is a copy of Wilkinson and Pickett's book about inequalities that she brought in to show a colleague. At home, she is steadily reading through Paul Mason's *Why It's Kicking Off Everywhere: the New Global Revolutions*.

Helen's intervention

Helen receives a telephone call from the psychiatrist asking her to become involved with Maureen. He has received reports from the community nurse who monitors her that she is probably not taking medication and is becoming paranoid. She may require hospital detention again. Helen does not know Maureen and agrees to take the call as an early warning and to be on standby for a possible legal intervention to secure hospital detention. She speaks to her supervisor and it is agreed that the case is allocated to her. Maureen writes up the referral and completes her day as the office closes. On her way home, she passes Maureen's house and notices the curtains are shut even though it is still daylight.

A week later, Helen receives a telephone call from Maureen's son, Paul. He went to see his mother at the weekend and is very concerned

Debbie's interactions

Debbie networks closely with the local community psychiatric nurses and they will often phone each other informally about individuals known to them. She receives a call from a CPN who wants to share concerns about Maureen. She is becoming increasingly socially isolated and is not looking after herself, or keeping as busy as she was. Maybe Debbie has some ideas about how she can be helped? Debbie agrees to look at the matter further.

On her way home that night, Debbie calls on Maureen, noticing the curtains are closed even though it is still daylight. They have met before when staff rallied around to help her move into her new home a few years previously. When Maureen answers the door, Debbie reminds her of this and asks how she is and can she come in for a chat? Maureen is initially suspicious but is won over by Debbie's smile and easy manner. Debbie notices the about her. Helen is a great believer in getting people to act for themselves and is happy to signpost to help them do that, so asks him to contact the Community Mental Health Team direct and pass on this information to them. She tells him Social Services will become involved if the psychiatrist requests but, in the meantime, the community psychiatric nurses are monitoring his mother's condition.

Over the next few weeks, Helen is busy with outstanding reports and does not think about Maureen again until she gets a telephone call from the psychiatrist. He has received further reports of deterioration and it is agreed that he and Helen will visit her home again a few days later. In the event of hospital detention being required, he will arrange for an ambulance to be on standby with staff from the hospital ward to which she will be going. He will also alert the police, as their help might be required. They remind themselves that, at the time of her admission four years previously, Maureen had been threatening to staff who had been involved.

Two days later, Helen and the psychiatrist call at Maureen's home. She refuses to admit them and the police are called. They gain access and between them try to explain that they are there to assess her mental health. Maureen is seen to be hostile and distressed, to lack insight into her condition, and to

house is cold, untidy and that there seems to be little food. In discussion, Maureen tells Debbie that she is finding it difficult to go out to the post office to collect her money and has no friends or family around who can help her with this. The only people who call are the CPNs, whose main concern, she says, is that she is taking her medication. Debbie agrees to call back the next day and take Maureen to the post office.

The next day, Debbie speaks to her supervisor and persuades him to allocate Maureen to her for further assessment. He trusts Debbie's judgement and respects her work, although he has concerns about her burgeoning caseload. She advises him that, if they intervene at this point, escalation might be avoided, including the possibility of compulsory hospital admission. Having rearranged her diary commitments, Debbie calls back to see Maureen and takes her to the post office to collect her benefit. They then call at a supermarket to buy some groceries and stop for a coffee before Maureen is dropped off at home. Debbie notices a change for the better in Maureen's mood.

The following day, Debbie calls back at Maureen's to talk to her about her situation. Debbie expresses worry that Maureen seems to be very isolated and that there are many others in her situation because follow up to hospital admission has suffered through cuts in service. Between them, Debbie explains, she would like to be displaying paranoid symptoms and ideations. A decision is made to detain her. Maureen becomes very distressed and is given intravenous injection to calm her down. She is taken to hospital. Helen feels the risks involved have been effectively dealt with through this action.

Maureen's situation in hospital takes some time to improve and, after legal involvement in her compulsory detention, Helen steps back until discharge planning commences a few months later.

work out a plan to improve Maureen's life and ensure that she is able, with the supports that can be put into place, to move forward. As a start, she offers to organize a planning meeting with the psychiatric nurse and Maureen's mother and son. Maureen thinks this would be a good idea. In the meantime, Maureen agrees that the next day she will go out to the shops and call in at Debbie's office on the way home.

(NB Debbie clearly spends more time on this case than Helen and issues about workload management will be addressed later in this chapter.)

Exercise 8.2

Think about these two scenarios:

First, consider from your experience if this comparison is believable.

Where and how has discretion by both workers been exercised?

How might Debbie be described as a 'streetwise bureaucrat'?

How might a Marxist perspective inform a view of Maureen's situation?

What are the merits, or otherwise, of these two approaches?

From a procedural and mainstream point of view, there is nothing wrong with Helen's practice but how might you criticize it from a radical perspective?

Working within state organizations

The list in Box 8.1 below concerns factors that will help ensure that the radical social worker does not draw adverse attention that might threaten employment and professional registration. It draws on the Canadians Mullaly (2010: 255–6) and Baines (2007: 60–5), and Hardcastle *et al.* (2011: 232–43). Its themes will be individually explored in this chapter.

A Survival Checklist

- Be good at the job.
- Be likeable! Be human!
- If looking for employment, seek out settings that offer good supervision and workload management.
- Use opportunities to promote radical and anti-oppressive practice.
- Understand your employer.
- Avoid adventurism, martyrdom and pointless confrontation.
- Confront behaviours that reflect negative stereotypes of service users.
- Join, and be active in, trade unions.
- Consider the role of professional associations and networks; use them positively to promote radical practice.

Being good at the job

Harry McShane (1892–1988) was an inspirational and legendary socialist and trade union activist who spent most of his life living and working in Glasgow. Harry, in a very principled rather than dogmatic way, gave over his life to the socialist movement in Scotland and was still addressing meetings well into his eighties. Over the years, he worked with some of the leading socialist figures of the day, such as the revolutionary John McLean at a time when Bolshevism threatened the British state after World War I. Harry had worked in the shipyards and industries of Clydeside as an engineer, skills he had carried abroad when no work was available to him in his native city. Despite his politics (which had been a full-time employment commitment for part of his life), he always described himself as an engineer, first, and a political activist, second: for him, pride in his work earned him respect when he argued with his workmates about politics. This is fundamental to radical practice in social work and one recognized by the Canadian Donna Baines (2007).

Social workers who take a pride in their work will value and seize further training and other opportunity for personal development. Respect will be accorded to those who are well-read and well-versed in practice developments and who can link what they do to grounded research and evidence. It is increasingly likely that this may not be recognized and appreciated by senior managers in organizations, who may have progressed on the basis of their managerial skills, rather than their practice skills. However, such respect will build an audience for radical ideas in the workplace. There is also a question here about what being a 'professional' means. Within the radical tradition this has been treated with scepticism, as it was seen to create barriers between social workers and working-class clients (Weinstein 2011). More recently, Mullaly discusses this in terms of the oppressive aspects of professionalism, especially the cultural norms of 'dress, speech, tastes and demeanour' and their association with white males (*ibid.*: 121). This was touched on in Chapter 4. It might be best to differentiate between *professionalism*, in the sense of good practice, and aspiring to *professional* status, which has the negative associations (if you aspire to radical practice) discussed by Mullaly. Terms associated with the 'profession' are very much part of the day-to-day language of social work and appear frequently in the pages of this book.

Be likeable! Be human!

Baines (2007) argues persuasively that humour, courtesy and associated people skills can achieve as much in certain circumstances as a willingness to become involved in conflict and struggle can in others. This mirrors the activist skills referred to by Alinsky in Chapter 6. Certainly, building support in the workplace will be helped by warmth and sensitivity to others, rather than dull (if politically-correct) activism. These tend to be skills that effective social workers have through the artistry referred to in Chapter 7.

Try to find work in settings likely to offer good support

The basis of effective organizational support has been covered in the first part of this chapter. There are frontline managers and supervisors who are more in tune with anti-oppressive values than the managerial agendas of their agencies. Supervisors who offer good support are likely to be known to students on placement and by reputation more widely; they are also more likely to be surrounded by committed teams. Recruitment advertisements for staff are unlikely to draw attention to such factors, or, if they do, they should not be taken at face value. Whilst it might be hard for newly-qualified workers to find employment in the first place, such considerations can save grief at a later stage.

Use opportunities to promote anti-oppressive practice

The book has demonstrated many opportunities to practice in an anti-oppressive and radical style. Each successful intervention based on such values and principles proves the inherent soundness of radical practice.

Know your employer

The underlying theme here was discussed in general terms in Chapter 3 in the examination of discretion and space for radical practice. Knowledge of an agency's implicit, as well as explicit, rules and boundaries will help locate areas where discretion is available and much of this will be picked up from colleagues observed in practice. This involves policies and procedures, as well as regulations and guidance, over such matters as the uses of new technology. It is worth getting to know managers and working out who are the allies and who the obstacles to progressive practice. All should be treated with courtesy and respect whatever their role and views: aggression and rudeness to managers will not achieve ends for clients and are likely to become disciplinary matters.

Avoid martyrdom

Radical practitioners will inevitably be frustrated by the restrictions imposed on them and the lack of resources available to benefit their clients. This book has looked at how a difference to people's lives that is in tune with social justice aims can, nonetheless, be accomplished. It may be tempting for some to consider 'making a stand' on a particular issue. Confrontation can be a useful weapon but the balance of forces has to be weighed up before considering such a tactic. It is no use standing alone over an issue, or even with one or two colleagues, if the majority of workmates are unwilling to go with you: such gestures are likely to end up as disciplinary matters and could even result in dismissal and professional de-registration. Ultimately, such gestures are futile as they are quickly forgotten by colleagues who will want to move on from anything that might have implicated them. On the other hand, an issue that has widespread support for action outside of normal processes, even within a single office, can be productive, especially if trade union support is forthcoming (see p. 156). Involvement at the sharp end of industrial action, or even simple campaigning activity, can be tremendously educational for participants, which is in line with the teachings of Freire discussed in Chapter 7.

Confronting oppressive behaviours

Negative stereotyping of individuals tends to be cultural within workplaces and even some agencies. Such beliefs should not be ridiculed, as they reflect commonly-held views propagated by sections of the media and certain politicians, so they require considered challenge. The exercises in Chapter 1 looked at this. If these are effectively challenged, this can change the culture. However, this may not be about getting into an argument with a new colleague on your first day: it might be wiser to talk over the matter with someone else you know who might share your views and then work out a strategy.

Trade unions

In the 1970s, trade unions were seen as essential vehicles for radical social workers (see, for example, Bailey and Brake (1975) and Corrigan and Leonard (1978)). The radical social workers of that time criticized trade unions for their bureaucracy and economism (being concerned more with immediate economic demands, rather than social ones). They nonetheless urged individuals to join them and then 'work very closely, long and hard with them' (Corrigan and Leonard 1978: 146) if trade unions were to be persuaded of the value of supporting particular causes. As we saw in Chapter 1, the trade unions at the start of the 1970s were at the peak of their power in the UK and elsewhere, but the rise of neoliberalism and its accompanying attempts to emasculate them have taken their toll across the advanced capitalist world. This, of course, means that trade unions no longer have the mass membership and attraction they might have had. I have personally lived through a period during which we have moved from a situation where most people automatically entered into a 'closed shop' agreement with the local government employer where everyone had to be in a union (this is now outlawed in the UK) to a situation now where hard work is needed to recruit and sustain union membership. Indeed, many individuals in trouble or with grievances now see ambulance-chasing 'no win, no fee' lawyers as offering better representation than trade unions. This is inevitable when the values of individualism and legal remedy through assertion of citizen rights are seen to have replaced solidarity and collective action. However, to paraphrase Mark Twain, the latter's demise has been much exaggerated and forms of collective action have risen to the fore again in recent years with anti-capitalist struggles, the Arab Spring and other forms of international resistance to the effects of neoliberalism (Mason 2012).

In the UK, there are various trade unions that represent social workers. Trade unions often represent members individually and, as such, are not unlike breakdown organizations for car owners: there when you want them and largely ignored when you do not need them. This, at least, has been the broad picture since the 1980s. However, most trade unions campaign around social justice issues at least as much (if not more, in some cases) as they did when they were stronger in power and influence. This aspect, as well as the exercise of industrial action over grievances, is of interest to radical social workers: collective possibilities for change – rather than simple insurance for an individual's bad times, important though that might be – offer opportunities to radicalize those who take part. The UNISON (2013) Conference Agenda included the following amongst its 105 motions for discussion put up by branches and regions from across the UK:

- *Stepping up the Campaign against Privatization*: calling, amongst other things, for support for a new national campaign 'We Own It'
- *The NHS and the Future of Social Care*: opposing austerity policies and calling for attention to the impact of personalization on the quality and reliability of services, and for the introduction of a public national care service integrated with the NHS
- *Defending the Welfare State*: opposing the introduction by government of 'welfare reforms' that will increase poverty when inequality is increasing
- *Strike against Austerity*: calling for planned and coordinated 24-hour strike action in conjunction with other trade unions against government austerity policies.

Using the preferred criteria, radical social workers should join the trade union that has the majority membership in their workplace, or across their agency. They should also join a trade union that unites them with other workers. In this sense, the specialist trade unions that emerge from time to time, usually through small groups of people who feel let down by the larger unions, are rarely able to provide a forum for effective collective action alongside other public sector colleagues. An anonymous letter-writer to the UK social work magazine *PSW* (2012) captured this when they stated that they did not want to be in a trade union that 'included bin men and dinner ladies'. The radical social worker will take an opposite view, on the basis that unity amongst public sector workers is more important than a pure and unique trade union voice for social workers in a relatively small union.

Research Box 8.3

Social workers in trade unions

Baines (2010) studied unionized social workers in Canada, where there was 38% density of trade union membership.

Her findings suggested to her that years of neoliberal policies in workplaces and agencies meant that 'critical skills have been phased out of most jobs and, hence, largely out of workplace consciousness' (*ibid.*: 941). This rather pessimistic conclusion was tempered by the social workers seeking social justice, who told her that they were turning to their trade unions to further such agendas.

In the UK, the trade union that represents the majority of social workers is UNISON, a member-led organization that has a national social work officer who provides support for the promotion of social work matters. Through its local regional bodies, UNISON brings social workers and social care workers together and, in Scotland, this involves direct representation to government over social work matters. UNITE the Union and the GMB also have social work members, the latter traditionally representing frontline social care workers at one end of the spectrum and social work managers at the other. Whilst trade unions are weak organizations compared with their past status, they are still recognized by most public sector employers for bargaining purposes and still represent millions of public sector workers in the western democracies. Workplace activists should help build their strength and influence, as their role is crucial in defending the welfare state, as discussed in Chapter 1.

Professional associations and other networks

These have been traditionally weak and unrepresentative in the UK and other western countries (Hughes and Wearing 2007) but, in the UK, BASW has consistently promoted practice development through professional networking (conferences and training events) and peer reviewed journals (*Practice* and the *British Journal of Social Work*). BASW also has a code of ethics referred to elsewhere in this book which is a worthy accompaniment to the codes of practice of the professional registration bodies. Recent attempts to improve the influence of the profession through the development in England and Wales of a College of Social Work have resulted in argument and ill-feeling, especially between UNISON and BASW. As one consequence, in 2011 the latter established its own trade union, the Social Workers Union. This move seems only to have served to marginalize BASW still further and it is hoped that their situation improves.

Some organizations promote practitioners' forums where ideas can be debated – at least, in theory. Some universities in the UK also invite practitioners to open social work forums (an example being the West of Scotland University). SWAN (the Social Work Action Network) has been mentioned elsewhere in this book and provides a home to those who want to learn more about radical social work.

Conclusions and prospects for radical practice

This book set out to prove, amongst other things, that radical social work is considerably more than just a critique of mainstream practice. As a form, it builds on anti-oppressive practice and concerns about social justice (this was illustrated in Figure 3.1). The add-ons include a belief that the defence of the welfare state against neoliberal-based attack is a fundamental precursor to the building of a better society based on socialist values. This theme was extensively covered in Chapter 1.

The history of radical social work since the 1970s was discussed in some detail in Chapter 2. Most of the theories underlying the methods discussed are of relevance today and contribute to a modern radical practice: these include feminism, anti-racist practice, anti-discriminatory practice and the broader spectrum of anti-oppressive practice. Twenty-first-century radical social work is a fusion of these methods and the critiques of the Radical Literature rooted in the realities of a neoliberal global context. It arises from resistance to neoliberalism and global capitalism without being tied to the fortunes of the organizations and movements involved. Radical social work practice is, in essence, the practical application of the values of the political left within the work context of social work. We saw in Chapter 2 that radical social work in the 1970s was criticized for being too concerned with macro-level concerns and ignoring micro matters. This critique has continued and has, rather unfairly, been levelled at the Radical Literature of recent years, probably as a consequence of somewhat tangential debates around post-modernism. Much of this book has been largely concerned with micro-level practice, carried out consciously because of macro-level concerns that can also be targeted by the radical social worker.

Social work is a helping occupation based on human relationships and therefore lends itself to 'mutual aid' – the everyday practice of socialism as detailed over a hundred years ago by the Russian socialist and anarchist Peter Kropotkin (1939 [1902]) in his description of the ways human beings naturally help one another without regard to profit or competition – the antithesis of the 'Big Society' of modern neoliberals discussed in Chapter 6. There is nothing grandiose about these ideas and ideals. The capacity of social workers to exercise discretion and find space for such practice was detailed in Chapter 3. The down-to-earth and day-to-day applicability of such ideas across the main spectrum of social work, particularly in the public sector, is demonstrated in Chapters 4 to 8.

A Manifesto for Radical Practice is proposed in the Appendix. This tries to capture the main ideas from the book in an easy form that workers can use to remind themselves of the possibilities they might have available, and the hope that things could be better and that their contribution might make a difference.

At the time of writing, I work in a children and family team in an area of high unemployment, deprivation, drug abuse and domestic violence. Over a recent year, with resources including ten full-time qualified social workers and one part-time, our team produced 150 full child protection investigation assessments amongst other (from a managerial standpoint) measureable outputs. This was achieved despite maternity leave, sickness absence and all the other matters that affect workplace units. You might think that ours was a setting that would be best avoided, but this is not the case: morale is high and staff tend to be committed and settled. Whilst few of my colleagues would describe themselves as 'radical social workers', there is an approach to the incongruences described in the Introduction to the book that fits with the type of practice described in these pages. My colleagues' down-to-earth approach to their clients' problems, their willingness to learn and work with, not against, service users and continually to look for better ways of working have given me inspiration and belief in the possibilities for radical practice.

My colleague Jamie, the children and family social worker whose thoughts about work were mentioned in the Introduction, was asked what helped him maintain his commitment to his job in the face of growing social problems and increasing pressure. He was clear that, for him, just seeing social work as a job was not enough. He felt that recognition of the roots of the poverty and deprivation encountered by the families he worked with was essential to maintain balance and ward off discrimination, prejudice and frustration. He was proud that the general culture in his workplace supported such explanations and attitudes. The children he was responsible for needed effective support and he would try to ensure it was provided. Jamie was also convinced that the job he felt he did well was not one that anyone could do and that much of this came down to communication skills that could not be learned: they were part of his heritage. This is the artistry discussed in Chapter 7.

This book has advocated for the role of the modern day streetwise bureaucrat who positively uses and extends the discretion that will always exist in anything other than a fully totalitarian system. This celebration of the concept accepts that the systems in which we operate and the organizations in which we work, which frontline workers did not construct (and in which they increasingly have little say), are often intrinsically oppressive and that we, as workers, should seek to empower our clients wherever and whenever we can. We can all operate as radical social workers to an extent, at least, and our work can be unassumingly, but proudly constructed and presented as offering an alternative practice.

Radical social work practice will not, in itself, change the world. However, that should not stop us wanting to stand alongside the victims, rather than the defenders, of the present system. We know we work within that system, and that means abiding by its general prescriptions and rules, but, if we can make things better for some of those oppressed within our society, then our efforts will be worth the making. This has therefore been an optimistic book in its belief that social work is still a very worthwhile activity.

- Good supervision and workload management are essential supports for social workers who want to avoid stress and burnout.

- The use of new technology and associated changes in working arrangements should be used to improve the lives of staff and not just to meet managerial objectives.

- Radical social workers need to be good at their jobs, if they are to win respect and influence others.

- Always join the majority trade union in your workplace or agency, and make building collective trade union strength and influence a priority.

- Other networks and forums (particularly SWAN) can promote discussion where there is opportunity to look at radical practice.

- SWAN (the Social Work Action Network) http://www.socialwork future.org/ This online resource requires the user to create an account. It has useful articles and notes, as well as information about SWAN conferences and events.
- UNISON online resources:
  http://www.unison.org.uk/socialwork/pages_view.asp?did=11458 (UK pages accessed 20 January 2013).
  http://www.unison-scotland.org.uk/socialwork/index.html (Scottish pages accessed 20 January 2013).
  The UK trade union UNISON has an abundance of online resources for social workers that can be accessed through the pages above.

A Manifesto for a Radical Social Work Practice

The book has contained ideas in each chapter that can be used to promote a radical practice. The manifesto presented here does not pretend to be original but tries to use the book's content to complement the Social Work Manifesto published several years ago by the authors of the Radical Literature and others (Jones *et al.* 2004). It includes the UK author Malcolm Payne's suggestions regarding resilience-building (Payne 2011) and the Australian Catherine McDonald's views (which deliberately mimic the language of managerialism) on the type of social worker needed effectively to carry forward a radical agenda within the constraints of a managerial environment (McDonald 2006).

A manifesto for a radical social work practice:

- A recognition that the circumstances of the majority of service users within western democracies are created through their place at the lower end of very unequal societies
- The use of the discretion that exists within the workplace to promote a social work practice that acknowledges social class and disadvantage, and seeks out opportunity to work alongside service users to improve their lives by challenging their oppression; this will involve winning the respect of colleagues for the quality of work undertaken
- Within practice, an emphasis on security, dignity and resilience-building rather than surveillance of risk
- As an antidote to managerialism and the neoliberal agenda, the creation of radical 'entrepreneurial and challenging leaders' in social work who take what the system gives and seek out opportunities to do so; ask for more, even if they have to settle for less; maintain ambiguity in order that responses from others (such as those who manage resources) are not predetermined; and network with other 'challenger' groups

- Assisting service users to navigate systems through advocacy, education, empowerment and capacity-building
- Engaging authentically and building good working relationships based on listening and learning, respect, agreement about goals and sharing of information, including written records
- Recognizing power imbalances and acknowledging them openly
- Small-scale resistance involving the diversion of resources to help the poor and disadvantaged
- Challenging oppressive language and culture wherever they arise, and replacing them with the language and pursuance of social justice
- Utilizing concepts such as SMARRT objectives and EBP to pursue goals of social justice
- Using new technologies to the advantage of service users and not just the systems required to manage their problems and issues
- Join and contribute to trade union activity that seeks to defend the welfare state and improve the conditions of those who work within it
- Using other collective opportunities to campaign for social justice and the creation of a truly socialist society.

Glossary of Keywords

Williams (1976) explains that keywords such as the ones interpreted below change their meaning in context and over time, and are contested. However, their use is so commonplace in the literature referred to in this book, and in its own pages (especially Chapters 1 and 2), that this short glossary is required so that at least the meaning here, which mirrors that found elsewhere in the Radical and Critical social work literature, is understood.

Alienation: In the Marxist sense, this refers to the powerlessness and estrangement from the process of work felt by those who work for others and are part of a larger process in the creation of a product or service from which another class benefits. Psychological explanations flow from this historical-materialist meaning based on the capitalist means of production.

Capitalism: An economic system where the ownership of the means of production is centralized in the ownership and control of a minority, creating wage labour.

Collectivism (and **anti-collectivism**): Associated with communism and socialism, it describes forms of social ownership and control in society that are exercised through groups of citizens acting together for the common good. Its antithesis is anti-collectivism, or individualism (see below).

Commodification of labour (and **de-commodification**): This is the notion that employment depends on the marketplace. Conversely, de-commodification occurs when the state assumes responsibility for provision of employment – as found in Communist systems and, to an extent, in the post-war welfare states.

Communism: As 'communism', this describes an economic system where the means of production are commonly owned and controlled. As 'Communism', this tends to be associated with the former Soviet Union and its satellite states in Eastern Europe. These states had full employment and extensive social provision but, as we now know, at the cost of individual freedoms.

Dialectic (and **dialectical materialism**): See Chapter 3 for an account of these concepts

Feminism (and **feminist**): Movements and ideologies aimed at defining, establishing and defending equal political, economic and social rights for women. Those who adhere to such ideas are known as *feminists*.

Hegemony: In this book, it describes the cultural control of society by its dominant class through the use of systems, including press, TV and marketing media, that effectively determine how and what the majority of citizens think – which allows for rule by consensus. This idea was developed by the early twentieth-century Italian Marxist Antonio Gramsci.

Individualist (and **individualism**): This describes the idea that it is the individual person's attributes that determine their place in society, rather than the way in which society is organized. Its proponents favour minimum state interventions and maximum freedom to make one's own way in the world. It is generally espoused by neoliberals (see below) and right-wing politicians, especially in the US.

Keynesian (and **Keynesianism**): This stems from the theories of John Maynard Keynes, a British economist who died in 1946. He believed that economic prosperity depended on state control through money, taxation and, when required, state provision of employment. His ideas dominated post-war thinking but have fallen into disfavour with the rise of neoliberal ideas since the 1970s.

Macro (and **micro**) **level**: Taken from sociology, macro focuses on forces at work within wider society whilst micro looks at the level of the individual.

Managerialism: Essentially a pejorative term used by critics of the style of management increasingly seen in public sector organizations with the advent of neoliberal market-based ideas. These refer to top-down, financially-led methods of control through prescribed eligibility criteria and interventions for services that remove professional discretion and autonomy.

Marxism (and **Marxist**): This describes those who either subscribe to the Marxist vision of a communist future for society based on the abolition of private property and state provision of work and the necessary requirements for subsistence, or the application of Marx's method to the study of history. These concepts are overlapping.

Modernism (and **post-modernism**): *Modernism* describes the ideas that accompanied the industrialization of society that occurred in the nineteenth century with the breakdown of old forms of social relationship and belief: it is a term that took on particular meaning in the arts. *Post-modernism* describes a range of diffuse ideas that have come to replace the ideologies based on modernism that characterized the twentieth century. The certainties of modernist thinking, especially the grand explanations such as Marxism, are replaced in post-modernism by a range of explanations that are based on different experiences. In social work, post-modernist adherents reject the class-based explanations for the oppression experienced by service users, and explain things from the point of view of the particular oppressions and how they are experienced. Critics of post-modernism in social work see it as reinforcing notions of individual explanation for problems and denying the impact of common themes such as poverty and inequality.

Neoliberalism (and **neoliberal**): The belief 'that free markets in which individuals maximize their material interests provide the best means for satisfying human aspirations, and that markets are in particular to be preferred over state and politics, which are at best inefficient and at worst threats to freedom' (Crouch 2011: vii). In the nineteenth century, such ideas were called *laissez-faire* and in the US they are known as *neo-Conservative*.

New public management: See *Managerialism*.

Quantitative (and **qualitiative**): Research terms that describe the origins of data. *Quantitative* tends to have numerical significance and is characterized by sets of comparative figures based on information gathered and analysed statistically. *Qualitative* data is based on people's perceptions and opinions, often in small samples but rich in detail and particularity. It, too, can be analysed statistically through coding. A major criticism of EBP in social work is that it is often based on quantitative data, which has limited applicability.

Socialist (and **socialism**): A generic term with wide application, being claimed by a spectrum from those whose beliefs are akin to communist ones (see above) to those *social democrats* who embrace the free market (in regulated form) but who want to maintain a strong welfare state.

Taylorist: Named after Frederick Taylor (1856–1915), this describes methods of scientific organization of work designed to extract maximum value and efficiency from labour.

Welfare state: 'The complex of social policies and programs that distribute economic resources disproportionly to a nation's vulnerable populations ... (including) progressive taxes, cash and near cash assistance, publicly funded services such as health care, public programs that guarantee economic security, and government programs to ensure social inclusion and economic capability' (Brady 2009: 7). Welfare states differ greatly in their emphasis: Esping-Anderson (1990) suggests three types: the 'liberal', where state provision is modest (such as the US, Canada and Australia – and, increasingly, the UK); the 'corporatist', where state provision is shaped by the values of the Church, represented by European countries such as France, Germany and Italy; and the 'social democratic', where state provision is at its most extensive and equality most pronounced, found in only a few countries, such as Sweden and Norway.

Workfare: The notion that benefit entitlement for the unemployed should be based on their ability to prove that they are willing to work and are actively seeking work. Workfare is now also being used to describe the expectation that those seeking work should also be prepared to work for nothing in order to be eligible for benefits. Workfare is associated with neoliberal ideas (see above). McDonald (2006) describes the 'workfare state' as one in which full employment has been abandoned as governments engage the unemployed in job preparation and job seeking instead of providing actual employment.

References

Adams, R., Dominelli, L. and Payne, M. (eds) (2002) *Critical Practice in Social Work*, Basingstoke, Palgrave Macmillan.

Alinsky, S. (1971) *Rules for Radicals: A Pragmatic Primer for Realistic Radicals*, New York, Random House.

Asylum Aid (2008) Women's Asylum Charter http://www.asylumaid.org.uk/data/files/publications/180/Charter.pdf (accessed 17 November 2012).

Baars, J., Dannefer, D., Phillipson, C. and Walker, A. (eds) (2006) *Ageing, Globalization and Inequality: The New Critical Gerontology*, New York, Baywood.

Bailey, D. (2002) Mental Health, in Adams, R., Dominelli, L. and Payne, M. (eds), *Critical Practice in Social Work*, Basingstoke, Palgrave Macmillan.

Bailey, R. and Brake, M. (eds) (1975) *Radical Social Work*, London, Edward Arnold.

Baines, D. (2010) 'If We Don't Get Back to Where We Were Before': Working in the Restructured Non-Profit Social Services, *British Journal of Social Work* 40, 928–45.

Baines, D. (ed.) (2007) *Doing Anti-Oppressive Practice: Building Transformative Politicized Social Work*, Nova Scotia, Fernwood.

Baldwin, M. (2011) Resisting the Easy Care Model: Building a More Radical, Community-Based, Anti-Authoritarian Social Work for the Future, in Lavalette, M. (ed.), *Radical Social Work Today: Social Work at the Crossroads*, Bristol, Policy Press.

Balloch, S., McLean, J. and Fisher, M. (1999) *Social Services: Working Under Pressure*, Bristol, Policy Press.

Banks, S. (2012) *Ethics and Values in Social Work*, 4th edn, Basingstoke, Palgrave Macmillan.

Barclay, P. (1982) *Social Work Roles, Tasks and Responsibilities*, London, Bedford Square Press.

Barnes, M. (2006) *Caring and Social Justice*, Basingstoke, Palgrave Macmillan.

Barnes, M. (1997) *Care, Communities and Citizens*, London, Longman.

Barnes, M. and Bowl, R. (2001) *Taking Over the Asylum: Empowerment and Mental Health*, Basingstoke, Palgrave.

BASW (British Association of Social Workers) (2012a) *The Code of Ethics for Social Work*, Birmingham, BASW.

BASW (British Association of Social Workers) (2012b) The State of Social Work 2012 http://cdn.basw.co.uk/upload/basw_23651-3.pdf (accessed 2 December 2012).

BBC News (2012a) David Cameron Holds Q&A in Leeds, 23 January, http://www.bbc.co.uk/news/uk-politics-16682190 (accessed 28 September 2012).

BBC News (2012b) Remploy Factory Closures: Hundreds More Face Redundancy, 6 December, http://www.bbc.co.uk/news/uk-england-20624552 (accessed 10 December 2012).

BBC News (2011) Mervyn King: Banks Putting Profits before Customers, 5 March, www.bbc.co.uk/news/business-12655035 (accessed 21 January 2012).

Beresford, P., Croft, S. and Adshead, L. (2008) 'We Don't See Her as a Social Worker': A Service User Case Study of the Importance of the Social Worker's Relationship and Humanity *British Journal of Social Work* 38, 1388–407.

Bhatti-Sinclair, K. (2011) *Anti-Racist Practice in Social Work*, Basingstoke, Palgrave Macmillan.

Boddy, J. (2011) The Supportive Relationship in 'Public Care': The Relevance of Social Pedagogy, in Cameron, C. and Moss, P. (eds), *Social Pedagogy and Working with Children and Young People: Where Care and Education Meet*, London, Jessica Kingsley.

Brady, D. (2009) *Rich Democracies, Poor People: How Politics Explain Poverty*, New York, Oxford University Press.

Braverman, H. (1974) *Labour and Monopoly Capital: The Degradation of Work in the 20th Century*, New York, Monthly Review Press.

Bricker-Jenkins, M. (1992) The Propositions and Assumptions of Feminist Practice, in Bricker-Jenkins, M., Hooyman, N. and Gottleib, N., *Feminist Practice in Clinical Settings*, Newbury Park, CA, Sage.

Brier-Thompson, C. (2006) Overlapping Behavioral Characteristics & Related Mental Health Diagnoses in Children, http://www.fasaware.co.uk/images/stories/documentation/7_Overlapping_Characteristics.pdf (accessed 11 November 2012).

Broadhurst, K., Hall, C., Wastell, D., White, S. and Pithouse, C. (2010) Risk, Instrumentalisation and the Humane Project in Social Work: Identifying the Informal Logics of Risk Management in Children's Statutory Services, *British Journal of Social Work*, 40, 1046–64.

Brophy Down, S. (2012) *Irena Sendler: Bringing Life to the Children of the Holocaust*, Hove, Crabtree.

Brown, A. (1994) *Groupwork*, 3rd edn, Aldershot, Ashgate.

Brown, K. (2010) The Older Person's Social Care and the Enabling Service, in Brown, K. (ed.), *Vulnerable Adults and Community Care*, 2nd edn, Exeter, Learning Matters.

Bruce, M. (1961) *The Coming of the Welfare State*, London, Batsford.

Buckley, E. and Decter, P. (2006) From Isolation to Community: Collaborating with Children and Families in Times of Crisis, *International Journal of Narrative Therapy and Community Work*, no. 2, http://www.dulwichcentre.com.au/from-isolation-to-community.pdf (accessed 6 January 2013).

Burghardt, S. (2010) *Macro Practice in Social Work for the 21st Century*, Thousand Oaks, CA, Sage.

Burghardt, S. (1996) A Materialist Framework for Social Work Theory and Practice, in Turner, F., *Social Work Treatment: Interlocking Theoretical Approaches*, 4th edn, New York, Free Press.

Cambridge, P. (2008) The Case for a New 'Case' Management in Services for People with Learning Disabilities *British Journal of Social Work* **38**(1), 91–116.

Cameron, C. and Moss, P. (eds) (2011) *Social Pedagogy and Working with Children and Young People: Where Care and Education Meet*, London, Jessica Kingsley.

Cameron, D. (2012) Welfare Speech, 25 June, http://www.number10.gov.uk/news/welfare-speech/ (accessed 14 October 2012).

Cameron, D. (2010) Big Society Speech Liverpool, 19 July, http://www.number10.gov.uk/news/big-society-speech/ (accessed 11 January 2012).

Carers UK (2012) Facts About Carers 2012 http://www.carersuk.org/media/k2/attachments/Facts_about_carers_Dec_2012.pdf (accessed 14 December 2012).

Carey, M. and Foster, V. (2011) Introducing 'Deviant' Social Work: Contextualising the Limits of Radical Social Work Whilst Understanding (Fragmented) Resistance Within the Social Work Labour Process *British Journal of Social Work* **41**, 576–93.

Cemlyn, S., Greenfields, M., Burnett, S., Matthews, K. and Whitwell, C. (2009) *Inequalities Experienced by Gypsy and Traveller Communities: A Review*, Manchester, Equality and Human Rights Commission.

Charles, M. and Butler, S. (2004) Social Workers' Management of Organisational Change, in Lymbery, M. and Butler, S. (eds), *Social Work: Ideals and Practice Realities*, Basingstoke, Palgrave MacMillan.

Clarke, J., Langan, M. and Williams, F. (2001) The Construction of the British Welfare State, 1945–1975, in Cochrane, A., Clarke, J. and Gewirtz, S. (eds), *Comparing Welfare States*, London, Sage.

Civil Exchange (2012) The Big Society Audit 2012, http://www.civilexchange.org.uk/the-big-society-audit (accessed 31 January 2012).

Cochrane, A., Clarke, J. and Gewirtz, S. (eds) (2001) *Comparing Welfare States*, London, Sage.

Collier, A. (2004) *Marx: A Beginner's Guide*, Oxford, One World.

Collins, S. (2008) Statutory Social Workers: Stress, Job Satisfaction, Coping, Social Support and Individual Differences *British Journal of Social Work* **38**(6), 1173–93.

Community Care (2011) Social workers forced to leave children in danger as cuts hit child protection, 13 April, http://www.communitycare.co.uk/static-pages/articles/child-protection-thresholds-survey/ (accessed 23 September 2012).

Community Care (2007) Hospital Social Work and How Less Bed Blocking Means More Emergencies, 12 December, http://www.communitycare.co.uk/articles/12/12/2007/106785/hospital-social-work-and-how-less-bed-blocking-means-more-emergencies.htm (accessed 2 December 2012).

Connell, R. (2005) *Masculinities*, 2nd edn, Cambridge, Polity Press.

Cooke, I. and Shaw, M. (eds) (1996) *Radical Community Work: Perspectives from Practice in Scotland*, Edinburgh, Moray House Publications.

Cooke, P. and Ellis, R. (2004) Exploitation, Protection and Empowerment of People with Learning Disabilities, in Lymbery, M. and Butler, S. (eds), *Social Work: Ideals and Practice Realities*, Basingstoke, Palgrave MacMillan.

Corrigan, P. and Leonard, P. (1978) *Social Work Practice under Capitalism: A Marxist Approach*, London, Macmillan.

Coulshed, V., Mullender, A., Jones, D. and Thompson, N. (2006) *Management in Social Work*, 3rd edn, Basingstoke, Palgrave MacMillan.

Coussee, F., Bradt, L., Roose, R. and Bouverne-De Bie, M. (2010) The Emerging Social Pedagogical Paradigm in UK Child and Youth Care: Deus Ex Machina or Walking the Beaten Path? *British Journal of Social Work* **40**(3), 789–805.

Crouch, C. (2011) *The Strange Non-Death of Neoliberalism*, Cambridge, Polity Press.

Crystal, S. (2006) Dynamics of Later-Life Inequality: Modeling the Interplay of Health Disparities, Economic Resources, and Public Policies, in Baars, J., Dannefer, D., Phillipson, C. and Walker, A. (eds), *Ageing, Globalization and Inequality: The New Critical Gerontology*, New York, Baywood.

Cunningham, I. and Nickson, D. (2010) Personalisation and its Implications for Work and Employment in the Voluntary Sector. http://www.ccpscotland.org/assets/files/vssswu/Articles%20and%20Reports/Personalisation%20Report%20Final%2015th%20November.pdf

Dalrymple, J. and Burke, B. (2006) *Anti-Oppressive Practice: Social Care and the Law*, 2nd edn, Maidenhead, Open University Press.

Davies, M. (1991) Sociology and Social Work: a Misunderstood Relationship, in Davies, M. (ed.), *The Sociology of Social Work*, London, Routledge.

Davis, A. and Garrett, P. (2004) Progressive Practice for Tough Times: Social Work, Poverty and Division in the 21st Century, in Lymbery, M. and Butler, S. (eds), *Social Work: Ideals and Practice Realities*, Basingstoke, Palgrave MacMillan.

Day, L. (1992) Women and Oppression: Sex, Class and Gender, in Langan, M. and Day, L., *Women, Oppression and Social Work: Issues in Anti-Discriminatory Practice*, London, Routledge.

Department for Education (2012a) Data Research and Statistics: Children looked after by local authorities in England (including adoption), September, http://www.education.gov.uk/researchandstatistics/statistics/a00213762/children-looked-after-las-england (accessed 25 November 2012).

Department for Education (2012b) Publication of the Two Serious Case Review Overview Reports – Peter Connelly, June, http://www.education.gov.uk/a0065483/serious-case-review (accessed 6 November 2012).

Department of Health (1998) *Modernising Social Services*, London, Stationary Office.

Dominelli, L. (1988) *Anti-Racist Social Work*, 1st edn, Basingstoke, BASW Macmillan.

Dominelli, L. (1998) Anti-Oppressive Practice in Context, in Adams, R., Dominelli, L. and Payne, M., *Social Work: Themes, Issues and Critical Debates*, Basingstoke, Macmillan Open University.

Dominelli, L. (2002) *Anti-Oppressive Social Work: Theory and Practice*, Basingstoke, Palgrave Macmillan.

Dorling, D. (2011) *Injustice: Why Social Inequality Persists*, Bristol, Policy Press.

Elliott, L. and Atkinson, D. (2012) *Going South: Why Britain Will Have a Third World Economy by 2014*, Basingstoke, Palgrave Macmillan.

Engels, F. (1978 [1884]) *The Origin of the Family, Private Property and the State*, Peking, Foreign Languages Press.

England, H. (1986) *Social Work as Art*, London, Allen & Unwin.

Esping-Anderson, G. (1990) *The Three Worlds of Welfare Capitalism*, Oxford, Polity Press.

Evans, T. (2011) Professionals, Managers and Discretion: Critiquing Street-Level Bureaucracy *British Journal of Social Work* **41**(2), 368–86.

Evans, T. and Harris, J. (2004) Street-Level Bureaucracy, Social Work and the (Exaggerated) Death of Discretion *British Journal of Social Work* **34**(6), 871–95.

Fanon, F. (1967) *The Wretched of the Earth*, Harmondsworth, Penguin.

Farmer, E. and Wijedasa, D. (2011) The Reunification of Looked After Children with Their Parents: What Contributes to Return Stability? *British Journal of Social Work*, Advanced Access (published online 11 June 2012).

Ferguson, H. (2011) *Child Protection Practice*, Basingstoke, Macmillan.

Ferguson, I. (2011) Why Class (Still) Matters, in Lavalette, M. (ed.) *Radical Social Work Today: Social Work at the Crossroads*, Bristol, Policy Press.

Ferguson, I. (2008) *Reclaiming Social Work*, London, Sage.

Ferguson, I. (2007) Increasing User Choice or Privatizing Risk? The Antinomies of Personalization *British Journal of Social Work* **37**(3), 387–403.

Ferguson, I. and Lavalette, M. (2013) Crisis, Austerity and the Future(s) of Social Work in the UK *Critical and Radical Social Work* **1**(1), 95–110.

Ferguson, I. and Lavalette, M. (2004) Beyond Power Discourse: Alienation and Social Work *British Journal of Social Work* **34**(3), 297–312.

Ferguson, I., Lavalette, M. and Mooney, G. (2002) *Rethinking Welfare: A Critical Perspective*, London, Sage.

Ferguson, I., Lavalette, M. and Whitmore, E. (2005) *Globalisation, Global Justice and Social Work*, London, Routledge.

Ferguson, I. and Woodward, R. (2009) *Radical Social Work in Practice – Making a Difference*, Bristol, Policy Press.

Fern, E. (2012) Child-Directed Social Work Practice: Findings from an Action Research Study Conducted in Iceland *British Journal of Social Work* Advanced Access (published online 10 July 2012).

Financial Times (2010) Council Cuts Widen Postcode Lottery, 12 December, www.ft.com/cms/s/0/0e1c2360-061f-11e0-976b-00144feabdc0.html (accessed 21 January 2012).

Fook, J. (2002) *Social Work: Critical Theory and Practice*, London, Sage.

Fook, J. (1993) *Radical Casework: A Theory of Practice*, St Leonards, NSW, Allen & Unwin.

Forgacs, D. (ed.) (1999) *The Antonio Gramsci Reader: Selected Writings 1916–1935*, London, Lawrence & Wishart.

Forrester, D. and Harwin, J. (2011) *Parents who Misuse Drugs and Alcohol: Effective Interventions in Social Work and Child Protection*, Chichester, Wiley-Blackwell.

Freese, B. (2006) *Coal: A Human History*, London, Arrow Books.

Freire, P. (1996) *Pedagogy of the Oppressed*, London, Penguin.

Friedman, M. (1962) *Capitalism and Freedom*, Chicago, University of Chicago Press.

Frost, N. (2000) Evaluating Practice, in Adams, R., Dominelli, L. and Payne, M. (eds), *Critical Practice in Social Work*, Basingstoke, Palgrave Macmillan.

Galper, J. (1980) *Social Work Practice: A Radical Perspective*, Englewood Cliffs, NJ, Prentice Hall.

Galpin, D. and Bates, N. (2009) *Social Work Practice with Adults*, Exeter, Learning Matters.

Gardner, A. (2011) *Personalisation in Social Work*, Bristol, Learning Matters.

Garrett, P.M. (2013) *Social Work and Social Theory*, Bristol, Policy Press.

General Social Care Council (GSCC) (2010) Codes of Practice for Social Care Workers, http://www.gscc.org.uk/cmsFiles/CodesofPracticeforSocialCareWorkers.pdf (accessed 17 November 2012).

Gilbert, M., Newns, M., Good, P., Evans, J. and Frampton, D. (2004) *Anarchists in Social Work: Known to the Authorities*, Ulverston, Gilbert.

Gilligan, P. (2007) Well Motivated Reformists or Nascent Radical: How Do Applicants to the Degree in Social Work See Social Problems, their Origins and Solutions? *British Journal of Social Work* 37(4), 735–60.

Gillingham, P. (2012) The Development of Electronic Information Systems for the Future: Practitioners, 'Embodied Structures' and 'Technologies-in-Practice' *British Journal of Social Work* Advanced Access (published online 12 January 12 2012).

Glyn, A. (2006) *Capitalism Unleashed: Finance, Globalisation and Welfare*, Oxford, Oxford University Press.

Goffman, E. (1968) *Asylums*, Harmondsworth, Penguin.

Goldberg-Wood, G. and Tully, C. (2006) *The Structural Approach to Direct Practice in Social Work: A Social Constructionist Approach*, 3rd edn, New York, Columbia University Press.

Gough, I. (1979) *The Political Economy of the Welfare State*, London, Macmillan.

Gramsci, A. (1982) *Selections from the Prison Notebooks*, London, Lawrence & Wishart.

Gray, M., Plath, D. and Webb, S. (2009) *Evidence Based Social Work: A Critical Stance*, Abingdon, Routledge.

Guardian, The (2012a) ATOS is doing a good job – as the Government's flak-catcher, 5 September, http://www.guardian.co.uk/commentisfree/2012/sep/05/atos-the-government-flakcatcher (accessed 1 January 2013).

Guardian, The (2012b) Conservative Conference: Return of the Nasty Party, 10 October, http://www.guardian.co.uk/politics/2012/oct/10/conservative-con-ference-return-nasty-party (accessed 14 October 2012).

Guardian, The (2012c) Michael Gove: Children at risk of abuse should be put in care more quickly, 16 November, http://www.guardian.co.uk/society/2012/nov/16/michael-gove-children-risk-care (accessed 1 January 2013).

Guardian, The (2011a) English Riots: Are Harsh Sentences for Rioters Justified?, 17 August, http://www.guardian.co.uk/uk/2011/aug/17/england-riots-harsh-sentences-justified (accessed 29 September 2012).

Guardian, The (2011b) From 'No Such Thing as Society' to 'Big Society'. Spot the Difference, 11 July, http://www.guardian.co.uk/society/joepublic/2011/jul/11/big-society-no-such-thing-as-society (accessed 31 January 2012).

Guardian, The (2008) Drop the Deadline: Computers can hinder child protection, warns Sue White, 19 November, http://www.guardian.co.uk/society/2008/nov/19/child-protection-computers-ics (accessed 19 January 2012).

Guardian, The and London School of Economics (2011) Reading the Riots: Investigating England's Summer of Disorder, www.guardian.co.uk/readingthe riots (accessed 29 September 2012).

Hadley, R., Cooper, M., Dale, P. and Stacy, G. (1987) *A Community Social Worker's Handbook*, London, Tavistock Publications.

Hammond, J. and Hammond, B. (1920) *The Town Labourer 1760–1832*, London, Longmans Green.

Hardcastle, D., Powers, P. and Wenocur, S. (2011) *Community Practice: Theories and Skills for Social Workers*, 3rd edn, New York, Oxford University Press.

Hardy, J. (2009) *Poland's New Capitalism*, London, Pluto.

Harlock, J. (2009) National Council for Voluntary Organisations: Personalisation: Rhetoric to Reality, http://www.ncvo-vol.org.uk (accessed 8 December 2012).

Harris, J. (2008) State Social Work: Constructing the Present from Moments in the Past *British Journal of Social Work* **38**(4), 662–79.

Harris, J. (2003) *The Social Work Business*, London, Routledge.

Harris, J. and White, V. (2009) *Modernising Social Work: Critical Considerations*, Bristol, Policy Press.

Hawkins, L., Fook, J. and Ryan, M. (2001) Social Workers' Use of the Language of Social Justice *British Journal of Social Work* **31**, 1–13.

Hawtin, M. and Percy-Smith, J. (2007) *Community Profiling: A Practical Guide*, 2nd edn, Buckingham, Open University.

Hay, C. (2006) (What's Marxist About?) Marxist State Theory, in Hay, C., Lister, M. and Marsh, D. (eds), *The State: Theories and Issues*, Basingstoke, Palgrave Macmillan.

Healy, K. (2000) *Social Work Practices: Contemporary Perspectives on Change*, London, Sage.

Herald (2012) Outcry at Illness Benefit Cut, 23 January, http://www.herald scotland.com/news/home-news/outcry-at-illness-benefit-cut.16548525 (accessed 29 September 2012).

Herald (2013) Tenants Warned over Bedroom Tax Rent Arrears Action, 2 November, http://www.heraldscotland.com/politics/wider-political-news/tenants-warned-over-bedroom-tax-rent-arrears-action.22584733 (accessed 3 November 2013).

Hernstein, R. and Murray, C. (1994) *The Bell Curve: Intelligence and Class Structure in American Life*, New York, Free Press.

Hobsbawm, E. (1995) *Age of Extremes: The Short Twentieth Century 1914–1991*, London, Abacus.

Howe, D. (2005) *Child Abuse and Neglect: Attachment, Development and Intervention*, Basingstoke, Palgrave Macmillan.

Howe, D. (1991) Knowledge, Power, and the Shape of Social Work Practice, in Davies, M. (ed.), *The Sociology of Social Work*, London: Routledge.

Howe, D. (1987) *An Introduction to Social Work Theory*, Aldershot (UK), Wildwood House.

Howe, D., Brandon, M., Hinings, D. and Schofield, G. (1999) *Attachment Theory, Child Maltreatment and Family Support*, Basingstoke, Palgrave.

Hughes, M. and Wearing, M. (2007) *Organisations and Management in Social Work*, London, Sage.

Hunt, L., Marshall, M. and Rowlings, C. (1997) *Past Trauma in Late Life: European Perspectives on Therapeutic Work with Older People*, London, Jessica Kingsley.

Ife, J. (2008) *Human Rights and Social Work: Towards Rights-Based Practice*, 2nd edn, Port Melbourne, Cambridge University Press.

IFSW (2012a) Statement of Principles, http://ifsw.org/policies/statement-of-ethical-principles/ (accessed 27 April 2013).

IFSW (2012b) Definition of Social Work, http://ifsw.org/policies/definition-of-social-work/ (accessed 15 October 2012).

Johns, R. (2011) *Using the Law in Social Work*, 5th edn, Exeter, Learning Matters.

Jones, C. (2011) The Best and Worst of Times: Reflections on the Impact of Radicalism on British Social Work in the 1970s, in Lavalette, M (ed.), *Radical Social Work Today: Social Work at the Crossroads*, Bristol, Policy Press.

Jones, C. (2001) Voices from the Front Line: Social Workers and New Labour *British Journal of Social Work* **31**(4), 547–62.

Jones, C., Ferguson, I., Lavalette, M. and Penketh, L. (2004) Social Work and Social Justice: a Manifesto for a New Engaged Practice, http://www.social workfuture.org/about-swan/national-organisation/manifesto (accessed 29 September 2012).

Jones, C. and Novak, T. (1999) *Poverty, Welfare and the Disciplinary State*, London, Routledge.

Jones, O. (2011) *Chavs: The Demonisation of the Working Class*, London, Verso.

Jordan, B. and Drakeford, M. (2012) *Social Work and Social Policy Under Austerity*, Basingstoke, Palgrave Macmillan.

Jordan, B. and Jordan, C. (2000) *Social Work and the Third Way: Tough Love as Social Policy*, London, Sage.

Keddell, E. (2011) Reasoning Processes in Child Protection Decision Making: Negotiating Moral Minefields and Risky Relationships *British Journal of Social Work* **41**(7), 1251–70.

Kemshall, H. and Pritchard, J. (2005) Introduction, in Kemshall, H. and Pritchard, J. (eds), *Good Practice in Risk Assessment and Risk Management 2: Protection, Rights and Responsibilities*, 7th impression, London, Jessica Kingsley.

Kilbrandon, Lord (1964) *Report of the Committee on Children and Young Persons*, Scotland, Edinburgh, HMSO.

Klein, A. (2012) More Police, Less Safety: Policing as a Causal Factor in the Outbreak of Riots and Public Disturbances, in Briggs, D. (ed.), *The English Riots of 2011: A Summer of Discontent*, Hook, Waterside Press.

Konrad, G. (1975) *The Case Worker*, London, Hutchinson.

Kropotkin, P. (1939 [1902]) *Mutual Aid*, London, Pelican edn.

Laing, R.D. (1969) *The Divided Self*, Harmondsworth, Penguin.

Lammy, D. (2011) *Out of the Ashes: Britain After the Riots*, London, Guardian Books.

Langan, M. (2011) Rediscovering Radicalism and Humanity in Social Work, in Lavalette, M. (ed.), *Radical Social Work Today: Social Work at the Crossroads*, Bristol, Policy Press.

Langan, M. (1998) Radical Social Work, in Adams, R., Dominelli, L. and Payne, M. *Social Work: Themes, Issues and Critical Debates*, Basingstoke, Macmillan Open University.

Lavalette, M. (ed.) (2011) *Radical Social Work Today: Social Work at the Crossroads*, Bristol, Policy Press.

Lavalette, M. and Ferguson, I. (2007) *International Social Work and the Radical Tradition*, Birmingham, Venture Press.

Leadbeater, C. and Lownsbrough, H. (2004) *Personalisation Through Participation: A New Script for Public Services*, London, DEMOS.

Leadbeater, C. and Lownsbrough, H. (2005) *Personalisation and Participation: The Future of Social Care in Scotland*, London, DEMOS www.socialworkscotland. org.uk/resources/cp-sd/ (accessed 29 November 2012).

Ledwith, M. (2012) *Community Development: A Critical Approach*, Bristol, Policy Press.

Lenin, V. (1973 [1919]) *The State: A Lecture Delivered at the Sverdlov University July 11th 1919*, Peking, Foreign Languages Press.

Lenin, V. (1920) *Left Wing Communism: An Infantile Disorder* http://www. marxists.org/archive/lenin/works/1920/lwc/index.htm (accessed 9 September 2012).

Leonard, P. (1997) *Post-Modern Welfare: Reconstructing an Emancipatory Project*, London, Sage.

Lewycka, M. (2010) *We Are All Made of Glue*, London, Penguin.

Lipsky, M. (1980) *Street Level Bureaucracy – Dilemmas of the Individual in Public Services*, New York, Russell Sage Foundation.

Lorenz, W. (2008) Paradigms and Politics: Understanding Methods Paradigms in an Historical Context: The Case of Social Pedagogy *British Journal of Social Work* 38(4), 625–44.

Lymbery, M. (2004) Responding to Crisis: The Changing Nature of Welfare Organisations, in Lymbery, M. and Butler, S. (eds), *Social Work: Ideals and Practice Realities*, Basingstoke, Palgrave MacMillan.

Lymbery, M. and Butler, S. (eds) (2004) *Social Work: Ideals and Practice Realities*, Basingstoke, Palgrave MacMillan.

Macintyre, S. (1980) *Little Moscows: Communism and Working-class Militancy in Inter-war Britain*, London, Croom Helm.

Manthorpe, J., Moriarty, J., Rapaport, J., Clough, R., Corries, M., Bright, L., Iliffe, S. and OPRI (Older People Researching Social Issues) (2008) 'There are Wonderful Social Workers but it's a Lottery': Older People's Views about Social Workers *British Journal of Social Work* 38, 1132–50.

Maracek, J. and Hare-Hustin, R. (2009) Clinical Psychology: The Politics of Madness, in Fox, D., Prilleltensky, I. and Austin, S. (eds), *Critical Psychology: An Introduction*, 2nd edn, Thousand Oaks, CA, Sage.

Marsh, P. and Fisher, M. (2005) Developing the evidence base for social work and social care practice: Using knowledge in social care report 10, Social Care Institute for Excellence http://www.scie.org.uk/publications/reports/report10. pdf (accessed 27 October 2012).

Marston, G. and McDonald, C. (2012) Getting Beyond 'Heroic Agency' in Conceptualising Social Workers as Policy Actors in the 21st Century *British Journal of Social Work* 42(6), 1022–38.

Martinez, D. (2005) Mental Health Care after Capitalism, *Radical Psychology*, winter http://www.radicalpsychology.org/vol4-2/Martinez4.html

Martinez-Brawley, E. (2000) *Close to Home: Human Services and the Small Community*, Washington, DC, NASW Press.

Martinez-Brawley, E. and Delevan, S. (1993) *Transferring Technology in the Personal Social Services*, Washington, DC, NASW Press.

Martinez-Brawley, E. and McKinlay, R. (2012) 'Revisiting Barra': Changes in the Structure and Delivery of Social Work Services in the Outer Hebrides – Are Rural Tenets Still Alive?, *British Journal of Social Work* 42(8), 1608–25.

Marx, K. (1847) *Wage Labour and Capital* http://www.marxists.org/archive/marx/ works/1847/wage-labour/ch06.htm (accessed 24 September 2012).

Marx, K. (1845) *Thesis on Feurebach* https://www.marxists.org/archive/marx/ works/1845/theses/theses.htm (accessed 24 April 2013).

Marx, K. and Engels, F. (1848) Manifesto of the Communist Party http://www.marxists.org/archive/marx/works/1848/communist-manifesto/ (accessed 20 April 2013).

Maslach, C. and Leiter, M. (1997) *The Truth About Burnout*, San Francisco, Jossey-Bass.

Mason, P. (2012) *Why It's Kicking Off Everywhere: The New Global Revolutions*, London, Verso.

McDonald, C. (2006) *Challenging Social Work: The Context of Practice*, Bristol, Policy Press.

McKeganey, N. (2011) *Controversies in Drugs Policies and Practice*, Basingstoke, Palgrave Macmillan.

Melling, J. (1983) *Rent Strikes: People's Struggle for Housing in West Scotland 1890–1916*, Edinburgh, Polygon.

Miles, L. (2011) LGBT Oppression, Sexualities and Radical Social Work Today, in Lavalette, M. (ed.) *Radical Social Work Today: Social Work at the Crossroads*, Bristol, Policy Press.

Miliband, R. (1969) *The State in Capitalist Society: The Analysis of the Western System of Power*, London, Weidenfeld & Nicolson.

Mishra, R. (1990) *The Welfare State and Capitalist Society*, Hemel Hempstead, Harvester Wheatsheaf.

Moane, G. (1999) *Gender and Colonialism: A Psychological Analysis of Oppression and Liberation*, New York, St Martin's Press.

Moreau, M.J. (1979) A Structural Approach to Social Work Practice, *Canadian Journal of Social Work Education* 5(1), 75–94.

Morleo, M., Woolfall, K., Dedman, D., Mukherjee, R., Bellis, M. and Cook, P. (2011) Under-reporting of Foetal Alcohol Spectrum Disorders: An Analysis of Hospital Episode Statistics, *BMC Paediatrics* Research Article 11(14), http://www.biomedcentral.com/content/pdf/1471-2431-11-14.pdf.

Moss, P. (2011) Early Childhood Education in Reggio Emilia and Social Pedagogy: Are They Related?, in Cameron, C. and Moss, P. (eds), *Social Pedagogy and Working with Children and Young People: Where Care and Education Meet*, London, Jessica Kingsley.

Mullaly, B. (2010) *Challenging Oppression and Confronting Privilege*, 2nd edn, Ontario, Oxford University Press.

Mullaly, B. (1997) *Structural Social Work: Ideology, Theory, and Practice*, 2nd edn, Ontario, Oxford University Press.

Mullender, A. (2002) Persistant Oppressions: The Example of Domestic Violence, in Adams, R., Dominelli, L. and Payne, M. (eds), *Critical Practice in Social Work*, Basingstoke, Palgrave Macmillan.

Mullender, A., Fleming, J. and Ward, D. (forthcoming) *Self-Directed Groupwork Revisited*, Basingstoke, Palgrave Macmillan.

Mullender A. and Hague, G. (2005) Giving Voice to Women Survivors of Domestic Violence through Recognition as a Service Group, *British Journal of Social Work* 35(8), 1121–341.

Mullender, A. and Ward, D. (1991) *Self-Directed Groupwork: Users Take Action for Empowerment*, London, Whiting & Birch.

Munro, E. (2011) *The Munro Review of Child Protection Final Report: A Child Centred System*, London, Stationary Office.

Munro, E. (2010) Learning to Reduce Risk in Child Protection *British Journal of Social Work* **40**, 1135–51.

Needham, C. (2012) What is Happening to Day Centre Services?: Voices from Frontline Staff, UNISON/University of Birmingham, http://www.unison.org.uk/socialwork/pages_view.asp?did=14463 (accessed 8 December 2012).

NHS (2012) *Statistics on Alcohol England 2012*, NHS, Information Centre for Health and Social Care, www.ic.nhs.uk (accessed 11 November 2012).

Observer, The (2011) How a big US Bank laundered billions from Mexico's murderous drugs gangs, 3 April, http://www.guardian.co.uk/world/2011/apr/03/us-bank-mexico-drug-gangs (accessed 7 November 2012).

Office for National Statistics (2012) *2011 Census: Key Statistics for England and Wales March 2011*, http://www.ons.gov.uk/ons/dcp171778_290685.pdf (accessed 14 December 2012).

Oliver, M., Sapey, B. and Thomas, P. (2012) *Social Work with Disabled People*, 4th edn, Basingstoke, Palgrave Macmillan.

Orme, J. (1998) Feminist Social Work, in Adams, R., Dominelli, L. and Payne, M. (eds), *Social Work: Themes, Issues and Critical Debates*, Basingstoke, Macmillan Open University.

Ostberg, F. (2012) Using 'Consensual Ideology': A Way to Sift reports in Child Welfare *British Journal of Social Work*, Advanced Access (published online 11 July 2011).

Parton, N. (1998) Risk, Advanced Liberalism and Child Welfare: The Need to Rediscover Uncertainty and Ambiguity *British Journal of Social Work* **28**, 5–27.

Parton, N. and O'Byrne, P. (2000) *Constructive Social Work: Towards a New Practice*, London, Palgrave Macmillan.

Pauwels, J. (2002) *The Myth of the Good War: America in the Second World War*, Toronto, James Lorimer.

Payne, M. (2011) *Humanistic Social Work*, Basingstoke, Palgrave Macmillan.

Payne, M. (2005) *Modern Social Work Theory*, 3rd edn, Basingstoke, Macmillan.

Penketh, L. (2011) Social Work and Women's Oppression Today, in Lavalette, M. (ed.) *Radical Social Work Today: Social Work at the Crossroads*, Bristol, Policy Press.

Petrie, S. (2009) Are the International and National Codes of Ethics for Social Work in the UK as Useful as a Chocolate Teapot? *Journal of Social Work Values and Ethics* 6(2), http://www.socialworker.com/jswve/content/view/123/68

Phillipson, C. (1982) *Capitalism and the Construction of Old Age*, London, Macmillan.

Pierson, J. (2008) *Going Local: Working in Communities and Neighbourhoods*, Abingdon, Routledge.

Pinkerton, J. (2002) Child Protection, in Adams, R., Dominelli, L. and Payne, M. (eds), *Critical Practice in Social Work*, Basingstoke, Palgrave Macmillan.

Piratin, P. (1978) *Our Flag Stays Red*, London, Lawrence & Wishart.

Policis (2012) *Optimising Welfare Reform Outcomes for Social Tenants*, http://www.housing.org.uk/publications/find_a_publication/general/social_tenants'_finances_and_v.aspx (accessed 2 January 2013).

Pollack, S. (2010) Labelling Clients Risky: Social Work and the Neo-liberal Welfare State *British Journal of Social Work* **40**, 1263–78.

Preston-Shoot (2007) *Effective Groupwork*, 2nd edn, Basingstoke, Palgrave Macmillan.

Prime Minister's Office (2010) Big Society Speech, 19 July, www.number10.gov. uk/news/big-society-speech/ (accessed 11 January 2012).

PSW (Professional Social Work) Magazine, Letters Page, June/July 2012.

Public and Commercial Services Union (PCS) (2011) *Welfare: An Alternative Vision*, London PCS.

Qubain, E. (2010) Intermediate Care: Implications for Service Users, in Brown, K (ed.), *Vulnerable Adults and Community Care*, 2nd edn, Exeter, Learning Matters.

Reichert, E. (2007) Human Rights in the 21st Century: Creating a New Paradigm for Social Work, in Reichert, E. (ed.), *Challenges in Human Rights: A Social Work Perspective*, New York, Columbia University Press.

Reisch, M. (2013) What is the Future of Social Work? *Critical and Radical Social Work* 1(1), 67–85.

Rinaldi, C. (2006) *In Dialogue With Reggio Emilia*, Abingdon, Routledge.

Roberts, J. (2011) Getting it Right for Older People, in Taylor, R., Hill, M. and McNeill, F. (eds), *Early Professional Development for Social Workers*, Birmingham, Venture Press.

Rogowski, S. (2013) *Critical Social Work with Children and Families: Theory, Context and Practice*, Bristol, Policy Press.

Rogowski, S. (2010) *Social Work – The Rise and Fall of a Profession?*, Bristol, Policy Press.

Roose, R., Roets, G. and Bouverne-De Bie (2011) Irony and Social Work: In Search of the Happy Sisyphus *British Journal of Social Work* Advanced Access (published online 23 November 2011).

Rowley, D. and Hunter, S. (2011) Creating Better Lives: Learning Disability, Early Professional Development and Social Work, in Taylor, R., Hill, M. and McNeill, F. (eds), *Early Professional Development for Social Workers*, Birmingham, Venture Press.

Roy, B. (2007) Radical Psychiatry: Therapeutic Change for Self and Society, http://www.jugglerpress.com/jockm/BethRoyRT_update2007.htm (accessed 9 December 2012).

Schon, D. (1983) *The Reflective Practitioner: How Professionals Think in Action*, New York, Basic Books.

Schur, E. (1973) *Radical Non-Intervention: Rethinking the Delinquency Problem*, Englewood Cliffs NJ, Prentice-Hall.

Scotsman (2013) Iain Duncan Smith £53 a week petition near 300,000, 2 April, http://www.scotsman.com/the-scotsman/uk/iain-duncan-smith-53-a-week-petition-near-300-000-1-2870419 (accessed 8 May 2013).

Scottish Executive (2006) *Changing Lives: Review of Social Work in the 21st Century*, Edinburgh, Scottish Executive, http://www.scotland.gov.uk/Resource/Doc/91931/0021949.pdf (accessed 2 January 2013).

Scottish Government (2011a) *Scotland's National Dementia Strategy*, http://www.scotland.gov.uk/Publications/2010/09/10151751/0 (accessed 11 November 2012).

Scottish Government (2011b) The Caledonian System: An integrated approach to address men's domestic abuse and to improve the lives of women, children and men, http://www.scotland.gov.uk/Topics/People/Equality/violence-women/CaledonianSystem (accessed 7 November 2012).

Scottish Government (2009) Personalisation – A Shared Understanding, www. scotland.gov.uk/publications/04/07112629/0 (accessed 27 November 2012).

Scourfield, J. (2003) *Gender and Child Protection*, Basingstoke, Palgrave Macmillan.

Seddon, D., Robinson, C., Reeves, C., Tommis, Y., Woods, B. and Russell, I. (2007) In Their Own Right: Translating the Policy of Carer Assessment into Practice *British Journal of Social Work* 37, 1335–52.

Seebohm, F. (1968) *Report of the Committee on Local Authority and Allied Personal Services*, London, HMSO.

Seniors Homecare LLC, St Louis Missouri (2012) Home Care Company Morale: 10 Warning Signs Yours is Dipping http://www.seniorshomecare.com/blog/ archives/2012/02/21/home-care-company-morale-10-warning-signs-yours-is-dipping/ (accessed 22 September 2012).

Simkin, M. (1979) *Trapped Within Welfare: Surviving Social Work*, London, Macmillan.

Slettebo, T. (2013) Partnership with Parents of Children in Care: A Study of Collective User Participation in Child Protection Services *British Journal of Social Work* 43(3), 579–95.

Smale, G., Tuson, G. and Statham, D. (2000) *Social Work and Social Problems: Working Towards Social Inclusion and Social Change*, Basingstoke, Macmillan.

Smidt, S. (2006) *The Developing Child in the 21st Century: A Global Perspective on Child Development*, Abingdon, Routledge.

Smith, K. (2007) Social Work, Restructuring and Everyday Resistance: 'Best Practices' Gone Underground, in Baines, D. (ed.) *Doing Anti-Oppressive Practice: Building Transformative Politicized Social Work*, Nova Scotia, Fernwood.

SSSC (2009) Codes of Practice for Social Services Workers and Employers, http://www.sssc.uk.com/doc_details/1020-sssc-codes-of-practice-for-social-service-workers-and-employers (accessed 27 April 2013).

Stanford, S. (2011) Constructing Moral Responses to Risk: A Framework for Hopeful Social Work Practice *British Journal of Social Work* 41, 1514–31.

Stanford, S. (2010) 'Speaking Back' to Fear: Responding to the Moral Dilemmas of Risk in Social Work Practice *British Journal of Social Work* 40, 1065–80.

Statham, D. (1978) *Radicals in Social Work*, London, Routledge & Kegan Paul.

Statham, J., Cameron, C. and Mooney, A. (2006) *The Tasks and Roles of Social Workers: A Focused Overview of Research Evidence*, Institute of Education University of London, Thomas Coram Research Unit http://eprints.ioe.ac.uk/ 59/ (accessed 10 November 2012).

Strega, S. (2007) Anti-Oppressive Practices in Child Welfare, in Baines, D. (ed.), *Doing Anti-Oppressive Practice: Building Transformative Politicized Social Work*, Nova Scotia, Fernwood.

Sullivan, M. (2009) Social Workers in Community Care Practice: Ideologies and Interactions with Older People *British Journal of Social Work* 39, 1306–25.

Telegraph Newspaper (2004) Pay Female Addicts Not To Have Children, 14 March, http://www.telegraph.co.uk/news/uknews/1456770/Pay-female-addicts-not-to-have-children.html (accessed 10 November 2012).

Thatcher, M. (1987) Interview for *Woman's Own*, http://www.margaretthatcher. org/document/106689 (accessed 31 December 2012).

Thompson, N. (2001) *Anti Discriminatory Practice*, 3rd edn, Basingstoke, BASW Palgrave.

Throssell, H. (ed.) (1975) *Social Work: Radical Essays*, St Lucia, University of Queensland Press.

Titmuss, R. (1968) *Commitment to Welfare*, London, George Allen & Unwin.

Trainor, B. (1996) *Radicalism, Feminism and Fanaticism: Social Work in the Nineties*, Aldershot, Avebury.

Trantor, D. (2005) Breaking the Connection Between Traditional Masculinity and Violence, in Brownlee, K. and Graham, J. (eds), *Violence in the Family: Social Work Readings and Research from Northern and Rural Canada*, Toronto, CSPI.

Trevithick, P. (2005) The Knowledge Base of Groupwork and its Importance within Social Work *Groupwork* **15**(2), 80–107.

Turbett, C. (2010) *Rural Social Work Practice in Scotland*, Birmingham, Venture Press.

Turbett, C. (2004) A Decade After Orkney: Towards a Practice Model for Social Work in the Remoter Areas of Scotland *British Journal of Social Work* **34**(7), 981–95.

Turney, D., Platt, D., Selwyn, J. and Farmer, E. (2012) *Improving Child and Family Assessments: Turning Research into Practice*, London, Jessica Kingsley.

ukpublicspending.co.uk (2012) *Public Spending Charts*, http://www.ukpublic spending.co.uk/ (accessed 2 December 2012).

Ungar, M. (2011) *The Social Worker: A Novel*, Lawrencetown Beach Nova Scotia, Pottersfield.

UNISON (2013) UNISON Preliminary Agenda 20th National Delegate Conference 18–21 June 2013, http://www.unison.org.uk/conference/ndc.asp (accessed 1 May 2013).

UNISON (2012a) UNISON'S Ethical Care Charter, http://www.unison.org.uk/ acrobat/21188.pdf (accessed 1 December 2012).

UNISON (2012b) Personalisation in Scotland – the Facts http://www.unison-scotland.org.uk/socialwork/Personalisation_01_2012.pdf (accessed 2 December 2012).

UNISON (2010) Not Waving but Drowning: Paperwork and Pressure in Adult Social Work Services, http://www.unison.org.uk/acrobat/B4710.pdf (accessed 24 September 2012).

UNISON (2009a) Still Slipping through the Net? Front-line Staff Assess Children's Safeguarding Progress, http://www.unison.org.uk/acrobat/B4416.pdf (accessed 24 September 2012).

UNISON (2009b) *Cash or Care: 10 Essential Questions for Councils on Personalisation*, London, UNISON.

UNISON Scotland (2010) Supervision and Workload Management for Social Work – A Negotiating Resource http://www.unison-scotland.org.uk/socialwork/ workloadmanagement.pdf (accessed 19 January 2012).

UNISON Scotland (2006) Asylum in Scotland: Child's Welfare Paramount? A guide for members from BASW and UNISON Scotland http://www. unison-scotland.org.uk/socialwork/asylumbooklet/asylumbooklet.pdf (accessed 2 June 2013).

Webb, S. (2010) (Re) Assembling the Left: The Politics of Redistribution and Recognition in Social Work *British Journal of Social Work* **40**, 2364–79.

Webber, F. (2012) *Borderline Justice: The Fight for Refugee and Migrant Rights*, London, Pluto Press.

Weiner, M. and Petrella, P. (2007) The Impact of New Technology: Implications for Social Work and Social Care Managers, in Aldgate, J., Healy, L., Malcolm, B, Pine, B., Rose, W. and Seden, J. (eds), *Enhancing Social Work Management: Theory and Best Practice from the UK and USA*, London, Jessica Kingsley.

Weinstein, J. (2011) Case Con and Radical Social Work in the 1970s: The Impatient Revolutionaries, in Lavalette, M. (ed.), *Radical Social Work Today: Social Work at the Crossroads*, Bristol, Policy Press.

Welbourne, P. (2012) *Social Work with Children and Families: Developing Advanced Practice*, Abingdon, Routledge.

Whelan, J., Stone, C., Lyons, M., Niamh-Wright, N., Long, A., Ryall, J., Whyte, G. and Harding-Smith, R. (2012) Big Society and Australia: How the UK Government is Dismantling the State and What it Means for Australia, http://cpd.org.au/2012/06/australian-policy-online-big-society-and-australia/ (accessed 1 January 2013).

White, M. and Epston, D. (1990) *Narrative Means to Therapeutic Ends*, New York, Norton.

White, V. (2009) Quiet Challenges? Professional Practice in Modernised Social Work, in Harris, J. and White, V. (eds), *Modernising Social Work: Critical Considerations*, Bristol, Policy Press.

White, V. (1999) Feminist Social Work and the State: A British Perspective, in Lesnik, B. (ed.), *International Perspectives on Social Work: Social Work and the State*, Brighton, Pavilion Publishing.

White, V. and Harris, J. (2001) *Developing Good Practice in Community Care: Partnership and Participation*, London, Jessica Kingsley.

Wilkinson, R. and Pickett, K. (2010) *The Spirit Level: Why Equality is Better for Everyone*, London, Penguin.

Willets, C. (2010) People with Learning Disabilities: Issues of Vulnerability, in Brown, K. (ed.), *Vulnerable Adults and Community Care*, 2nd edn, Exeter, Learning Matters.

Williams, C. (2011) The Jester's Joke, in Lavalette, M. (ed.), *Radical Social Work Today: Social Work at the Crossroads*, Bristol, Policy Press.

Williams, R. (1976) *Keywords: A Vocabulary of Culture and Society*, Glasgow, Fontana.

Winlow, S. and Hall, S. (2012) Gone Shopping: Inarticulate Politics in the English Riots of 2011, in Briggs, D. (ed.), *The English Riots of 2011: A Summer of Discontent*, Hook, Waterside Press.

Wolfenstein, E. (1993) *Psychoanalytic Marxism: Groundwork*, New York, Guilford Press.

Woodward, R. (2013) Some Reflections on Critical and Radical Social Work Literature, *Critical and Radical Social Work* 1(1), 135–40.

Younghusband, E. (1964) *Social Work and Social Change*, London, George Allen & Unwin.

Index